Freedom

FUNDAMENTAL ISSUES IN PHILOSOPHY SERIES

Freedom

A Study Guide with Readings

edited by
William L. Reese

Humanity
Books

an imprint of Prometheus Books
59 John Glenn Drive, Amherst, New York 14228-2197

Published 2000 by Humanity Books, an imprint of Prometheus Books

04 03 02 01 00   5 4 3 2 1

Library of Congress Cataloging-in-Publication Data

Freedom: a study guide with readings / edited by William L. Reese.
      p.   cm. — (Fundamental issues in philosophy series)
  Includes bibliographical references and index.
  ISBN 1–57392–736–8 (pbk.)
  1. Liberty. I. Reese, William L. II. Series.
B824.4 .F725 1999
123'.5—dc21   99-046411
                                                  CIP

Printed in the United States of America on acid-free paper

Preface

The volume at hand belongs to a series of eight volumes on Fundamental Issues in Philosophy, making up a body of material capable of supporting both individual and course study in the beginning ranges of philosophy. Each volume features one of the eight unavoidable philosophical problems. The essential texts for interpreting the problems have been selected from thinkers, both classical and modern, Western and Eastern, allowing the student to experience the problem in something like its historical depth and complexity within a volume of modest size.

The eight unavoidable problems are:

(1)   the nature and extent of one's personal freedom;
(2)   one's value profile and its underlying theory of value;
(3)   the nature of the self;
(4)   one's relation to truth, and one's theory of truth;
(5)   one's view of the nature and function of beauty;
(6)   one's way of distinguishing between right and wrong, and its underlying theory;
(7)   the principles making up one's social philosophy, and their defense;
(8)   God and immortality—affirmation and denial producing contrasts in one's sensed relation to the universe. .

Although in the above list only freedom is said to be personal, in fact all eight problems are personal in the Socratic sense of encouraging self-knowledge and the examined life. When the great philosophers are viewed as purveyors of final truth, that somehow closes them off from our experience. But when we think of them as engaged in working out their own personal philosophies, as must we, they become our associates and friends engaged in a common quest. Philosophers come to different conclusions, discovering different standing grounds. That is sometimes pointed to as a weakness in philosophy. I think it a strength. It means that their work offers us a set of important and well-reasoned alternatives, allowing us to philosophize from a state more informed than theirs, since we have their thought in addition to our own. What is at issue here is discovery of our personal truth about ourselves, the universe, and how the two relate. Final truth is at issue only indirectly. In the first place we do not expect to find it. In the second place, if we did find it and philosophers agreed in every way, life would be less interesting. To be sure we would like our personal truths to be flecked with final truth. So taken, all philosophy—ours and that of the past—deals with options which are, as William James (*q.v.* D4) put it, "forced, living, and momentous." In that sense philosophy is the most practical of all disciplines, for how can one live an ordered and rational life of self-knowledge without a standing ground?

The series has been ordered on the principle of increasing range. Although each volume is intelligible, standing alone, the volumes are mutually supporting. One can begin anywhere, with any problem. The independent reader, whose interest we heartily encourage, might select any volume of central interest, along with the *Dictionary of Philosophy and Religion: Eastern and Western Thought* (Amherst, N.Y.: Humanity Books, 2d ed., 1996) as interpretive supplement.

Each of the eight volumes contains a Study Guide preceding the Readings, and on its special topic. The readings provide exposure to the arguments and explanations of philosophers in their own words, and are structured in terms of their role as alternative interpretations of the concept under investigation. The Study Guide shows how these sources may be utilized in thinking out one's position on this concept. The *Dictionary* supplements the Study Guide and Readings, providing background information on philosophers, concepts, and movements. The volumes of the series are keyed to the *Dictionary* and each other, and are to be considered as companion volumes. In each volume of the series the Table of Contents, the Study Guide, and the Readings are keyed to each other (as further explained in the Introduction to this volume). In the Study Guide alternatives proposed in the Readings are further clarified, and the relevance of various moves discussed; this is done in an open-structured manner leaving final decision to the student/reader.

Where the individual reader makes a personal selection, in formal instruction the selection is made by the instructor in order to achieve the objectives of the course. The principle of maximum flexibility allows the series to be relevant to many, if not all, philosophy courses in the beginning range. Introductory courses in philosophy are organized around problems, history, selected readings, or some combination of the three. When organized around problems or selected readings, this series is especially relevant. Given the customary limitation of philosophy courses to one semester, the total series contains more material than can ordinarily be used in a single course. The instructor might well, however, select two or three of the volumes, deemed to be most appropriate to the design of the given course, along with the *Dictionary* to be used for other topics (*q.v.* the Appendix for the entry listings in the *Dictionary* appropriate to each of the eight problems). Should the instructor utilize a group approach, the entire series might be used. The class would be divided into subgroups working with some independence, each subgroup assigned, e.g., two of the problems for intensive work during the semester, the groups taking turns in presenting their results to the rest of the class. For courses whose orientation is historical, the *Dictionary* can provide historical background for periods of philosophy not covered by the primary material (a text in the history of ancient, medieval, or modern philosophy, or philosophical classics within a period, such as, for ancient philosophy, Plato's *Republic* or Aristotle's *Nicomachean Ethics*). Greater variety can be added to any course through the selection of one of the Readings volumes. Finally, since each study guide can serve as the outline of a problem-solving paper, a writing component can be introduced into any course by having the student select a volume appropriate to the course as the basis of a paper. For ethics courses the volumes on *Freedom*, *Value*, and *Right and Wrong* would be appropriate. For epistemology courses, the *Truth* volume; for aesthetics courses the nature and function of *Beauty*; for political philosophy the volumes on *Right and Wrong* and *Social Philosophy*; for philosophy of religion or metaphysics courses the volumes on *God and Immortality*, *Freedom*, or the *Self*. We invite your attention to the consideration of these possibilities.

How might the Study Guide be used? It might be used to strengthen the skills by whose means one gains an education. One educates oneself by listening, reading, thinking, writing, and talking. The stronger these skills the better one's education.

In the stereotypical course one listens to the instructor, reads the text, attempting to isolate possible examination questions, and then checks the appropriate box in multiple choice exams, or writes short answers. Here listening, reading, and writing are involved, but hardly in their most intensive forms.

In courses stressing quizzes, sections of the Study Guide can be assigned, along with the related readings, and quizzes administered. There is at once, however, the possibility of class and group discussion prior to any quiz, taking advantage of the reading and note taking which occurred in preparing the assignment. In discussion the fourth of the skills acquires a place, talking, representing oneself before others.

It is possible to make discussion more pointed if group discussion with defined goals is added to class discussion, where both talking and listening are practiced.

Thinking in some form goes on most of the time; but it can be encouraged. According to the philosopher John Dewey (*q.v.* D2) thinking, properly so-called, requires that one have a problem in mind, and is working toward its solution. Thinking can be encouraged, then, by directing the student's attention to the Study Guide as a problem to be solved in a rational manner. That can be done by the instructor taking the class through the steps of the Study Guide. It can be done by having the students keep journals in which they work for clarity, understanding, and personal response. The journals would then be submitted to the instructor at stated times during the semester for evaluation and feedback. The words directed to the independent student below on journal writing apply to the formal instruction-based journal as well. Finally, since each Study Guide has a problem solving structure, requiring student decision at each step, it can become the basis of a problem-solving student paper on the topic of the volume under consideration.

In participative education each of the five skills will be promoted. Students will listen not only to their instructor in class, but to their fellow students in discussion groups. They will read the material, and think about its implications. They will participate in class discussion, as well as in discussion groups. They will write out their positions and think out the reasons which support them, either in journals or in problem-solving papers. There will be times when they will present their positions in class, or in discussion groups, and defend them against the questions of their fellow students.

But where does this leave the independent student who has chosen one of the volumes and wishes to study it? One can envision several individuals with shared interests and perhaps circumstances working together on these problems. But whether one establishes an informal group or chooses to work in splendid isolation the Study Guide becomes the sole instructor. By choosing to keep a journal of the responses which occur in working through the Study Guide and Readings, if not in preparation of a formal paper, the skills of reading, thinking, and writing are developed. As for the missing skills of listening and talking, one can talk with one's friends about new ideas, and listen to their responses. One talks to oneself in any case while working out the articulation of one's ideas. One also listens to the voices of inner dialogue as one works to establish one's own standing ground. Plato believed this internal dialogue to be as significant as conversation with another person. Perhaps in the conflict of voices one may find one's own voice, a goal of which writers—especially novelists—often speak. If this is not enough, let the independent student write the author. This has happened not infrequently in the past; it has enriched my experience, and perhaps that of those writing to me.

I wish to thank the students of my Introduction to Philosophy courses, most recently those of my courses at the State University of New York at Albany, for their help through class participation in the analysis of these problems. I am grateful to Keith Ashfield and Paul Kurtz for their support. My special thanks to W.L.R. III for his contributions as Editorial and Research Assistant; many of the features of the series developed in the course of a continuing dialogue between us.

William L. Reese
Slingerlands, New York

Acknowledgments

Oxford University Press.

Aristotle, *Nicomachean Ethics, The Basic Works of Aristotle*, ed. R. Mckeon. Reprinted by permission of Oxford University Press.

John Locke, *An Essay Concerning Human Understanding*, 1894. By permission of Oxford University Press.

David Hume, *A Treatise of Human Nature*, 1888. By permission of Oxford University Press.

C. A. Campbell, "Is 'Freewill' a Pseudo Problem?" *Mind* LX, no. 240, October, 1951. Reprinted by permission of Oxford University Press.

Philosophical Library.

Jean-Paul Sartre, *Being and Nothingness*, tr. Hazel Barnes, 1956. Reprinted by permission of Philosophical Library, N.Y.

Yale University Press.

Jonathan Edwards, *Freedom of the Will*, Yale University Press. Copyright © 1957 by Yale University Press.

Dutton Signet.

From *Essentials of Zen Buddhism* by Daisetz T. Suzuki, Bernard Phillips, editor. Copyright © 1962 by Bernard Phillips. Used by permission of Dutton Signet, a division of Penguin Books USA Inc.

Burns and Oates, Ltd.

St. Thomas Aquinas, *Summa Theologica*, tr. Fathers of the English Dominican Province, Burns Oates and Washbourne Ltd., 1922. Reprinted by permission of Burns and Oates, Ltd.

Ernest B. Hook.

Brand Blanshard, "The Case for Determinism," from *Determinism and Freedom in the Age of Modern Science*, ed. Sidney Hook, New York University Press, 1958. Reprinted by permission of Ernest B. Hook.

HarperCollins.

Anselm, selected excerpts from *Truth, Freedom and Evil by Anselm of Canterbury*, edited by Jasper Hopkins. Copyright © 1967 by Jasper Hopkins and Herbert Richardson. Reprinted by permission of HarperCollins Publishers, Inc.

Paul Edwards.

"Hard and Soft Determinism" from *Determinism and Freedom in the Age of Modern Science*, ed. Sidney Hook, New York University Press, 1958. Reprinted by permission of Paul Edwards.

Introduction

The subject of this volume, the first of the series, is the concept of personal freedom. We say "personal" because it concerns the problem of exercising freedom in one's life, that is, in one's own person. But if, as we have argued, one can begin philosophizing with any one of the eight concepts of the series, why should the series begin with freedom? Freedom seems to have a methodological primacy, examining one's power to control one's own life, including the power to settle questions. In a sense, then, one's power to settle any of the other questions is implicit in this one.

To gain an initial feel for the subject matter of the volume, consider the following summary version of the Study Guide's detailed outline on freedom.

SUMMARY OUTLINE

(1) Question: What freedom have I to control my life?
(2) Definitions of freedom.
  (a) The capacity in a moment of decision to take any one of two or more alternatives
  (b) Doing what one wants to do
  (c) Acting in terms of internal, rather than external, factors

       (d) Doing what one ought to do

(3)   Discussion of the definitions and concluding with a workable definition.

(4)   In terms of this workable definition, what freedom have I to control my life?

(5)   There are three possible solutions:

       (a) A great deal of freedom

       (b) A limited amount of freedom

       (c) No freedom at all

(6)   Evaluation of the three possibilities, giving your reasons for choosing one of them.

Brief comments on the Summary Outline:

On (1) the question, "What freedom have I to control my life?" is not intended to prejudge its answer. It does not suggest that we have some freedom, since one of the possible answers to the question is that we have a zero degree of freedom (5c). If that answer stands at one end of the spectrum, at its other end is the answer that our freedom is total (whatever that would mean); (5a) would be a reasonable approach to total freedom. Most of us, including Aristotle, are inclined to flee extremes, finding our answer in some mean between extremes. Between the extremes are other positions. In any event we don't know what to look for until we have an adequate definition of freedom.

On the definitions of freedom (2), finding an adequate definition is not a simple matter. Look up "freedom" in a standard dictionary, and you are likely to find as the first definition: "the quality or state of being free." There will be other suggestions, and along with them a sense of circularity and ambiguity. Sometimes it is claimed that everyone has a different definition of freedom. But we find that four definitions of freedom have been advanced in the history of philosophy, and that anyone's definition of freedom can be related to one (or more) of these four definitions. Sometimes one hears the claim, expressed at times admiringly, at times belligerently, "This is a free country." The claim is surely expressed in many countries, but perhaps nowhere more frequently than in the fifty states, perhaps because they constitute a democracy. Plato suggested in the *Republic* that democracies are "ready to burst with freedom." The definition of freedom in use when such claims are made is the second definition. The speaker is saying that the America so defined is a country where one can do what one wants to do; or at least more of what one wants to do than in any other country. On further consideration it will be admitted that such freedom is more extensive in speech than in action, and that there are necessary limits to such freedom, at least in action, and probably also in speech. The statement of a definition calls for analysis of its adequacy; and that requires consideration of alternative definitions.

The heart of the outline is contained in steps (2) through (6), and the entire volume is constructed to help one move through these steps to an informed answer: the Keyed Table of Contents, the Study Guide, the Readings themselves, the Appendix, and the Index. No part of the book should be ignored. Referring now to the Keyed Table of Contents you will find an unusual variety of important thinkers selected to represent the four definitions. An attempt has been made to provide the richest concentration of material possible in a volume of modest size. In the Study Guide, which takes one through a detailed version of the outline, the thinkers and readings defending each of these definitions are considered, and their strengths and weaknesses noted. It is pointed out that sometimes more than one definition is held by a given thinker. And, to be sure, several of the definitions, or parts of them, can be affirmed together, while some cannot. It is important to be able to know the difference.

The Keyed Table of Contents, the Study Guide, and the Readings are keyed to each other. The numbers (2) through (5c) of the Table of Contents refer to divisions both of the Study Guide and of the Readings. All of the (2)s in the Table of Contents, Study Guide, and Readings refer to considerations of definitions of freedom. (2a) through (2d) refer to consideration of the four different definitions of freedom. If one looks back to (2) in the Summary Outline (a), (b), (c), and (d) give brief definitions of the four usages. (2a1) through (2a5) in the Table of Contents, reflecting both the Study Guide and the Readings, refer to the five readings on the first definition of freedom. (2b1) through (2b4) refer to the 4 readings on the second definition of freedom, etc. (3d1) deals with a thinker critical of the second definition, who contrasts the fourth definition with the second, and finds creative action requiring the first definition. (5c1) through (5c3) refer to the three readings dealing with determinism since that is, in most interpretations, the zero degree of freedom. In the Table of Contents the Readings are also graced with a page number. One can thus move back and forth among the Keyed Table of Contents, the Study Guide, and the Readings to the precise section of material one wishes to consider.

Having discussed all of the other keyed features of the book, it is also appropriate to mention that the index can guide one to information on freedom not referred to elsewhere, *e.g.*, in C. A. Campbell (3d1), a summary of Moritz Schlick's view; in Paul Edwards (5c3), statements by and about Mill, Schopenhauer, Holbach; the represented authors also make significant points about each other.

Key

Q.v.—literally "which see," thus "refer to." Descartes (*q.v.* D7) means "refer to the 7th point under Descartes in the *Dictionary of Philosophy and Religion.*" All (*q.v.* D's) are to be so interpreted, including those to William James, on page 6 of the Preface, and to John Dewey on page 8.

Especially within the text of the Study Guide, but also in the introductions to the Readings, many *q.v.* references contain additional detail. For example, when Aristotle is mentioned, and we wish to indicate that the point is covered in the Aristotle reading, we do so by the notation (R2a1). "Aristotle (*q.v.* R2a1)" thus means *q.v.* the Reading on Aristotle, mentioned in point (2) of the Guide, representing the "a" definition of freedom, and the first selection of the readings. "Descartes (*q.v.* R2a2)" means *q.v.* the Reading on Descartes, mentioned in point 2 of the Guide, representing the "a" definition of freedom and the 2nd Reading. Since the *Dictionary of Philosophy and Religion* is considered a companion volume to the Readings, it is also desirable to refer to the *Dictionary* for supplementary material. The complete Descartes reference mentioned above in fact reads "Descartes (*q.v.* D7 and R2a2)." That instructs us to look up Descartes in two places: in the *Dictionary*, point 7 under Descartes, as well as in the 2nd reading. Such dual references are not uncommon; and of course many references take one to the *Dictionary* or Readings alone.

The Table of Contents is keyed to the various divisions of the volume as described at the end of the Introduction; hence its name, "Keyed Table of Contents." The keying between the Study Guide and Readings results from both following the structure of the Summary and Detailed Outlines. The Study Guide, in addition to considering the Readings, has sections setting the problems, evaluating the possible solutions, and coming to one's own reasonable conclusions. This being so, there are sections of the Keyed Table of Contents, *i.e.*, sections (1) and (4) through (5b), reflecting the Study Guide alone.

SG stands for "Study Guide," and R for "Reading" when a contraction is desirable.

The narrative comment preceding each reading, and between some sections, supplied by us, is always in a larger typeface than the text of the Readings.

The section notes at the end of each Reading guide the reader to the precise location of that section in the author's work. The section headings, if in italics, were supplied by the editors; if not in italics, or if in quotes, they were in the source; if in both italics and quotes, they were in the source and in italics.

All footnotes are indicated by superscript numbers, even when the author used some other convention, *e.g.*, asterisks. Our footnotes appear in the 1 to n sequence along with theirs; but ours are identifiable by "[Ed.]" following each of our footnotes. Sometimes the author's work has already received editorial attention. These original editors, or in some cases the authors themselves, offer clarifying comments, as do we. In these cases their comments, when retained, also appear in the sequence with ours; once again, ours are set apart by "[Ed.]."

Keyed
Table of Contents

(1)
Study Guide
The Problem of Personal Freedom

(1) Question. What are the extent and nature of my power to control my life?

(2) This is a problem in which we must work our way to an adequate definition of freedom before we can interpret the question. Only within the context of an adequate definition can the question be interpreted. Reference to the freedom entry in the *Dictionary* shows us that its four sections relate to four distinct definitions of freedom: (a) the ability in a moment of decision to accept any one of two or more alternatives; (b) the ability to do as one wishes; (c) acting in terms of one's inner nature; (d) doing what one ought to do. The four definitions are also featured in (2a–d) of the Summary Outline and the Keyed Table of Contents. Reference to the latter and to the Readings themselves makes it clear that well-regarded thinkers have held each of these. How, then, will the student decide on a definition? Only by working through each of the four alternatives.

(2a) Let us begin with freedom as the ability in a moment of decision to select any one of two or more alternatives. This is perhaps the most common definition of freedom. Held by many philosophers, it is infused by now into common sense.

Aristotle (*q.v.* R2a1)[1] defines voluntary actions as those whose moving principle comes from within. Since he holds that such actions are within our power we can choose to do them or not to do them. Descartes (*q.v.* D7 and

R2a2)[2] situates freedom as choice in the power of the will to extend beyond reason, enabling us to do or not to do a given thing. John Locke (*q.v.* D3 and R2a3) defines freedom as "a power to do or not to do," and finds its most likely provenance in the choosing of remote goods as ends to be pursued.

We shall center here, however, on William James' (*q.v.* D8 and R2a4) treatment of a difficulty in the first definition of freedom. Lecturing in Lowell Hall, James pointed out that upon finishing the lecture he would walk out of the Hall and face the choice of two paths to his home. He could go home by way of Oxford St. or Divinity Ave. Having made the choice of Oxford St., this first definition requires that he could just as well have chosen Divinity Ave. The first definition is considered as supposing that one's capacity to choose means that one could have done otherwise, everything remaining the same except the decision itself. James pointed out that one could prove or disprove this only if the powers governing the universe were to wipe out the ten minutes of time it took to walk home, put him back on the steps of Lowell Hall, so that he could see if he would be able this time to choose Divinity Avenue. Three problems: (1) the ten minutes can't be wiped out, therefore, (2) his second choice must always be at a later time, and under different circumstances; (3) most alternatives, perhaps not a quickly made decision to go home by way of Oxford Street but most alternatives, have careers and there is no such thing as the situation remaining the same except for the choice itself. In James' simple example the criterion governing the choice may have been "the prospect which seems most pleasant on this occasion"; but in weighty decisions there are numerous criteria in terms of which one chooses. An example which fits many of the students at SUNY-Albany is that each of them has chosen SUNYA as one alternative out of at least four. The spread of alternatives might well be:

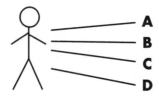

for Albany, Binghamton, Cornell, Dartmouth. Every student also has a set
of criteria governing this choice. These criteria typically include: the
school can't be too near home or too far away, it can't be too expensive, it
must have a "good reputation," and a strong department in the student's
major field. The student's grade point average must also be high enough to
be admitted. The last factor is not one of the criteria, but a circumstance.
Criteria and the circumstances of the student's life either reduce the alternative to a single one, or else two remain and the student has no clue why
s/he is at one place rather than the other. In the latter case, the student is
at SUNY-Albany rather than, *e.g.*, Binghamton by chance, not choice.

Whatever else one might want to say about this, it seems clear that in
choosing, neither James nor SUNYA students are able to show that they
could have done otherwise. James wants a pleasing walk home, and the
students want to make the best choice, given the circumstances of their
lives. In fact, the students seem in the SUNYA example to be following the
fourth definition, where freedom means doing what one ought to do, that
is, what is best for one to do. Before moving toward this definition, however, it would be well to consider the position of a philosopher who
believes that the amount of first-definition freedom we possess is virtually
unlimited. The philosopher is Jean-Paul Sartre (*q.v.* D1–2 and R2a5). The
argument has many facets; but its central thought is that our first definition
freedom is awesome in extent, because we not only choose among possibilities, but also create the possibilities among which we choose.

(2b) Given the difficulties of the first definition many philosophers
shift to the second definition, in which freedom means doing what one
wants to do. Hobbes (*q.v.* D2 and R2b1) defines freedom as the absence of
opposition which, he further says, exists when one is not hindered from
doing what one has the will to do. In his view, and that of others with this
position, "liberty, and necessity are consistent." Voltaire (*q.v.* D4 and R2b2)
gives the same hard-edged interpretation of this definition, saying we can
do what we choose, but what we choose we choose necessarily. He has
made the definition compatible with determinism (*q.v.* D and R5c3). The
term, compatibilism, has appeared to name this hard-edged version. Hume
(*q.v.* D4 and R2b3) states clearly that freedom (he, too, uses "liberty")
should be contrasted with restraint, although compatible with necessity.
His psychological notion of necessity and his skepticism suggest that

Hume (*q.v.* D2–3, 7) should say that we don't know that everything is physically determined (although it may be). We do know when constraints prevent us from doing things we want to do, and when we are able to do them.
In this way the problem of freedom can avoid the metaphysical level and
become an empirical problem. We have some freedom because we can
sometimes do what we wish. We lack some freedom because sometimes we
can't. The mixture would vary with the individuals concerned. Edwards
(*q.v.* D3 and R2b4) takes the hard-edged view theologically, so that it is
compatible with predestination.

On the second definition we have some freedom. But should Voltaire
(and Laplace, *q.v.* D3 and R5c1) be correct, and everything in fact be determined, then we have been shaped by the world to do what we want to do,
and appear to move through life as robots. That possibility might direct
one to the third definition.

(2c) If the specter of being a robot determined by the outer world is
unattractive, the third definition of freedom, acting in terms of one's inner,
or real, or essential, nature may be more appealing. We are sometimes told
to "be natural, be yourself." If there are ways of behaving which are "natural" to one, if there is a self for one to be, then acting from internal
sources may be a preferred definition of freedom. Philosophers from Aristotle to Hegel (*q.v.* D Freedom 16–20) speak of a basic nature which is what
we are. We sample this rich vein, referring first to the Stoic philosopher
Epictetus (*q.v.* D and R2c1), for whom freedom is complete independence.
Such independence is to be found in following one's inner reason. There
are other aspects of the position, including the presence of a universal
reason in nature, and a destiny for one's life. Second, there is Spinoza (*q.v.*
D9 and R2c2) for whom freedom consists in following the guidance of
one's reason. The view grants necessity, and ends in the blessedness of the
wise man "scarcely at all disturbed in spirit." Hegel (*q.v.* D10, 17; and R2c3)
finds freedom in the independent consciousness, taking many forms in its
development through the ages, and finally appearing as the Absolute
Spirit, inclusive of us and our striving.

For the third definition we can perhaps take as canonical Nietzsche's
(*q.v.* D6 and R2c4) description in *Ecce Homo*, coming at the end of the
Romantic age. You are a self in two senses. In the first place you are all the
things your culture has determined that you be, including the herd

morality which (in Nietzsche's view) had shaped all of Europe. This is one's empirical (or phenomenal) self. There is also a potential self, which exists in the depths of one's nature. What Nietzsche wants us to do is separate ourselves from conventional society in order to feel our own feelings and think our own thoughts. Nietzsche doesn't tell us there is an optimal time when such critical appraisal can occur, but of course there is—as one approaches the age of accountability. He does tell us that in such reappraisal "the idea which is destined to be master," which has grown and continues to grow in the depths, begins to command. On this definition one is free when the potential self, which is your inner nature, is allowed to actualize. The conception fits much of the language of freedom such as the desirability of our being inner-directed, and of self-determination. Note, too, however, that while he sometimes uses the language of choice (selections 8 and 9) in describing this alternative, he most often (sections 10–17) opposes "freedom of the will" as an error, and opts for (section 16) a view of eternal return.

If there is evidence for an *Ecce Homo* potential self which is one's inner nature, the further question is whether it can be related to the first definition freedom of sections 8 and 9, and separated from the eternal return of section 16. The inner nature view could be related to our having capacities from birth—intellectual, manual, musical, etc.—whose development actualizes something which is one's birthright. If these capacities can be said to be the origin of an inner self then one could argue that in addition to inputs from the outer world there can be an internal input, and that the claim of self-determination makes good sense. In the twentieth century one would have to answer Freud's (*q.v.* D3–4 and Self volume) challenge that the unconscious consists of conscious experiences now repressed, and B. F. Skinner's (*q.v.* D1 and R2c5) view that every output of the psyche is the sum of all the inputs. Notice that Skinner, while essentially second definition determinist, does grant in the first section of his reading that one feels happier and freer when one's genetic endowment is brought into play. That is very close to the third definition view, when potential self is taken as one's set of capacities. Also, one might consider a fact running through all of these views that a first definition choice keeps struggling to the surface.

For Epictetus and Spinoza one will follow one's inner reason or not; for Hegel one will seek to have an independent consciousness or not. For

Nietzsche one will be one's phenomenal self, or encourage one's potential self. For Skinner there is the life not allowing exercise of one's genetic endowments, and the life that does. Since the latter is in every case preferable, is there not some kind of presumption that one can elect it? If so, that would undermine the claim made for the Skinner box that output is the sum of the inputs; for now it is possible to add to the mix an input which comes from inside oneself, from one's inner nature. In the case where this inner factor is decisive we are self-determined.

Daisetz Suzuki (*q.v.* D3–6 and R2c6) interprets freedom as gaining self-knowledge. That achievement is freedom from bondage, self-realization, or *satori* (*q.v.* D) in the language of Zen Buddhism. This is self-realization in the fullest sense, including fulfillment of our creative capacities.

(2d) The fourth definition holds we are free when doing what we ought to do. One could perhaps derive this fourth definition from the third by arguing that when it is possible to follow our inner nature we ought to do so. This seems to be the case. We can come to this by noting that from the eternal standpoint, that of God, freedom is going to mean doing what ought to be done. So claimed St. Augustine (*q.v.* D12 and R2d1), and the argument is worth considering. God would have no interest in doing other than he has done since he always chooses the good. Augustine didn't discuss the second and third meanings of freedom; but clearly on Augustine's terms the good is what God would always want to do, and precisely that would also reflect his inner nature. He also argues that God's foreknowledge is compatible with this definition of freedom. Thomas Aquinas (*q.v.* D3 and R2d3) accepts the position of St. Augustine. While basically fourth definition, his position allows validity to the other definitions as well. In this connection St. Anselm's (*q.v.* R2d2) powerful argument for freedom as rectitude of will should not be ignored. A simpler version of the fourth definition is that of Governor John Winthrop (*q.v.* R2d4) of Massachusetts who in 1645 held that the ability to do as one pleases is a "natural corrupt liberty . . . common to man [and] beasts," while moral liberty, the liberty to do what is "good, just, and honest" is the only liberty worth taking seriously. He also believed such liberty came from faith in Christ. Religious associations aside, when it comes to human beings the argument is less straight forward, but nonetheless more or less present. A final version of the fourth definition is that of Montesquieu (*q.v.* D9 and R2d5) who defined freedom as "doing what we ought to will," while identifying this "ought" with what the laws oblige. Notice that when we explored the first definition it turned out that smaller choices tended to follow the second definition, but in significant choices we establish criteria for choosing in order to end up with the alternative which will best serve our purposes, and this means our goal is what is best for us. Significant choice, in other words, is governed by some version of the fourth definition.

(3) In gaining one's own adequate definition of freedom you may want to recognize an overlap in these definitions.

(3a) You may want to avoid claiming that the first definition requires being able to do otherwise, everything being the same except the choice itself. You may wish to relate definitions (1) and (4), and think of choice as the use of reason to reach the best decision. Dewey (*q.v.* D7) did so, while also stressing the third definition.

(3b) On the other hand, you may think the first definition so fundamental that you want it to remain central. If you have an analysis, or case, which shows you can do otherwise, produce it and that may provide direct support for the first definition. Ethics seems to suppose that when we say an individual should not have done a certain thing s/he could at that moment have avoided doing it. Similarly, epistemology seems to suppose that when we say an individual has discovered some truth, we do not believe this person was driven by forces beyond his or her control to accept a given proposition. If our example is Einstein developing the theory of relativity, we believe on the one hand that he was subject to all of the influences playing upon him, but we do not believe that his final theory was the output dictated by the sum of those influences. Instead, we believe that Einstein could accept or reject possible hypotheses at every point on the basis of reasonable criteria. Dewey's (see (3a) above) view that freedom is the ability to make intelligent choices may require some first-definition freedom in just this sense. By way of contrast, we do believe that some individuals are driven by irrational influences, and do not exhibit the capacity of reasoned choice to any marked degree. Similarly, to take an example from another field, in aesthetic creativity we believe the artist, Beethoven for example, is in control, and makes his choices on the basis of aesthetic ideals, not driven by influence and circumstance alone, or in large part. C. A. Campbell (*q.v.* R3e1, sec. 2 and (3d) below) identifies free will with creative activity. Since creative activity brings something novel into being it may not be subject to the determining influence of the established world. Perhaps you want to argue that if ethics, epistemology, and aesthetics require first definition freedom, that is reason enough to accept it. This would be indirect but, possibly, powerful support.

(3c) If that is what you want, while having in your philosophy an omniscient God, there is another problem. If God knows the total future, including every detail of your future life, then when you arrive at the point where that detail becomes actual, there would seem to be no question of your doing otherwise. How could one do something other than what God knows you will do? At least, you need to explain how you can be free in the first definition when God knew at the beginning of the world all of these details (*q.v.* D Omniscience; Hartshorne 5; Socinus 4). St. Augustine (R2d1, sec. 1) argues that God's foreknowledge does not deprive us of free will. St. Thomas Aquinas (*q.v.* D4) agrees with St. Augustine on this point as on many others.

(3d) At the end of his essay C. A. Campbell cites the instance of the internal clash between the strongest desire and what one recognizes as one's duty. His point is that one's character, as so far formed, is to follow one's strongest desire, yet one also senses one can rise to duty. From our standpoint this is a conflict between second definition freedom, doing what one wants to do, and fourth-definition freedom, doing what one senses one ought to do. The conflict looks very much like a first-definition choice between the two. Compare this to the empirical/potential self distinction in (2c) above.

(3e) Similarly, third definition freedom supposes a conflict between the desire of our inner nature (*q.v.* (3c) above), and what the world around wishes for us. Once again, it is one's inner sense that it is possible to stand against the world, but often more comfortable to let the world have its way. Here it seems that within third definition freedom there is a first definition choice which can go either way, and sometimes goes first one way and then the other.

(3f) You may find ways to combine other of these definitions. We have already suggested that in choosing an alternative according to criteria you are using the fourth definition, as well as a revised first definition. But will not what you choose also be what you want to do (the second definition), and might it not also reflect your inner nature (third definition) in case, of course, you can show you have an inner nature?

(4) Once you have the definition of freedom which satisfies all the objections you can see, it is time to restate the question about the amount of freedom, if any, you have to control your life. This question now allows us to state the alternative positions among which you have to decide: Either you have (a) a vast amount of freedom, (b) a limited amount of freedom, or (c) no freedom at all.

(5) You have to evaluate these alternatives in relation to your life. Does your life feel free according to your definition?

(5a) If you opt for a vast amount of freedom, you are agreeing with Jean-Paul Sartre (*q.v.* D1–2 and R2a5) who subscribed to this view, or perhaps Descartes (*q.v.* D7 and R2a2), for whom freedom was substantial. But it would be inconsistent to claim a vast amount of freedom in your life, but be unable to point to any decisions you have made which reflect your individuality, or the power of your will to stand against peer pressure, or break addictive habits (maintain a diet, interrupt a chemical dependence, stop smoking, establish a new lifestyle).

(5b) If you opt for freedom, but feel a substantial weight of influence, circumstance, accumulated habit, chance happenings, and even established set purposes (no longer subject to review), it may be that you will wish to hold to a view of real but limited freedom in your life, and perhaps in human life generally.

(5c) If you feel that you have no control over your life, but that everything is determined, there is point in exploring the nature of the determinism which you sense. If you sense a causal determinism, the view of Laplace (*q.v.* D3 and R5c1) may be what you have in mind. He posits a hypothetical superhuman intelligence, able to know the position and velocity of every particle in the universe. As a result nothing, either past or future, would be hidden from its eyes. If you think in terms of reasons as well as causes, holding that nothing happens without a reason, then the view of Spinoza (*q.v.* D8–9 and R2c2, esp. sec. 3) may accord with your point of view. A modern version of determinism, both mechanical and rational, is that of Brand Blanshard (*q.v.* D2 and R5c2). If the determining agent is God, then *q.v.* D predestination and Jonathan Edwards (D3). The reading from Jonathan Edwards (*q.v.* R2b4, esp. secs. 3 and 4) explores this position. Paul Edwards (*q.v.* R5c3) discusses the distinction between hard and soft determinism, claiming that only the former has any clarity.

NOTES

1. For "*q.v.* Readings, 2a1." The convention will be followed throughout.

2. For "*q.v.* Dictionary 7, and Readings 2a2." The convention will be followed throughout.

(2)
Selected Readings
for Personal Freedom

Freedom as the ability in a moment of decision to select any one of two or more alternatives

(2a1)
Aristotle
384–322 B.C.E.

Nicomachean Ethics
bk. 3, ch. 1–3, *The Basic Works of Aristotle*

For Aristotle freedom is to be found in voluntary actions, *i.e.*, those whose moving principle is in the agent himself. Choice is voluntary, and generally relates to what is within one's power. He finally defines it as "deliberate desire of things within our power." The implication is that within the range of the voluntary we can do or not do a given thing, although the other definitions, especially the third, are also involved.

THE VOLUNTARY AND CHOICE

Ch. 1. Since virtue is concerned with passions and actions, and on voluntary passions and actions praise and blame are bestowed, on those that are involuntary pardon, and sometimes also pity, to distinguish the voluntary and the involuntary is presumably necessary for those who are studying the nature of virtue, and useful also for legislators with a view to the assigning both of honors and of punishments.

Those things, then, are thought involuntary, which take place under compulsion or owing to ignorance; and that is compulsory of which the moving principle is outside, being a principle in which nothing is contributed by the person who is acting or is feeling the passion, e.g., if he were to be carried somewhere by a wind, or by men who had him in their power.

But with regard to the things that are done from fear of greater evils or for some noble object (e.g., if a tyrant were to order one to do something base, having one's parents and children in his power, and if one did the action they were to be saved, but otherwise would be put to death), it may be debated whether such actions are involuntary or voluntary. Something of the sort happens also with regard to the throwing of goods overboard in a storm; for in the abstract no one throws goods away voluntarily, but on condition of its securing the safety of himself and his crew any sensible man does so. Such actions, then, are mixed, but are more like voluntary actions; for they are worthy of choice at the time when they are done, and the end of an action is relative to the occasion. Both the terms, then, 'voluntary' and 'involuntary', must be used with reference to the moment of action. Now the man acts voluntarily; for the principle that moves the instrumental parts of the body in such actions is in him, and the things of which the moving principle is in a man himself are in his power to do or not to do. Such actions, therefore, are voluntary, but in the abstract perhaps involuntary; for no one would choose any such act in itself.

For such actions men are sometimes even praised, when they endure something base or painful in return for great and noble objects gained; in the opposite case they are blamed, since to endure the greatest indignities for no noble end or for a trifling end is the mark of an inferior person. On some actions praise indeed is not bestowed, but pardon is, when one does what he ought not under pressure which overstrains human nature and which no one could withstand. But some acts, perhaps, we cannot be forced to do, but ought rather to face death after the most fearful sufferings; for the things that 'forced' Euripides' Alcmaeon to slay his mother seem absurd. It is difficult sometimes to determine what should be chosen at what cost, and what should be endured in return for what gain, and yet more difficult to abide by our decisions; for as a rule what is expected is painful, and what we are forced to do is base, whence praise and blame are bestowed on those who have been compelled or have not.

What sort of acts, then, should be called compulsory? We answer that without qualification actions are so when the cause is in the external circumstances and the agent contributes nothing. But the things that in themselves are involuntary, but now and in return for these gains are worthy of choice, and whose moving principle is in the agent, are in themselves involuntary, but now and in return for these gains voluntary. They are more like voluntary acts; for actions are in the class of particulars, and the particular acts here are voluntary. What sort of things are to be chosen, and in return for what, it is not easy to state; for there are many differences in the particular cases.

But if some one were to say that pleasant and noble objects have a compelling power, forcing us from without, all acts would be for him compulsory; for it is for these objects that all men do everything they do. And those who act under compulsion and unwillingly act with pain, but those who do acts for their pleasantness and nobility do them with pleasure; it is absurd to make external circumstances responsible, and not oneself, as being easily caught by such attractions, and to make oneself responsible for noble acts but the pleasant objects responsible for base acts. The compulsory, then, seems to be that whose moving principle is outside, the person compelled contributing nothing.

Everything that is done by reason of ignorance is *not* voluntary; it is only what produces pain and repentance that is *in*voluntary. For the man who has done something owing to ignorance, and feels not the least vexation at his action, has not acted voluntarily, since he did not know what he was doing, nor yet involuntarily, since he is not pained. Of people, then, who act by reason of ignorance, he who repents is thought an involuntary agent, and the man who does not repent may, since he is different, be called a not voluntary agent; for, since he differs from the other, it is better that he should have a name of his own.

Acting by reason of ignorance seems also to be different from acting *in* ignorance; for the man who is drunk or in a rage is thought to act as a result not of ignorance but of one of the causes mentioned, yet not knowingly but in ignorance.

Now every wicked man is ignorant of what he ought to do and what he ought to abstain from, and it is by reason of error of this kind that men become unjust and in general bad; but the term 'involuntary' tends to be used not if a man is ignorant of what is to his advantage—for it is not mistaken purpose that causes involuntary action (it leads rather to wickedness), nor ignorance of the universal (for *that* men are *blamed*), but ignorance of particulars, i.e., of the circumstances of the action and the objects with which it is concerned. For it is on these that both pity and pardon depend, since the person who is ignorant of any of these acts involuntarily.

Perhaps it is just as well, therefore, to determine their nature and number: A man may be ignorant, then, of who he is, what he is doing, what or whom he is acting on, and sometimes also what (e.g., what instrument) he is doing it with, and to what end (e.g., he may think his act will conduce to some one's safety), and how he is doing it (e.g., whether gently or violently). Now of all of these no one could be ignorant unless he were mad, and evidently also he could not be ignorant of the agent; for how could he not know himself? But of what he is doing a man might be ignorant, as for instance people say 'it slipped out of their mouths as they were speaking,' or 'they did not know it was a secret,' as Aeschylus said of the mysteries, or a man might say he 'let it go off when he merely wanted to show its working,' as the man did with the catapult. Again, one might think one's son was an enemy, as Merope did, or that a pointed spear had a button on it, or that a stone was pumice-stone; or one might give a man a draught to save him, and really kill him; or one might want to touch a man, as people do in sparring, and really wound him. The ignorance may relate, then, to any of these things, i.e., of the circumstances of the action, and the man who was ignorant of any of these is thought to have acted involuntarily, and especially if he was ignorant on the most important points; and these are thought to be the circumstances of the action and its end. Further, the doing of an act that is called involuntary in virtue of ignorance of this sort must be painful and involve repentance.

Since that which is done under compulsion or by reason of ignorance is involuntary, the voluntary would seem to be that of which the moving principle is in the agent himself, he being aware of the particular circumstances of the action. Presumably acts done by reason of anger or appetite are not rightly called involuntary.[1] For in the first place, on that showing none of the other animals will act voluntarily, nor will children; and secondly, is it meant that we do not do voluntarily *any* of the acts that are due to appetite or anger, or that we do the noble acts voluntarily and the base acts involuntarily? Is not this absurd, when one and the same thing is the cause? But it would surely be odd to describe as involuntary the things one ought to desire; and we ought both to be angry at certain things and to have an appetite for certain things, e.g., for health and for learning. Also what is involuntary is thought to be painful, but what is in accordance with appetite is thought to be pleasant. Again, what is the difference in respect of involuntariness between errors committed upon calculation and those committed in anger? Both are to be avoided, but the irrational passions are thought not less human than reason is, and therefore also the actions which proceed from anger or appetite are the man's actions. It would be odd, then, to treat them as involuntary.

Ch. 2. Both the voluntary and the involuntary having been delimited, we must next discuss choice; for it is thought to be most closely bound up with virtue and to discriminate characters better than actions do.

Choice, then, seems to be voluntary, but not the same thing as the voluntary; the latter extends more widely. For both children and the lower animals share in voluntary action, but not in choice, and acts done on the spur of the moment we describe as voluntary, but not as chosen.

Those who say it is appetite or anger or wish or a kind of opinion do not seem to be right. For choice is not common to irrational creatures as well, but appetite and anger are. Again, the incontinent man acts with appetite, but not with choice; while the continent man on the contrary acts with choice, but not with appetite. Again, appetite is contrary to choice, but not appetite to appetite. Again, appetite relates to the pleasant and the painful, choice neither to the painful nor to the pleasant.

Still less is it anger; for acts due to anger are thought to be less than any others objects of choice.

But neither is it wish, though it seems near to it; for choice cannot relate to impossibles, and if any one said he chose them he would be thought silly; but there may be a wish even for impossibles, e.g., for immortality. And wish may relate to things that could in no way be brought about by one's own efforts, e.g., that a particular actor or athlete should win in a competition; but no one chooses such things, but only the things that he thinks could be brought about by his own efforts. Again, wish relates rather to the end, choice to the means; for instance, we wish to be healthy, but we choose the acts which will make us healthy, and we wish to be happy and say we do, but we cannot well say we choose to be so; for, in general, choice seems to relate to the things that are in our own power.

For this reason, too, it cannot be opinion; for opinion is thought to relate to all kinds of things, no less to eternal things and impossible things than to things in our own power; and it is distinguished by its falsity or truth, not by its badness or goodness, while choice is distinguished rather by these.

Now with opinion in general perhaps no one even says it is identical. But it is not identical even with any kind of opinion; for by choosing what is good or bad we are men of a certain character, which we are not by holding certain opinions. And we choose to get or avoid something good or bad, but we have opinions about what a thing is or whom it is good for or how it is good for him; we can hardly be said to opine to get or avoid anything. And choice is praised for being related to the right object rather than for being rightly related to it, opinion for being truly related to its object. And we choose what we best know to be good, but we opine what we do not quite know; and it is not the same people that are thought to make the best choices and to have the best opinions, but some are thought to have fairly good opinions, but by reason of vice to choose what they should not. If opinion precedes choice or accompanies it, that makes no difference; for it is not this that we are considering, but whether it is *identical* with some kind of opinion.

What, then, or what kind of thing is it, since it is none of the things we have mentioned? It seems to be voluntary, but not all that is voluntary to be an object of choice. Is it, then, what has been decided on by previous deliberation? At any rate choice involves a rational principle and thought. Even the name seems to suggest that it is what is chosen before other things.

Ch. 3. Do we deliberate about everything, and is everything a possible subject of deliberation, or is deliberation impossible about some things? We ought presumably to call not what a fool or a madman would deliberate about, but what a sensible man would deliberate about, a subject of deliberation. Now about eternal things no one deliberates, e.g., about the material universe or the incommensurability of the diagonal and the side of a square. But no more do we deliberate about the things that involve movement but always happen in the same way, whether of necessity or by nature or from any other cause, e.g., the solstices and the risings of the stars; nor about things that happen now in one way, now in another, e.g., droughts and rains; nor about chance events, like the finding of treasure. But we do not deliberate even about all human affairs; for instance, no Spartan deliberates about the best constitution for the Scythians. For none of these things can be brought about by our own efforts.

We deliberate about things that are in our power and can be done; and these are in fact what is left. For nature, necessity, and chance are thought to be causes, and also reason and everything that depends on man. Now every class of men deliberates about the things that can be done by their own efforts. And in the case of exact and self-contained sciences there is no deliberation, e.g., about the letters of the alphabet (for we have no doubt how they should be written); but the things that are brought about by our own efforts, but not always in the same way, are the things about which we deliberate, e.g., questions of medical treatment or of money-making. And we do so more in the case of the art of navigation than in that of gymnastics, inasmuch as it has been less exactly worked out, and again about other things in the same ratio, and more also in the case of the arts than in that of the sciences; for we have more doubt about the former. Deliberation is concerned with things that happen in a certain way for the most part, but in which the event is obscure, and with things in which it is indeterminate. We call in others to aid us in deliberation on important questions, distrusting ourselves as not being equal to deciding.

We deliberate not about ends but about means. For a doctor does not deliberate whether he shall heal, nor an orator whether he shall persuade, nor a statesman whether he shall produce law and order, nor does any one else deliberate about his end. They assume the end and consider how and by what means it is to be attained; and if it seems to be produced by several means they consider by which it is most easily and best produced, while if it is achieved by one only they consider how it will be achieved by this and by what means *this* will be achieved, till they come to the first cause, which in the order of discovery is last. For the person who deliberates seems to investigate and analyze in the way described as though he were analyzing a geometrical construction[2] (not all investigation appears to be deliberation—for instance mathematical investigations—but all deliberation is investigation), and what is last in the order of analysis seems to be first in the order of becoming. And if we come on an impossibility, we give up the search, e.g., if we need money and this cannot be got; but if a thing appears possible we try to do it. By 'possible' things I mean things that might be brought about by our own efforts; and these in a sense include things that can be brought about by the efforts of our friends, since the moving principle is in ourselves. The subject of investigation is sometimes the instruments, sometimes the use of them; and similarly in the other cases—sometimes the means, sometimes the mode of using it or the means of bringing it about. It seems, then, as has been said, that man is a moving principle of actions; now deliberation is about the things to be done by the agent himself, and actions are for the sake of things other than themselves. For the end cannot be a subject of deliberation, but only the means; nor indeed can the particular facts be a subject of it, as whether this is bread or has been baked as it should; for these are matters of perception. If we are to be always deliberating, we shall have to go on to infinity.

The same thing is deliberated upon and is chosen, except that the object of choice is already determinate, since it is that which has been decided upon as a result of deliberation that is the object of choice. For every one ceases to inquire how he is to act when he has brought the moving principle back to himself and to the ruling part of himself; for this is what chooses. This is plain also from the ancient constitutions, which Homer represented; for the kings announced their choices to the people. The object of choice being one of the things in our own power which is desired after deliberation, choice will be deliberate desire of things in our own power; for when we have decided as a result of deliberation, we desire in accordance with our deliberation.

We may take it, then, that we have described choice in outline, and stated the nature of its objects and the fact that it is concerned with means.

NOTES

1. A reference to Plato *Laws* 863 B, ff., where anger and appetite are coupled with ignorance as sources of wrong action.

2 Aristotle has in mind the method of discovering the solution of a geometrical problem. The problem being to construct a figure of a certain kind, we suppose it constructed and then analyze it to see if there is some figure by constructing which we can construct the required figure, and so on till we come to a figure which our existing knowledge enables us to construct.

[Aristotle, *Nicomachean Ethics*, bk. 3, ch. 1–3, *The Basic Works of Aristotle*, ed. R. Mckeon (New York: Random House, 1941). (1) Pp. 964–71.]

René Descartes

1596–1650

Descartes' Philosophical Writings
Meditation IV, pp. 215–21

Descartes locates freedom in the power of the will to do a thing or not to do it "with no feeling of being constrained" by any external force. In this matter "the strong light of understanding" and a "strong inclination of the will" work together.

THE WILL MORE AMPLE THAN THE UNDERSTANDING

(1) . . . on regarding myself more closely, and on examining what are my errors (for they alone testify to there being imperfection in me), I find that they depend on two concurrent causes, on my power of knowing and on the power of choice, that is, of free will—in other words, on the cooperation of the understanding and the will. For by the understanding alone, I neither affirm nor deny anything, but merely apprehend the ideas of things I can affirm or deny. Viewing the understanding thus precisely, we can say that no error is ever to be found in it. And although there may be an infinity of things in the world of which I have in my understanding no ideas, we cannot on this account say that it is deprived of those ideas as of something which its nature requires, but only that it does not have them, there being indeed no sufficient proof that God ought to have given me a greater power of knowing than He has given me. However skilled an arti-

ficer I represent Him to be, I have no reason to think of Him as bound to place in each of His works all the perfections which He can place in some of them. Nor again can I complain that God has not given me a will ample and perfect, that is, a free will. I am conscious of a will so extended as to be subject to no limits. What here, as it seems to me, is truly noteworthy, is that of all the other things which are in me, no one is so perfect and so extensive that I do not recognize it as allowing of being yet greater and more perfect. To take, for example, my faculty of understanding, I at once recognize it as being in me of small extent and extremely limited; and at the same time I frame the idea of another faculty, much more extended and even infinite; and from this alone, that I can represent the latter, idea in this way [i.e., as being a faculty that is infinite],[1] I have no difficulty in likewise recognizing that it pertains to the nature of God. If in the same way I examine my memory, my imagination, or any other of my faculties, I do not find any which is not in me small and circumscribed, and in God infinite. Free will alone, that is liberty of choice, do I find to be so great in me that I can entertain no idea of any such power possibly greater, so that it is chiefly my will which enables me to know that I bear a certain image and similitude of God. The power of will is indeed incomparably greater in God than in man; the knowledge and the potency which in God are conjoined with it, render it more constant and more efficacious, and in respect of its object extend it to a greater number of things; nevertheless it does not seem to be greater, considered formally and precisely in itself [i.e., as a faculty]. The power of will consists solely in this, that we have the power to do a thing or not to do it (that is to say, to affirm or to deny, to pursue or to shun it), or rather in this alone, that in affirming or denying, pursuing or shunning, what is proposed to us by the understanding, we so act that we have no feeling of being constrained to it by any external force. For in order to be free it is not necessary that I should be indifferent in the choice between alternatives; on the contrary, the more I am inclined toward one of them, whether because I approve it as evidently good and true, or because God in this inward manner determines my inward thinking, the more freely do I choose and embrace it. Divine grace and natural knowledge, so far from diminishing liberty, augment and confirm it. The indifference of which I am aware when for want of a reason I am not carried to one side rather than to another, is the lowest grade of liberty, testifying to a lack of knowledge, i.e., to a certain negation, not to a perfection in the will. Were the true and the good always clear to me, I should never need to deliberate as to what I ought to judge or choose, and I should thus be entirely free, without ever being indifferent.

All this enables me to recognize that the power of will which I have received from God is not of itself the cause of my errors; in its kind it is altogether ample and perfect. Nor is the cause of my errors traceable to my power of understanding or thinking; for since I understand nothing save by the power of understanding which God has given me, undoubtedly all that I apprehend I apprehend rightly, and it is impossible that I should be deceived regarding it. What then is the source of my errors? This alone, that the will is of wider range than the understanding, and that I do not restrain it within the same limits as the understanding, but extend it to things which I do not understand; and as the will is of itself, in respect of such things, indifferent, it is easily deflected from the true and the good, and readily falls into error and sin, choosing the evil in place of the good, or the false in place of the true.

For example, in our recent inquiry as to whether there is any existing world, finding that inasmuch as this inquiry is being made by me it manifestly follows that I myself exist, I could not but judge to be true what I thus clearly apprehend—not that I was forced to do so by any external power, but simply because the strong light of understanding was followed by a strong inclination of the will. My act of belief was thus the more spontaneous and free in proportion as I was the less indifferent in the matter. But not only do I know that I exist inasmuch as I am a thinking thing; there is likewise present to my mind a certain idea of corporeal nature, and I thereupon find myself doubting whether this thinking nature which is in me, or rather by which I am what I am, differs from this corporeal nature, or whether both are not one and the same thing. In so doing I am supposing that I do not as yet know of any reason which should persuade me to give preference to one view over the other. Certainly, in such circumstances, it is a matter of indifference to me which of the two I affirm or deny, or even as to whether I form any judgment at all on this issue.

Moreover this indifference extends not only to things regarding which the understanding has no knowledge, but in general to all those which are not known quite perspicuously at the moment when the will is deliberating upon them; for however probable the conjectures which dispose me to judge in a particular manner, the very awareness that they are only conjectures, and not certain and indubitable reasons, is sufficient to impel me to judge them in the directly opposite manner. I have of late had considerable experience of this, setting aside as false all that I had hitherto unquestioningly held, and doing so for no other reason than that I had come to be aware that they could in some degree be doubted.

Now if I abstain from all judging of a thing which I do not apprehend sufficiently clearly and distinctly, it is evident that I am acting rightly and am not deceived. Should I, on the other hand, decide to deny or affirm, I am not in that case making a right use of my free will, and should I in so deciding choose the wrong alternative, it is evident that I am deceived. Even should I decide for what is true, it is by chance only that I shall be doing so, and still shall not be free from the fault of misusing my freedom. The natural light teaches us that knowledge, by way of the understanding, ought always to precede the determination of the will; and it is in the failure to do so that the privation, which constitutes the form of error, consists. Privation is then, I say, there in the act, in so far as it proceeds from me; it is not to be found in the faculty as I have it from God, nor even in the act in so far as it depends on Him [through His continued upholding of me in existence].

Nor have I any ground for complaint that God has not given me a greater power of understanding or a natural light stronger than that which He has actually given, since it is of the very nature of a finite understanding not to apprehend all things, and of a created understanding to be finite. Having every reason to render thanks to God who owes me nothing, and who has yet given me all the perfections I possess, I should be far from thinking Him to have been unjust in depriving me of, or in keeping back, the other perfections which He has not given me.

Nor have I ground to complain in that He has given me a will more ample than my understanding. Since the will consists entire in one single thing, and is, so to speak, indivisible, it would appear that its nature is such that nothing can be taken from it without destroying it; and certainly the more ample it is, the more reason I have to be grateful.

Nor, finally, ought I to complain that God concurs with me in framing those [wrongful] acts of the will, that is to say, the judgments in which I suffer deception. In so far as they depend on God they are entirely true and good and my ability to form them is, in its own way, a greater perfection in me than if I were unable to do so. The privation in which alone the formal [i.e., actual] reason of error or sin consists has no need of concurrence from God since it is not a thing; and if referred to God as to its cause, it ought (in conformity with the usage of the Schools)[2] to be entitled negation, not privation. For it is not in truth an imperfection in God that He has given me the freedom of assenting or not assenting to things of which He has not placed a clear and distinct knowledge in my understanding. On the other hand, unquestionably, it is an imperfection in me that I do not use this freedom aright, rashly passing judgment on things which I apprehend only obscurely and confusedly. I recognize, indeed, that God could easily have so created me that, while still remaining free and while still with only limited knowledge, I should yet not err, viz., by endowing my understanding with a clear and distinct knowledge of all the things upon which I shall ever have to deliberate, or simply by so deeply engraving on my memory the resolution never to pass judgment on anything of which I have no clear and distinct understanding, that I shall never lose hold on that resolution. And I easily understand that in so far as I consider myself alone, as if in the world there were only myself, I should have been much more perfect than I now am, had God created me in that fashion. But this does not justify me in refusing to recognize that in respect of the universe as a whole it is a greater perfection that certain of its parts should not be exempt from defect than that they should all be exactly alike. And I have, therefore, no right to complain because God, in placing me in the world, has not willed to assign me the nobler, more perfect role. If He has not done so by the first of the means above noted, that which would depend on my having a clear and evident knowledge of all the things upon which I may have to deliberate, at least He has left within my power the other means, viz., that of firmly adhering to the resolution never to pass judgment on things not clearly known to me. For although I am aware of a certain weakness in my nature which prevents me from continuously concentrating my mind on any one thought, I can yet by attentive and oft-repeated meditation so imprint it on my memory that I shall never fail to recall it as often as I have need of it, and so can acquire the habit of not erring.

Inasmuch as it is in this habit that the highest and chief perfection of man consists, I have, I consider, gained not a little by this day's meditation, discovering, as I have done, the cause of error and falsity. Certainly there can be no other cause than that which I have now explained; for so long as I so restrain my will within the limits of my knowledge that it frames no judgment save on things which are clearly and distinctly apprehended by the understanding, I can never be deceived. Since all clear and distinct awareness is undoubtedly something, it cannot owe its origin to nothing, and must of necessity have God as its author—God, I say, who being supremely perfect, cannot be the cause of any error. Consequently, as we have to conclude, all such awareness is true. Nor have I today learned merely what, to escape error, I should avoid, but also what I must do to arrive at knowledge of the truth. Such knowledge is assured to me provided I direct my attention sufficiently to those things which I perfectly understand, separating them from those which I apprehend only confusedly and obscurely. To this task I shall, from now on, give diligent heed.

NOTES

1. Cf. Descartes' Reply to Burman (*A.T.* v, p. 158; Adam's edition, p. 46).
2. Added in French version.

[René Descartes, *Meditations*, from *Descartes' Philosophical Writings*, sel. and trans., N. K. Smith (New York: The Modern Library, a division of Random House, 1958). (1) Meditation IV, pp. 215–21.]

(2a3)

John Locke

1632–1704

An Essay Concerning Human Understanding
vol. I, bk. II, ch XXI, sec. 57

Locke gives two somewhat different statements of the first definition, one in the first edition of his *Essay, q.v.* (1) immediately below, where he stresses the remoteness of the goal; the other in the second edition, *q.v.* (2) below. The discussion of indifferency appears in a French version of the *Essay.* Some had argued that freedom required one to be indifferent to one's motives as well as one's understanding. Since that idea put liberty "in a state of darkness," Locke searches for an intelligible use of indifferency. He finds it in the indifference of one's "operative power" to whether or not the will orders one's hand to move or rest. He also calls on the help of the philosophical community to "clear" the subject from any difficulties he has not removed.

OF LIBERTY AND POWER

(1) Liberty, it is plain, consists in a power to do, or not to do; to do, or forbear doing, *as we will.* This cannot be denied But this seeming to comprehend only the actions of a man consecutive to volition, it is further inquired,—Whether he be at liberty to will or no? And to this it has been answered, that, in most cases, a man is not at liberty to forbear the act of volition: he must exert an act of his will, whereby the action proposed is

53

made to exist or not to exist. But yet there is a case wherein a man is at liberty in respect of willing; and that is the choosing of a *remote* good as an end to be pursued. Here a man may *suspend* the act of his choice from being determined for or against the thing proposed, till he has examined whether it be really of a nature, in itself and consequences, to make him happy or not. For, when he has once chosen it, and thereby it is become a part of his happiness, it raises desire, and that proportionably gives him uneasiness; which determines his will, and sets him at work in pursuit of his choice on all occasions that offer. And here we may see how it comes to pass that a man may justly incur punishment, though it be certain that, in all the particular actions that he wills, he does, and necessarily does, will that which he then judges to be good. For, though his will be always determined by that which is judged good by his understanding, yet it excuses him not; because, by a too hasty choice of his own making, he has imposed on himself wrong measures of good and evil; which, however false and fallacious, have the same influence on all his future conduct, as if they were true and right. He has vitiated his own palate, and must be answerable to himself for the sickness and death that follows from it. The eternal law and nature of things must not be altered to comply with his ill-ordered choice. If the neglect or abuse of the liberty he had, to examine what would really and truly make for his happiness, misleads him, the miscarriages that follow on it must be imputed to his own election. *He had a power to suspend his determination*[1]; it was given him, that he might examine, and take care of his own happiness, and look that he were not deceived. And he could never judge, that it was better to be deceived than not, in a matter of so great and near concernment.

❦   ❦   ❦

(2) *Liberty* is a power to act or not to act, according as the mind directs. A power to direct the operative faculties to motion or rest in particular instances is that which we call the *will*. That which in the train of our voluntary actions determines the will to any change of operation is *some present uneasiness*, which is, or at least is always accompanied with that of *desire*. Desire is always moved by evil, to fly it: because a total freedom from pain always makes a necessary part of our happiness: but every good, nay, every greater good, does not constantly move desire, because it may not make, or

may not be taken to make, any necessary part of our happiness. For all that we desire, is only to be happy. But, though this general desire of happiness operates constantly and invariably, yet the satisfaction of any particular desire *can be suspended* from determining the will to any subservient action, till we have maturely examined whether the particular apparent good which we then desire makes a part of our real happiness, or be consistent or inconsistent with it. The result of our judgment upon that examination is what ultimately determines the man; who could not be *free* if his will were determined by anything but his own desire, guided by his own judgment. I know that liberty, by some, is placed in an indifferency of the man; antecedent to the determination of his will.[2] I wish they who lay so much stress on such an antecedent indifferency, as they call it, had told us plainly, whether this supposed indifferency be antecedent to the thought and judgment of the understanding, as well as to the decree of the will. For it is pretty hard to state it between them, i.e., immediately *after* the judgment of the understanding, and *before* the determination of the will: because the determination of the will immediately follows the judgment of the understanding: and to place liberty in an indifferency, antecedent to the thought and judgment of the understanding, seems to me to place liberty in a state of darkness, wherein we can neither see nor say anything of it; at least it places it in a subject incapable of it, no agent being allowed capable of liberty, but in consequence of thought and judgment. I am not nice about phrases, and therefore consent to say with those that love to speak so, that liberty is placed in indifferency; but it is an indifferency which remains after the judgment of the understanding, yea, even after the determination of the will: and that is an indifferency not of the *man* (for after he has once judged which is best, viz. to do or forbear, he is no longer indifferent), but an indifferency of *the operative powers of the man*, which remaining equally able to operate or to forbear operating after as before the decree of the will, are in a state, which, if one pleases, may be called indifferency; and as far as this indifferency reaches, a man is free, and no further: e.g., I have the ability to move my hand, or to let it rest; that operative power is indifferent to move or not to move my hand. I am then, in that respect perfectly free; my will determines that operative power to rest: I am yet free, because the indifferency of that my operative power to act, or not to act, still remains; the power of moving my hand is not at all impaired by the determination of my will, which at present orders rest; the indifferency of that power to act, or not to act, is just as it was before, as will appear, if the will puts it to the trial, by ordering the contrary. But if, during the rest of my hand, it be seized with a sudden palsy, the indifferency of that operative power is gone, and with it my liberty ; I have no longer freedom in that respect, but am under a necessity of letting my hand rest. On the other side, if my hand be put into motion by a convulsion, the indifferency of that operative faculty is taken away by that motion; and my liberty in that case is lost, for I am under a necessity of having my hand move. I have added this, to show in what sort of indifferency liberty seems to me to consist, and not in any other, real or imaginary.

[³True notions concerning the nature and extent of *liberty* are of so great importance, that I hope I shall be pardoned this digression, which my attempt to explain it has led me into.⁴ The ideas of will, volition, liberty, and necessity, in this Chapter of Power, came naturally in my way. In a former edition of this Treatise I gave an account of my thoughts concerning them, according to the light I then had. And now, as a lover of truth, and not a worshipper of my own doctrines, I own some change of my opinion; which I think I have discovered ground for. In what I first writ, I with an unbiassed indifferency followed truth, whither I thought she led me. But neither being so vain as to fancy infallibility, nor so disingenuous as to dissemble my mistakes for fear of blemishing my reputation, I have, with the same sincere design for truth only, not been ashamed to publish what a severer inquiry has suggested. It is not impossible but that some may think my former notions right; and some (as I have already found) these latter ; and some neither. I shall not at all wonder at this variety in men's opinions: impartial deductions of reason in controverted points being so rare, and exact ones in abstract notions not so very easy, especially if of any length. And, therefore, I should think myself not a little beholden to any one, who would, upon these or any other grounds, fairly clear this subject of *liberty* from any difficulties that may yet remain.⁵]

[⁶Before I close this chapter, it may perhaps be to our purpose, and help to give us clearer conceptions about *power*, if we make our thoughts take a little more exact survey of *action*. I have said above, that we have ideas but of two sorts of action, viz. motion and thinking. These, in truth, though called and counted actions, yet, if nearly considered, will not be found to be always perfectly so. For, if I mistake not, there are instances of both kinds, which, upon due consideration, will be found rather passions than actions; and consequently so far the effects barely of *passive powers* in those subjects, which yet on their accounts are thought agents. For, in these instances, the substance that hath motion or thought receives the impression, whereby it is put into that action, purely from without, and so acts merely by the capacity it has to receive such an impression from some external agent; and such a power is not properly an active power, but a mere passive capacity in the subject. Sometimes the substance or agent puts itself into action by its own power, and this is properly *active power*. Whatsoever modification a substance has, whereby it produces any effect, that is called action: e.g. a solid substance, by motion, operates on or alters the sensible ideas of another substance, and therefore this modification of motion we call action. But yet this motion in that solid substance is, when rightly considered, but a passion, if it received it only from some external agent. So that the active power of motion is in no substance which cannot begin motion in itself or in another substance when at rest. So likewise in thinking, a power to receive ideas or thoughts from the operation of any external substance is called a power of thinking: but this is but a passive power, or capacity. But to be able to bring into view ideas out of sight at one's own choice, and to compare which of them one thinks fit, this is an active power.]

NOTES

1. This 'power' is the essence of moral freedom according to the *Essay*.

2. What follows, in objection to the 'liberty' of ' indifferency,' was introduced in Comte's French version of the *Essay*. This appears in Locke's letter to Limborch, 12th August, 1701. Free agency, suggested by the chapter on ' Power,' was a subject of correspondence between Locke and Limborch in the course of that year. This and other arguments of Locke's in this chapter are criticized in Law's notes to his translation of Archbishop King's *Essay on the Origin of Evil*.

3. This section was introduced in the second edition.

4. 'I do not wonder,' writes Locke to Molyneux (Jan. 20, 1693), 'You think my discourse about liberty a little too fine spun. I had so much that thought of it

myself, that I said the same thing of it myself to some of my friends, before it was printed, and told them that upon that account, I judged it best to leave it out; but they persuaded me to the contrary. When the connection of the parts of my subject brought me to the consideration of *power*, I had no desire to meddle with the question of *liberty*, but barely pursued my thoughts in the contemplation of that power in man of choosing or preferring which we call the *will*, as far as they would lead me, without any the least bias to one side or the other; or if there was any leaning in my mind, it was rather to the contrary side of that where I found myself at the end of my pursuit. But doubting that it bore a little too hard on man's liberty, I showed it to a very ingenious but professed Arminian, and desired him, after he had considered it, to tell me his objections, if he had any; who frankly confessed he could carry it no further.' (Familiar Letters.)

5. This and the preceding sentence suggested a tract entitled:—*A Vindication of Mankind, or Free Will, asserted in answer to a Philosophical Inquiry concerning Human Liberty. To which is added an examination of Mr. Locke's Scheme of Freedom* (1717).

6. What follows to the end of the section was added in the fourth edition.

[John Locke, *An Essay Concerning Human Understanding* (Oxford: Clarendon Press, 1894). Vol. 1, bk. 11, ch. XXI, sec. 57. (1) Pp. 352–53. (2) Pp. 367–71.]

(2a4)

William James

1842–1910

"The Dilemma of Determinism"
Essays on Faith and Morals

If free choice exists, then James can choose either Divinity Ave. or Oxford Street to reach his home. And if, after having chosen one of the two, say Divinity Ave., for the ten minute walk, those ten minutes were to be annihilated leaving him back on the steps of the lecture hall, everything being the same except the choice itself, he could now choose Oxford St. But this would require an indeterministic universe, pluralistic, containing real contingency, harboring the real chance that the future can not only be other, but also better, than the past. In a deterministic universe he would make the same choice. The former supports optimism; the latter, pessimism.

"THE DILEMMA OF DETERMINISM"

(1) What is meant by saying that my choice of which way to walk home after the lecture is ambiguous and matter of chance as far as the present moment is concerned? It means that both Divinity Avenue and Oxford Street are called; but that only one, and that one *either* one, shall be chosen. Now, I ask you seriously to suppose that this ambiguity of my choice is real; and then to make the impossible hypothesis that the choice is made twice over, and each time falls on a different street. In other words, imagine that I first walk through Divinity Avenue, and then imagine that the powers

governing the universe annihilate ten minutes of time with all that it contained, and set me back at the door of this hall just as I was before the
choice was made. Imagine then that, everything else being the same, I now
make a different choice and traverse Oxford Street. You, as passive spectators, look on and see the two alternative universes,—one of them with me
walking through Divinity Avenue in it, the other with the same me walking
through Oxford Street. Now, if you are determinists you believe one of
these universes to have been from eternity impossible: you believe it to
have been impossible because of the intrinsic irrationality or accidentality
somewhere involved in it. But looking outwardly at these universes, can
you say which is the impossible and accidental one, and which the rational
and necessary one? I doubt if the most ironclad determinist among you
could have the slightest glimmer of light on this point. In other words,
either universe *after the fact* and once there would, to our means of observation and understanding, appear just as rational as the other. There would
be absolutely no criterion by which we might judge one necessary and the
other matter of chance. Suppose now we relieve the gods of their hypothetical task and assume my choice, once made, to be made forever. I go
through Divinity Avenue for good and all. If, as good determinists, you now
begin to affirm, what all good determinists punctually do affirm, that in the
nature of things I *couldn't* have gone through Oxford Street,—had I done so
it would have been chance, irrationality, insanity, a horrid gap in nature,—
I simply call your attention to this, that your affirmation is what the Ger-
mans call a *Machtspruch*, a mere conception fulminated as a dogma and
based on no insight into details. Before my choice, either street seemed as
natural to you as to me. Had I happened to take Oxford Street, Divinity
Avenue would have figured in your philosophy as the gap in nature; and
you would have so proclaimed it with the best deterministic conscience in
the world.

But what a hollow outcry, then, is this against a chance which, if it were
present to us, we could by no character whatever distinguish from a
rational necessity! I have taken the most trivial of examples, but no possible
example could lead to any different result. For what are the alternatives
which, in point of fact, offer themselves to human volition? What are those
futures that now seem matters of chance? Are they not one and all like the
Divinity Avenue and Oxford Street of our example? Are they not all of

them *kinds* of things already here and based in the existing frame of nature? Is any one ever tempted to produce an *absolute* accident, something utterly irrelevant to the rest of the world? Do not all the motives that assail us, all the futures that offer themselves to our choice spring equally from the soil of the past; and would not either one of them, whether realized through chance or through necessity, the moment it was realized, seem to us to fit that past, and in the completest and most continuous manner to interdigitate with the phenomena already there?[1]

The more one thinks of the matter, the more one wonders that so empty and gratuitous a hubbub as this outcry against chance should have found so great an echo in the hearts of men. It is a word which tells us absolutely nothing about what chances, or about the *modus operandi* of the chancing; and the use of it as a war-cry shows only a temper of intellectual absolutism, a demand that the world shall be a solid block, subject to one control,—which temper, which demand, the world may not be bound to gratify at all. In every outwardly verifiable and practical respect, a world in which the alternatives that now actually distract *your* choice were decided by pure chance would be by *me* absolutely undistinguished from the world in which I now live. I am, therefore, entirely willing to call it, so far as your choices go, a world of chance for me. To *yourselves*, it is true, those very acts of choice, which to me are so blind, opaque, and external, are the opposites of this, for you are within them and effect them. To you they appear as decisions; and decisions, for him who makes them, are altogether peculiar psychic facts. Self-luminous and self-justifying at the living moment at which they occur, they appeal to no outside moment to put its stamp upon them or make them continuous with the rest of nature. Themselves it is rather who seem to make nature continuous; and in their strange and intense function of granting consent to one possibility and withholding it from another, to transform an equivocal and double future into an inalterable and simple past.

But with the psychology of the matter we have no concern this evening. The quarrel which determinism has with chance fortunately has nothing to do with this or that psychological detail. It is a quarrel altogether metaphysical. Determinism denies the ambiguity of future volitions, because it affirms that nothing future can be ambiguous. But we have said enough to meet the issue. Indeterminate future volitions *do* mean chance. Let us not fear to shout it from the house-tops if need be; for we now know that the idea of chance is, at bottom, exactly the same thing as the idea of gift,—the one simply being a disparaging, and the other a eulogistic, name for anything on which we have no effective *claim*. And whether the world be the better or the worse for having either chances or gifts in it will depend altogether on *what* these uncertain and unclaimable things turn out to be.

And this at last brings us within sight of our subject. We have seen what determinism means: we have seen that indeterminism is rightly described as meaning chance; and we have seen that chance, the very name of which we are urged to shrink from as from a metaphysical pestilence, means only the negative fact that no part of the world, however big, can claim to control absolutely the destinies of the whole. But although, in discussing the word 'chance,' I may at moments have seemed to be arguing for its real existence, I have not meant to do so yet. We have not yet ascertained whether this be a world of chance or no; at most, we have agreed that it seems so. And I now repeat what I said at the outset, that, from any strict theoretical point of view, the question is insoluble. To deepen our theoretic sense of the *difference* between a world with chances in it and a deterministic world is the most I can hope to do; and this I may now at last begin upon, after all our tedious clearing of the way.

I wish first of all to show you just what the notion that this is a deterministic world implies. The implications I call your attention to are all bound up with the fact that it is a world in which we constantly have to make what I shall, with your permission, call judgments of regret. Hardly an hour passes in which we do not wish that something might be otherwise; and happy indeed are those of us whose hearts have never echoed the wish of Omar Khayam—

> That we might clasp, ere closed, the book of fate,
> And make the writer on a fairer leaf
> Inscribe our names, or quite obliterate.
>
> Ah! Love, could you and I with fate conspire
> To mend this sorry scheme of things entire,
> Would we not shatter it to bits, and then
> Remould it nearer to the heart's desire?

Now, it is undeniable that most of these regrets are foolish, and quite on a par in point of philosophic value with the criticisms on the universe of that friend of our infancy, the hero of the fable The Atheist and the Acorn,—

"Fool! had that bough a pumpkin bore,
Thy whimsies would have worked no more," etc.

Even from the point of view of our own ends, we should probably make a botch of remodelling the universe. How much more then from the point of view of ends we cannot see! Wise men therefore regret as little as they can. But still some regrets are pretty obstinate and hard to stifle,—regrets for acts of wanton cruelty or treachery, for example, whether performed by others or by ourselves. Hardly any one can remain *entirely* optimistic after reading the confession of the murderer at Brockton the other day: how, to get rid of the wife whose continued existence bored him, he inveigled her into a desert spot, shot her four times, and then, as she lay on the ground and said to him, "You didn't do it on purpose, did you, dear?" replied, "No, I didn't do it on purpose," as he raised a rock and smashed her skull. Such an occurrence, with the mild sentence and self-satisfaction of the prisoner, is a field for a crop of regrets, which one need not take up in detail. We feel that, although a perfect mechanical fit to the rest of the universe, it is a bad moral fit, and that something else would really have been better in its place.

But for the deterministic philosophy the murder, the sentence, and the prisoner's optimism were all necessary from eternity; and nothing else for a moment had a ghost of a chance of being put into their place. To admit such a chance, the determinists tell us, would be to make a suicide of reason; so we must steel our hearts against the thought. And here our plot thickens, for we see the first of those difficult implications of determinism and monism which it is my purpose to make you feel. If this Brockton murder was called for by the rest of the universe, if it had to come at its preappointed hour, and if nothing else would have been consistent with the sense of the whole, what are we to think of the universe? Are we stubbornly to stick to our judgment of regret, and say, though it *couldn't* be, yet it *would* have been a better universe with something different from this

Brockton murder in it? That, of course, seems the natural and spontaneous thing for us to do; and yet it is nothing short of deliberately espousing a kind of pessimism. The judgment of regret calls the murder bad. Calling a thing bad means, if it mean anything at all, that the thing ought not to be, that something else ought to be in its stead. Determinism, in denying that anything else can be in its stead, virtually defines the universe as a place in which what ought to be is impossible,—in other words, as an organism whose constitution is afflicted with an incurable taint, an irremediable flaw. The pessimism of a Schopenhauer says no more than this,—that the murder is a symptom; and that it is a vicious symptom because it belongs to a vicious whole, which can express its nature no otherwise than by bringing forth just such a symptom as that at this particular spot. Regret for the murder must transform itself, if we are determinists and wise, into a larger regret. It is absurd to regret the murder alone. Other things being what they are, *it* could not be different. What we should regret is that whole frame of things of which the murder is one member. I see no escape whatever from this pessimistic conclusion, if, being determinists, our judgment of regret is to be allowed to stand at all.

The only deterministic escape from pessimism is everywhere to abandon the judgment of regret. That this can be done, history shows to be not impossible. The devil, *quoad existentiam*, may be good. That is, although he be a *principle* of evil, yet the universe, with such a principle in it, may practically be a better universe than it could have been without. On every hand, in a small way, we find that a certain amount of evil is a condition by which a higher form of good is brought. There is nothing to prevent anybody from generalizing this view, and trusting that if we could but see things in the largest of all ways, even such matters as this Brockton murder would appear to be paid for by the uses that follow in their train. An optimism *quand même*, a systematic and infatuated optimism like that ridiculed by Voltaire in his *Candide*, is one of the possible ideal ways in which a man may train himself to look on life. Bereft of dogmatic hardness and lit up with the expression of a tender and pathetic hope, such an optimism has been the grace of some of the most religious characters that ever lived.

> Throb thine with Nature's throbbing breast,
> And all is clear from east to west.

Even cruelty and treachery may be among the absolutely blessed fruits of time, and to quarrel with any of their details may be blasphemy. The only real blasphemy, in short, may be that pessimistic temper of the soul which lets it give way to such things as regrets, remorse, and grief.

Thus, our deterministic pessimism may become a deterministic optimism at the price of extinguishing our judgments of regret.

But does not this immediately bring us into a curious logical predicament? Our determinism leads us to call our judgments of regret wrong, because they are pessimistic in implying that what is impossible yet ought to be. But how then about the judgments of regret themselves? If they are wrong, other judgments, judgments of approval presumably, ought to be in their place. But as they are necessitated, nothing else *can* be in their place; and the universe is just what it was before,—namely, a place in which what ought to be appears impossible. We have got one foot out of the pessimistic bog, but the other one sinks all the deeper. We have rescued our actions from the bonds of evil, but our judgments are now held fast. When murders and treacheries cease to be sins, regrets are theoretic absurdities and errors. The theoretic and the active life thus play a kind of see-saw with each other on the ground of evil. The rise of either sends the other down. Murder and treachery cannot be good without regret being bad: regret cannot be good without treachery and murder being bad. Both, however, are supposed to have been foredoomed; so something must be fatally unreasonable, absurd, and wrong in the world. It must be a place of which either sin or error forms a necessary part. From this dilemma there seems at first sight no escape. Are we then so soon to fall back into the pessimism from which we thought we had emerged? And is there no possible way by which we may, with good intellectual consciences, call the cruelties and the treacheries, the reluctances and the regrets, *all* good together?

Certainly there is such a way, and you are probably most of you ready to formulate it yourselves. But, before doing so, remark how inevitably the question of determinism and indeterminism slides us into the question of optimism and pessimism, or, as our fathers called it, 'the question of evil.' The theological form of all these disputes is the simplest and the deepest, the form from which there is the least escape,—not because, as some have sarcastically said, remorse and regret are clung to with a morbid fondness by the theologians as spiritual luxuries, but because they are existing facts of the world, and as such must be taken into account in the deterministic interpretation of all that is fated to be. If they are fated to be error, does not the bat's wing of irrationality still cast its shadow over the world?

The refuge from the quandary lies, as I said, not far off. The necessary acts we erroneously regret may be good, and yet our error in so regretting them may be also good, on one simple condition; and that condition is this: The world must not be regarded as a machine whose final purpose is the making real of any outward good, but rather as a contrivance for deepening the theoretic consciousness of what goodness and evil in their intrinsic natures are. Not the doing either of good or of evil is what nature cares for, but the knowing of them. Life is one long eating of the fruit of the tree of *knowledge*. I am in the habit, in thinking to myself, of calling this point of view the *gnostical* point of view. According to it, the world is neither an optimism nor a pessimism, but a *gnosticism*. But as this term may perhaps lead to some misunderstandings, I will use it as little as possible here, and speak rather of *subjectivism*, and the *subjectivistic* point of view.

Subjectivism has three great branches,—we may call them scientificism, sentimentalism, and sensualism, respectively. They all agree essentially about the universe, in deeming that what happens there is subsidiary to what we think or feel about it. Crime justifies its criminality by awakening our intelligence of that criminality, and eventually our remorses and regrets; and the error included in remorses and regrets, the error of supposing that the past could have been different, justifies itself by its use. Its use is to quicken our sense of *what* the irretrievably lost is. When we think of it as that which might have been ('the saddest words of tongue or pen'), the quality of its worth speaks to us with a wilder sweetness; and, conversely, the dissatisfaction wherewith we think of what seems to have driven it from its natural place gives us the severer pang. Admirable artifice of nature! we might be tempted to exclaim,—deceiving us in order the better to enlighten us, and leaving nothing undone to accentuate to our consciousness the yawning distance of those opposite poles of good and evil between which creation swings.

We have thus clearly revealed to our view what may be called the dilemma of determinism, so far as determinism pretends to think things out at all. A merely mechanical determinism, it is true, rather rejoices in not thinking them out. It is very sure that the universe must satisfy its postulate of a physical continuity and coherence, but it smiles at any one who comes forward with a postulate of moral coherence as well. I may suppose, however, that the number of purely mechanical or hard determinists among you this evening is small. The determinism to whose seductions you are most exposed is what I have called soft determinism,—the determinism which allows considerations of good and bad to mingle with those of cause and effect in deciding what sort of a universe this may rationally be held to be. The dilemma of this determinism is one whose left horn is pessimism and whose right horn is subjectivism. In other words, if determinism is to escape pessimism, it must leave off looking at the goods and ills of life in a simple objective way, and regard them as materials, indifferent in themselves, for the production of consciousness, scientific and ethical, in us.

To escape pessimism is, as we all know, no easy task. Your own studies have sufficiently shown you the almost desperate difficulty of making the notion that there is a single principle of things, and that principle absolute perfection, rhyme together with our daily vision of the facts of life. If perfection be the principle, how comes there any imperfection here? If God be good, how came he to create—or, if he did not create, how comes he to permit—the devil? The evil facts must be explained as seeming: the devil must be whitewashed, the universe must be disinfected, if neither God's goodness nor his unity and power are to remain impugned. And of all the various ways of operating the disinfection, and making bad seem less bad, the way of subjectivism appears by far the best.[2]

For, after all, is there not something rather absurd in our ordinary notion of external things being good or bad in themselves? Can murders and treacheries, considered as mere outward happenings, or motions of matter, be bad without any one to feel their badness? And could paradise properly be good in the absence of a sentient principle by which the goodness was perceived? Outward goods and evils seem practically indistinguishable except in so far as they result in getting moral judgments made about them. But then the moral judgments seem the main thing, and the outward facts mere perishing instruments for their production. This is subjectivism. Every one must at some time have wondered at that strange paradox of our moral nature, that, though the pursuit of outward good is the breath of its nostrils, the attainment of outward good would seem to be its suffocation and death. Why does the painting of any paradise or utopia, in heaven or on earth, awaken such yawnings for nirvana and escape? The whiterobed harp-playing heaven of our sabbath-schools, and the ladylike tea-table elysium represented in Mr. Spencer's Data of Ethics, as the final consummation of progress, are exactly on a par in this respect,—lubberlands, pure and simple, one and all. We look upon them from this delicious mess of insanities and realities, strivings and deadnesses, hopes and fears, agonies and exultations, which forms our present state, and *tedium vitae* is the only sentiment they awaken in our breasts. To our crepuscular natures, born for the conflict, the Rembrandtesque moral chiaroscuro, the shifting struggle of the sunbeam in the gloom, such pictures of light upon light are vacuous and expressionless, and neither to be enjoyed nor understood. If *this* be the whole fruit of the victory, we say; if the generations of mankind suffered and laid down their lives; if prophets confessed and martyrs sang in the fire, and all the sacred tears were shed for no other end than that a race of creatures of such unexampled insipidity should succeed, and protract *in saecula saeculorum* their contented and inoffensive lives,—why, at such a rate, better lose than win the battle, or at all events better ring down the curtain before the last act of the play, so that a business that began so importantly may be saved from so singularly flat a winding-up.

All this is what I should instantly say, were I called on to plead for gnosticism; and its real friends, of whom you will presently perceive I am not one, would say without difficulty a great deal more. Regarded as a stable finality, every outward good becomes a mere weariness to the flesh. It must be menaced, be occasionally lost, for its goodness to be fully felt as such. Nay, more than occasionally lost. No one knows the worth of innocence till he knows it is gone forever, and that money cannot buy it back. Not the saint, but the sinner that repenteth, is he to whom the full length and breadth, and height and depth, of life's meaning is revealed. Not the absence of vice, but vice there, and virtue holding her by the throat, seems the ideal human state. And there seems no reason to suppose it not a permanent human state. There is a deep truth in what the school of Schopenhauer insists on,—the illusoriness of the notion of moral progress. The more brutal forms of evil that go are replaced by others more subtle and more poisonous. Our moral horizon moves with us as we move, and never do we draw nearer to the far-off line where the black waves and the azure meet. The final purpose of our creation seems most plausibly to be the greatest possible enrichment of our ethical consciousness, through the intensest play of contrasts and the widest diversity of characters. This of course obliges some of us to be vessels of wrath, while it calls others to be vessels of honor. But the subjectivist point of view reduces all these outward distinctions to a common denominator. The wretch languishing in the felon's cell may be drinking draughts of the wine of truth that will never pass the lips of the so-called favorite of fortune. And the peculiar consciousness of each of them is an indispensable note in the great ethical concert which the centuries as they roll are grinding out of the living heart of man.

So much for subjectivism! If the dilemma of determinism be to choose between it and pessimism, I see little room for hesitation from the strictly theoretical point of view. Subjectivism seems the more rational scheme. And the world may, possibly, for aught I know, be nothing else. When the healthy love of life is on one, and all its forms and its appetites seem so unutterably real; when the most brutal and the most spiritual things are lit by the same sun, and each is an integral part of the total richness,—why, then it seems a grudging and sickly way of meeting so robust a universe to shrink from any of its facts and wish them not to be. Rather take the strictly dramatic point of view, and treat the whole thing as a great unending romance which the spirit of the universe, striving to realize its own content, is eternally thinking out and representing to itself.[3]

No one, I hope, will accuse me, after I have said all this, of underrating the reasons in favor of subjectivism. And now that I proceed to say why those reasons, strong as they are, fail to convince my own mind, I trust the presumption may be that my objections are stronger still.

I frankly confess that they are of a practical order. If we practically take up subjectivism in a sincere and radical manner and follow its consequences, we meet with some that make us pause. Let a subjectivism begin in never so severe and intellectual a way, it is forced by the law of its nature to develop another side of itself and end with the corruptest curiosity. Once dismiss the notion that certain duties are good in themselves, and that we are here to do them, no matter how we feel about them; once consecrate the opposite notion that our performances and our violations of duty are for a common purpose, the attainment of subjective knowledge and feeling, and that the deepening of these is the chief end of our lives,— and at what point on the downward slope are we to stop? In theology, subjectivism develops as its 'left wing' antinomianism. In literature, its left wing is romanticism. And in practical life it is either a nerveless sentimentality or a sensualism without bounds.

Everywhere it fosters the fatalistic mood of mind. It makes those who are already too inert more passive still; it renders wholly reckless those whose energy is already in excess. All through history we find how subjectivism, as soon as it has a free career, exhausts itself in every sort of spiritual, moral, and practical license. Its optimism turns to an ethical indifference, which infallibly brings dissolution in its train. It is perfectly safe to say now that if the Hegelian gnosticism, which has begun to show itself here and in Great Britain, were to become a popular philosophy, as it once was in Germany, it would certainly develop its left wing here as there, and produce a reaction of disgust. Already I have heard a graduate of this very school express in the pulpit his willingness to sin like David, if only he might repent like David. You may tell me he was only sowing his wild, or rather his tame, oats; and perhaps he was. But the point is that in the subjectivistic or gnostical philosophy oat-sowing, wild or tame, becomes a systematic necessity and the chief function of life. After the pure and classic truths, the exciting and rancid ones must be experienced; and if the stupid virtues of the philistine herd do not then come in and save society from the influence of the children of light, a sort of inward putrefaction becomes its inevitable doom.

Look at the last runnings of the romantic school, as we see them in that strange contemporary Parisian literature, with which we of the less clever countries are so often driven to rinse out our minds after they have become clogged with the dulness and heaviness of our native pursuits. The romantic school began with the worship of subjective sensibility and the revolt against legality of which Rousseau was the first great prophet: and through various fluxes and refluxes, right wings and left wings, it stands to-day with two men of genius, M. Renan and M. Zola, as its principal exponents,—one speaking with its masculine, and the other with what might be called its feminine, voice. I prefer not to think now of less noble members of the school, and the Renan I have in mind is of course the Renan of latest dates. As I have used the term gnostic, both he and Zola are gnostics of the most pronounced sort. Both are athirst for the facts of life, and both think the facts of human sensibility to be of all facts the most worthy of attention. Both agree, moreover, that sensibility seems to be there for no higher purpose—certainly not, as the Philistines say, for the sake of bringing mere outward rights to pass and frustrating outward wrongs. One dwells on the sensibilities for their energy, the other for their sweetness; one speaks with a voice of bronze, the other with that of an Æolian harp; one ruggedly ignores the distinction of good and evil, the other plays the coquette between the craven unmanliness of his Philosophic Dialogues and the butterfly optimism of his Souvenirs de Jeunesse. But under the pages of both there sounds incessantly the hoarse bass of *vanitas vanitatum, omnia vanitas*, which the reader may hear, whenever he will, between the lines. No writer of this French romantic school has a word of rescue from the hour of satiety with the things of life,—the hour in which we say, "I take no pleasure in them,"—or from the hour of terror at the world's vast meaningless grinding, if perchance such hours should come. For terror and satiety are facts of sensibility like any others; and at their own hour they reign in their own right. The heart of the romantic utterances, whether poetical, critical, or historical, is this inward remedilessness, what Carlyle calls this faroff whimpering of wail and woe. And from this romantic state of mind there is absolutely no possible *theoretic* escape. Whether, like Renan, we look upon life in a more refined way, as a romance of the spirit; or whether, like the friends of M. Zola, we pique ourselves on our 'scientific' and 'analytic' character, and prefer to be cynical, and call the world a 'roman expérimental' on an infinite scale,—in either case the world appears to us potentially as what the same Carlyle once called it, a vast, gloomy, solitary Golgotha and mill of death.

The only escape is by the practical way. And since I have mentioned the nowadays much-reviled name of Carlyle, let me mention it once more, and say it is the way of his teaching. No matter for Carlyle's life, no matter for a great deal of his writing. What was the most important thing he said to us? He said: "Hang your sensibilities! Stop your snivelling complaints, and your equally snivelling raptures! Leave off your general emotional tomfoolery, and get to WORK like men!" But this means a complete rupture with the subjectivist philosophy of things. It says conduct, and not sensibility, is the ultimate fact for our recognition. With the vision of certain works to be done, of certain outward changes to be wrought or resisted, it says our intellectual horizon terminates. No matter how we succeed in doing these outward duties, whether gladly and spontaneously, or heavily and unwillingly, do them we somehow must; for the leaving of them undone is perdition. No matter how we feel; if we are only faithful in the outward act and refuse to do wrong, the world will in so far be safe, and we quit of our debt toward it. Take, then, the yoke upon our shoulders; bend our neck beneath the heavy legality of its weight; regard something else than our feeling as our limit, our master, and our law; be willing to live and die in its service,—and, at a stroke, we have passed from the subjective into the objective philosophy of things, much as one awakens from some feverish dream, full of bad lights and noises, to find one's self bathed in the sacred coolness and quiet of the air of the night.

But what is the essence of this philosophy of objective conduct, so old-fashioned and finite, but so chaste and sane and strong, when compared with its romantic rival? It is the recognition of limits, foreign and opaque to our understanding. It is the willingness, after bringing about some external good, to feel at peace; for our responsibility ends with the performance of that duty, and the burden of the rest we may lay on higher powers.[4]

> Look to thyself, O Universe,
> Thou art better and not worse,

we may say in that philosophy, the moment we have done our stroke of conduct, however small. For in the view of that philosophy the universe belongs to a plurality of semi-independent forces, each one of which may help or hinder, and be helped or hindered by, the operations of the rest.

But this brings us right back, after such a long detour, to the question of indeterminism and to the conclusion of all I came here to say tonight. For the only consistent way of representing a pluralism and a world whose parts may affect one another through their conduct being either good or bad is the indeterministic way. What interest, zest, or excitement can there be in achieving the right way, unless we are enabled to feel that the wrong way is also a possible and a natural way,—nay, more, a menacing and an imminent way? And what sense can there be in condemning ourselves for taking the wrong way, unless we need have done nothing of the sort, unless the right way was open to us as well? I cannot understand the willingness to act, no matter how we feel, without the belief that acts are really good and bad. I cannot understand the belief that an act is bad, without regret at its happening. I cannot understand regret without the admission of real, genuine possibilities in the world. Only *then* is it other than a mockery to feel, after we have failed to do our best, that an irreparable opportunity is gone from the universe, the loss of which it must forever after mourn.

(2) The world is enigmatical enough in all conscience, whatever theory we may take up toward it. The indeterminism I defend, the free-will theory of popular sense based on the judgment of regret, represents that world as vulnerable, and liable to be injured by certain of its parts if they act wrong. And it represents their acting wrong as a matter of possibility or accident, neither inevitable nor yet to be infallibly warded off. In all this, it is a theory devoid either of transparency or of stability. It gives us a pluralistic, restless universe, in which no single point of view can ever take in the whole scene; and to a mind possessed of the love of unity at any cost, it will, no doubt, remain forever inacceptable.

(3) Make as great an uproar about chance as you please, I know that chance means pluralism and nothing more. If some of the members of the pluralism are bad, the philosophy of pluralism, whatever broad views it may deny me, permits me, at least, to turn to the other members with a clean breast of affection and an unsophisticated moral sense. And if I still wish to think of the world as a totality, it lets me feel that a world with a *chance* in it of being altogether good, even if the chance never come to pass, is better than a world with no such chance at all. That 'chance' whose very notion I am exhorted and conjured to banish from my view of the future as the suicide of reason concerning it, that 'chance' is—what? just this,— the chance that in moral respects the future may be other and better than the past has been. This is the only chance we have any motive for supposing to exist.

(4) But now you will bring up your final doubt. Does not the admission of such an unguaranteed chance or freedom preclude utterly the notion of a Providence governing the world? Does it not leave the fate of the universe at the mercy of the chance-possibilities, and so far insecure? Does it not, in

short, deny the craving of our nature for an ultimate peace behind all tempests, for a blue zenith above all clouds?

To this my answer must be very brief. The belief in free-will is not in the least incompatible with the belief in Providence, provided you do not restrict the Providence to fulminating nothing but *fatal* decrees. If you allow him to provide possibilities as well as actualities to the universe, and to carry on his own thinking in those two categories just as we do ours, chances may be there, uncontrolled even by him, and the course of the universe be really ambiguous; and yet the end of all things may be just what he intended it to be from all eternity.

An analogy will make the meaning of this clear. Suppose two men before a chessboard,—the one a novice, the other an expert player of the game. The expert intends to beat. But he cannot foresee exactly what any one actual move of his adversary may be. He knows, however, all the *possible* moves of the latter; and he knows in advance how to meet each of them by a move of his own which leads in the direction of victory. And the victory infallibly arrives, after no matter how devious a course, in the one predestined form of checkmate to the novice's king.

Let now the novice stand for us finite free agents, and the expert for the infinite mind in which the universe lies. Suppose the latter to be thinking out his universe before he actually creates it. Suppose him to say, I will lead things to a certain end, but I will not *now*[5] decide on all the steps thereto. At various points, ambiguous possibilities shall be left open, *either* of which, at a given instant, may become actual. But whichever branch of these bifurcations become real, I know what I shall do at the *next* bifurcation to keep things from drifting away from the final result I intend.[6]

The creator's plan of the universe would thus be left blank as to many of its actual details, but all possibilities would be marked down. The realization of some of these would be left absolutely to chance; that is, would only be determined when the moment of realization came. Other possibilities would be *contingently* determined; that is, their decision would have to wait till it was seen how the matters of absolute chance fell out. But the rest of the plan, including its final upshot, would be rigorously determined once for all. So the creator himself would not need to know *all* the details of actuality until they came; and at any time his own view of the world would be a view partly of facts and partly of possibilities, exactly as ours is now. Of one thing, however, he might be certain; and that is that his world was safe, and that no matter how much it might zigzag he could surely bring it home at last.

Now, it is entirely immaterial, in this scheme, whether the creator leave the absolute chance-possibilities to be decided by himself, each when its proper moment arrives, or whether, on the contrary, he alienate this power from himself, and leave the decision out and out to finite creatures such as we men are. The great point is that the possibilities are really *here*. Whether it be we who solve them, or he working through us, at those soul-trying moments when fate's scales seem to quiver, and good snatches the victory from evil or shrinks nerveless from the fight, is of small account, so long as we admit that the issue is decided nowhere else than *here* and *now*. *That* is what gives the palpitating reality to our moral life and makes it tingle, as Mr. Mallock says, with so strange and elaborate an excitement. This reality, this excitement, are what the determinisms, hard and soft alike, suppress by their denial that *anything* is decided here and now, and their dogma that all things were foredoomed and settled long ago. If it be so, may you and I then have been foredoomed to the error of continuing to believe in liberty.[7] It is fortunate for the winding up of controversy that in every discussion with determinism this *argumentum ad hominem* can be its adversary's last word.

NOTES

1. A favorite argument against free-will is that if it be true, a man's murderer may as probably be his best friend as his worst enemy, a mother be as likely to strangle as to suckle her first-born, and all of us be as ready to jump from fourth-story windows as to go out of front doors, etc. Users of this argument should properly be excluded from debate till they learn what the real question is. 'Free-will' does not say that everything that is physically conceivable is also morally possible. It merely says that of alternatives that really *tempt* our will more than one is really possible. Of course, the alternatives that do thus tempt our will are vastly fewer than the physical possibilities we can coldly fancy. Persons really tempted often do murder their best friends, mothers do strangle their first-born, people do jump out of fourth-story windows, etc.

2. To a reader who says he is satisfied with a pessimism, and has no objection to thinking the whole bad, I have no more to say: he makes fewer demands on the world than I, who, making them, wish to look a little further before I give up all hope of having them satisfied. If, however, all he means is that the badness of some parts does not prevent his acceptance of a universe whose *other* parts give him satisfaction, I welcome him as an ally. He has abandoned the notion of the *Whole*, which is the essence of deterministic monism, and views things as a pluralism, just as I do in this paper.

3. Cet univers est un spectacle que Dieu se donne à lui-même. Servons les intentions du grand chorège en contribuant à rendre le spectacle aussi brillant, aussi varié que possible.—Renan.

4. The burden, for example, or seeing to it that the *end* of all our righteousness be some positive universal gain.

5. This of course leaves the creative mind subject to the law of time. And to any one who insists on the timelessness of that mind I have no reply to make. A mind to whom all time is simultaneously present must see all things under the form of actuality, or under some form to us unknown. If he thinks certain moments as ambiguous in their content while future, he must simultaneously know how the ambiguity will have been decided when they are past. So that none of his mental judgments can possibly be called hypothetical, and his world is one from which chance is excluded. Is not, however, the timeless mind rather a gratuitous fiction? And is not the notion of eternity being given at a stroke to omniscience only just another way of whacking upon us the block-universe, and of denying that possibilities exist?—just the point to be proved. To say that time is an illusory appearance is only a roundabout manner of saying there is no real plurality, and that the frame of things is an absolute unit. Admit plurality, and time may be its form.

6. And this of course means 'miraculous' interposition, but not necessarily of the gross sort our fathers took such delight in representing, and which has so lost its magic for us. Emerson quotes some Eastern sage as saying that if evil were really done under the sun, the sky would incontinently shrivel to a snakeskin and cast it out in spasms. But, says Emerson, the spasms of Nature are years and centuries; and it will tax man's patience to wait so long. We may think of the reserved possibilities God keeps in his own hand, under as invisible and molecular and slowly self-summating a form as we please. We may think of them as counteracting human agencies which he inspires *ad hoc*. In short, signs and wonders and convulsions of the earth and sky are not the only neutralizers of obstruction to a god's plans of which it is possible to think.

7. As long as languages contain a future perfect tense, determinists, following the bent of laziness or passion, the lines of least resistance, can reply in that tense, saying, "It will have been fated," to the still small voice which urges an opposite course; and thus excuse themselves from effort in a quite unanswerable way.

[William James, "The Dilemma of Determinism," *Essays on Faith and Morals*, sel. R. B. Perry (A Meridian Book, Cleveland, Ohio: The World Publishing, 1962). (1) Pp. 145–76. (2) Pp. 176–77. (3) Pp. 178–79. (4) Pp. 180–83.]

(2a5)
Jean-Paul Sartre
1905–1980

"Being and Doing: Freedom,"
Being and Nothingness
selections from ch. 1

Where most supporters of the first definition of freedom believe in a limited power to choose, Sartre held to a view of radical freedom. We not only choose among the possibilities, we create them for ourselves. We also have the power of nihilation. We can reduce the past to nothing, and choose in terms of a past differently projected. All of this is possible because we are *pour-soi*, a restless, changing for-itself, not *en-soi*, something in itself.

SUMMARY OF THE ARGUMENT

(1) In our attempt to reach to the heart of freedom we may be helped by the few observations which we have made on the subject in the course of this work and which we must summarize here. In the first chapter we established the fact that if negation comes into the world through human-reality, the latter must be a being who can realize a nihilating rupture[1] with the world and with himself; and we established that the permanent possibility of this rupture is the same as freedom. But on the other band, we stated that this permanent possibility of nihilating what I am in the form of "having-been" implies for man a particular type of existence. We were able then to determine by means of analyses like that of bad faith that human reality is its own nothingness. For the for-itself,[2] to be is to nihilate

the in-itself which it is. Under these conditions freedom can be nothing other than this nihilation. It is through this that the for-itself escapes its being as its essence; it is through this that the for-itself is always something other than what can be *said* of it. For in the final analysis the for-itself is the one which escapes this very denomination, the one which is already beyond the name which is given to it, beyond the property which is recognized in it. To say that the for-itself has to be what it is, to say that it is what it is not while not being what it is, to say that in it existence precedes and conditions essence or inversely according to Hegel, that for it "Wesen ist was gewesen ist"—all this is to say one and the same thing: to be aware that man is free. Indeed by the sole fact that I am conscious of the causes which inspire my action, these causes are already transcendent objects for my consciousness; they are outside. In vain shall I seek to catch hold of them; I escape them by my very existence. I am condemned to exist forever beyond my essence, beyond the causes and motives of my act. I am condemned to be free. This means that no limits to my freedom can be found except freedom itself or, if you prefer, that we are not free to cease being free. To the extent that the for-itself wishes to hide its own nothingness from itself and to incorporate the in-itself³ as its true mode of being, it is trying also to hide its freedom from itself.

The ultimate meaning of determinism is to establish within us an unbroken continuity of existence in itself. The motive conceived as a psychic fact—*i.e.*, as a full and given reality—is, in the deterministic view, articulated without any break with the decision and the act, both of which are equally conceived as psychic givens. The in-itself has got hold of all these "data"; the motive provokes the act as the physical cause its effect; everything is real, everything is full. Thus the refusal of freedom can be conceived only as an attempt to apprehend oneself as being-in-itself; it amounts to the same thing. Human reality may be defined as a being such that in its being its freedom is at stake because human reality perpetually tries to refuse to recognize its freedom. Psychologically in each one of us this amounts to trying to take the causes and motives as *things*. We try to confer permanence upon them. We attempt to hide from ourselves that their nature and their weight depend each moment on the meaning which I give to them; we take them for constants. This amounts to considering the meaning which I gave to them just now or yesterday—which is irremediable because it is *past*—and extrapolating from it a character fixed still in the present. I attempt to persuade myself that the cause *is* as it was. Thus it would pass whole and untouched from my past consciousness to my present consciousness. It would inhabit my consciousness. This amounts to trying to give an essence to the for-itself. In the same way people will posit ends as transcendences, which is not an error. But instead of seeing that the transcendences there posited are maintained in their being by my own transcendence, people will assume that I encounter them upon my surging up in the world; they come from God, from nature, from "my" nature, from society. These ends ready made and prehuman will therefore define the meaning of my act even before I conceive it, just as causes as pure psychic givens will produce it without my even being aware of them.

Cause, act, and end constitute a *continuum*, a *plenum*. These abortive attempts to stifle freedom under the weight of being (they collapse with the sudden upsurge of anguish before freedom) show sufficiently that freedom in its foundation coincides with the nothingness which is at the heart of man. Human-reality is free because it *is not enough*. It is free because it is perpetually wrenched away from itself and because it has been separated by a nothingness from what it is and from what it will be. It is free, finally, because its present being is itself a nothingness in the form of the "reflection-reflecting." Man is free because he is not himself but presence to himself. The being which is what it is can not be free. Freedom is precisely the nothingness which *is made-to-be* at the heart of man and which forces human-reality *to make itself* instead of *to be*. As we have seen, for human reality, to be is to *choose oneself*; nothing comes to it either from the outside or from within which it can *receive or accept*. Without any help whatsoever, it is entirely abandoned to the intolerable necessity of making itself be—down to the slightest detail. Thus freedom is not a being; it is *the being* of man—*i.e.*, his nothingness of being. If we start by conceiving of man as a plenum, it is absurd to try to find in him afterwards moments or psychic regions in which he would be free. As well look for emptiness in a container which one has filled beforehand up to the brim! Man can not be sometimes slave and sometimes free; he is wholly and forever free or he is not free at all.

DASEIN

(2) Human reality can not receive its ends, as we have seen, either from outside or from a so-called inner "nature." It chooses them and by this very choice confers upon them a transcendent existence as the external limit of its projects. From this point of view—and if it is understood that the existence of the *Dasein*[4] precedes and commands its essence—human reality in and through its very upsurge decides to define its own being by its ends. It is therefore the positing of my ultimate ends which characterizes my being and which is identical with the sudden thrust of the freedom which is mine. And this thrust is an *existence*; it has nothing to do with an essence or with a property of a being which would be engendered conjointly with an idea.

THREE INDISSOLUBLE TERMS

(3) ...the cause, the motive, and the end are the three indissoluble terms of the thrust of a free and living consciousness which projects itself toward its possibilities and makes itself defined by these possibilities.

FREEDOM AND THE FOR-ITSELF

(4) Let us consider more closely however the few certain results which our analysis has enabled us to attain. We have shown that freedom is actually one with the being of the for-itself; human reality is free to the exact extent that it has to be its own nothingness. It has to be this nothingness, as we have seen, in multiple dimensions: first, by temporalizing itself—*i.e.*, by being always at a distance from itself, which means that it can never let itself be determined by its past to perform this or that particular act; second, by rising up as consciousness of something and (of) itself—*i.e.*, by being presence to itself and not simply self, which implies that nothing exists in consciousness which is not consciousness of existing and that consequently nothing external to consciousness can motivate it; and finally, by being transcendence—*i.e.*, not something which would *first* be in order subsequently

to put itself into relation with this or that end, but on the contrary, a being which is originally a project—*i.e.*, which is defined by its end.

(5) I choose myself as a whole in the world which is a whole. Just as I come from the world to a particular "this," so I come from myself as a deto-talized totality to the outline of one of my particular possibilities since I can apprehend a particular "this" on the ground of the world only on the occa-sion of a particular project of myself. But in this case just as I can apprehend a particular "this" only on the ground of the world by surpassing it toward this or that possibility, so I can project myself beyond the "this" toward this or that possibility only on the ground of my ultimate and total possibility. Thus my ultimate and total possibility, as the original integration of all my particular possibles, and the world as the totality which comes to existents by my upsurge into being are two strictly correlative notions. I can perceive the hammer (*i.e.*, outline a plan of "hammering" with it) only on the ground of the world; but conversely I can outline this act of "hammering" only on the ground of the totality of myself and in terms of that totality.

(6) It should be observed first of all that the choice of total ends although totally free is not necessarily nor even frequently made in joy. We must not confuse our necessity of choosing with the will to power. The choice can be effected in resignation or uneasiness; it can be a flight; it can be realized in bad faith. We can choose ourselves as fleeing, as inapprehensible, as indecisive, *etc.* We can even choose not to choose ourselves. In these various instances, ends are posited beyond a factual situation, and the responsibility for these ends falls on us. Whatever our being may be, it is a choice; and it depends on us to choose ourselves as "great" or "noble" or "base" and "humiliated." If we have chosen humiliation as the very stuff of our being, we shall realize ourselves as humiliated, embittered, inferior, etc. We are not dealing here with *givens* with no further meaning. But the man who realizes himself as humiliated thereby constitutes himself as a *means* of attaining certain ends: the humilia-tion chosen can be, for example, identified like masochism with an instrument designed to free us from existence-for-itself; [if] it be a project of getting rid of our anguishing freedom to the advantage of others, our project can be to cause our being-for-itself to be entirely absorbed by our being-for-others. At all events the "inferiority complex" can arise only if it is founded on a free

apprehension of our being-for-others. This being-for-others as a *situation* will act in the capacity of a cause, but all the same it must be discovered by a *motive* which is nothing but our free project. Thus the inferiority which is felt and lived is the chosen instrument to make us comparable to a *thing*; that is, to make us exist as a pure outside in the midst of the world. But it is evident that it must be lived in accordance with the *nature* which we confer on it by this choice—*i.e.*, in shame, anger, and bitterness. Thus to *choose* inferiority does not mean to be sweetly contented with an *aurea mediocritas*; it is to produce and to assume the rebellion and despair which constitute the revelation of this inferiority. For example, I can persist in manifesting myself in a certain kind of employment *because* I am inferior in it, whereas in some other field I could without difficulty show myself equal to the average. It is this fruitless effort which I have chosen, simply because it is fruitless—either because I prefer to be the last rather than to be lost in the mass or because I have chosen discouragement and shame as the best means of attaining *being*.

(7) Since freedom is a being-without-support and without-a-springboard, the project in order to be must be constantly renewed. I choose myself perpetually and can never be merely by virtue of having-been-chosen; otherwise I should fall into the pure and simple existence of the in-itself. The necessity of perpetually choosing myself is one with the pursued-pursuit which I am. But precisely because here we are dealing with a *choice*, this choice as it is made indicates in general other choices as possibles. The possibility of these other choices is neither made explicit nor posited, but it is lived in the feeling of unjustifiability; and it is this which is expressed by the fact of the *absurdity* of my choice and consequently of my being. Thus my freedom eats away my freedom. Since I am free, I project my total possible, but I thereby posit that I am free and that I can always nihilate this first project and make it past.

Thus at the moment at which the for-itself thinks to apprehend itself and make known to itself by a projected nothingness what it *is*, it escapes itself; for it thereby posits that it can be other than it is. It will be enough for it to make explicit its unjustifiability in order to cause the *instant* to arise; that is, the appearance of a new project on the collapse of the former. Nevertheless this upsurge of the new project has for its express condition the nihilation of the former, and hence the for-itself can not confer on itself a new existence. As soon as it rejects the project which has lapsed into the past, it has to be this project in the form of the "was"; this means that this lapsed project belongs henceforth to the for-itself's situation. No law of being can assign an *a priori* number to the different projects which I am. The existence of the for-itself in fact conditions its essence. But it is necessary to consult each man's history in order to get from it a particular idea with regard to each individual for-itself. Our particular projects, aimed at the realization in the world of a particular end, are united in the global project which we are. But precisely because we are wholly choice and act, these partial projects are not determined by the global project. They must themselves be choices; and a certain margin of contingency, of unpredictability, and of the absurd is allowed to each of them although each project as it is projected is the specification of the global project on the occasion of particular elements in the situation and so is always understood in relation to the totality of my being-in-the-world.

THE FACTICITY OF FREEDOM

(8) We have established that the for-itself is free. But this does not mean that it is its own foundation. If to be free meant to be its own foundation, it would be necessary that freedom should decide the *existence* of its being. And this necessity can be understood in two ways. First, it would be necessary that freedom should decide its being-free; that is, not only that it should be a choice of an end, but that it should be a choice of itself as freedom. This would suppose therefore that the possibility of being-free and the possibility of not-being-free exist equally before the free choice of either one of them—*i.e.*, before the free choice of freedom. But since then a previous freedom would be necessary which would choose to be free—*i.e.*, basically, which would choose to be what it is already—we should be referred to infinity; for there would be need of another prior freedom in order to choose this and so on. In fact we are a freedom which chooses, but we do not choose to be free. We are condemned to freedom, as we said earlier, thrown into freedom or, as Heidegger says, "abandoned." And we can see that this abandonment has no other origin than the very existence of freedom. If, therefore, freedom is defined as the escape from the given, from fact, then there is a *fact* of escape from fact. This is the facticity of freedom.

(9) We said that freedom is not free not to be free and that it is not free not to exist. This is because the fact of not being able not to be free is the *facticity* of freedom, and the fact of not being able not to exist is its *contingency.* Contingency and facticity are really one; there is a being which freedom has to be in the form of *non-being* (that is, of nihilation). To exist as *the fact* of freedom or to have to be a being in the midst of the world are one and the same thing, and this means that freedom is originally a *relation to the given.*

(10) The given in no way enters into the constitution of freedom since freedom is interiorized as the internal negation of the given. It is simply the pure contingency which freedom exerts by denying the given while making itself a choice; the given is the plenitude of being which freedom colors with insufficiency and with *négatité* by illuminating it with the light of an end which does not exist. The given is freedom itself in so far as freedom *exists*; and whatever it does, freedom can not escape its existence. The reader will have understood that this given is nothing other than the in-itself nihilated by the for-itself which has to be it, that the body as a point of view on the world, that the past as the *essence* which the for-itself was—that these are three designations for a single reality. By its nihilating withdrawal, freedom causes a whole system of relations to be established, from the point of view of the end, between *all* in-itselfs; that is, between the *plenum* of being which is revealed then as the *world* and the being which it has to be in the midst of this *plenum* and which is revealed as *one* being, as *one* "this" which it has to be.

Thus by its very projection toward an end, freedom constitutes as a being in the midst of the world a particular *datum* which it has to be. Freedom does not choose it, for this would be to choose its own existence; but by the choice which it makes of its end, freedom causes the *datum* to be revealed in this or that way, in this or that light in connection with the revelation of the world itself. Thus the very contingency of freedom and the world which surrounds this contingency with its own contingency will appear to freedom only in the light of the end which it has chosen; that is, not as brute existents but in the unity of the illumination of a single nihilation. And freedom would never be able to reapprehend this ensemble as a pure *datum*, for in that case it would be necessary that this freedom be outside of all choice and therefore that it should cease to be freedom.

(11) Thus it must be said that the facticity of my place is revealed to me only in and through the free choice which I make of my end. Freedom is indispensable to the discovery of my facticity. I learn of this facticity from all the points of the future which I project; it is from the standpoint of this chosen future that facticity appears to me with its characteristics of impotence, of contingency, of weakness, of absurdity. It is in relation to my dream of seeing New York that it is absurd and painful for me to live at Mont-de-Marsan. But conversely facticity is the only reality which freedom can discover, the only one which it can nihilate by the positing of an end, the only thing in terms of which it is meaningful to posit an end. For if the end can illuminate the situation, this is because the end is constituted as a projected modification *of* this situation.

◦   ◦   ◦

It is only in the act by which freedom has revealed facticity and apprehended it as *place* that this place thus defined is manifested as an *impediment* to my desires, an obstacle, *etc.*

(12) Thus our freedom itself creates the obstacles from which we suffer. It is freedom itself which by positing its end and by choosing this end as inaccessible or accessible with difficulty, causes our placing to appear to our projects as an insurmountable resistance or a resistance to be surmounted with difficulty. It is freedom again which establishes the spatial connections between objects as the first type of a relation of instrumentality, which decides on techniques permitting distances to be measured and cleared, and thus constitutes its own *restriction*. But to be precise, freedom can exist only as *restricted* since freedom is choice. Every choice, as we shall see, supposes elimination and selection; every choice is a choice of finitude. Thus freedom can be truly free only by constituting facticity as its own restriction.

(13) Thus I shall apprehend myself at any moment whatsoever as engaged in the world at my contingent place. But it is precisely this engagement which gives meaning to my contingent place and which is my freedom. To be sure, in being born I *take a place*, but I am responsible for the place which I take. We can see clearly here the inextricable connection

of freedom and facticity in the situation. Without facticity freedom would not exist—as a power of nihilation and of choice—and without freedom facticity would not be discovered and would have no meaning.

FREEDOM AND THE PAST

(14) It is because this human-reality was a free project eaten away by an unpredictable freedom that it becomes "in the past" a tributary of the further projects of the for-itself. Human-reality is condemned to make-itself-past and hence to wait forever for the confirmation which it expected from the future. Thus the past is indefinitely in suspense because human-reality "was" and "will be" perpetually expecting. Expectation and suspense only succeed in affirming still more plainly that freedom is their original constituent. To say that the past of the for-itself is in suspense, to say that its present is an expecting, to say that its future is a free project, or that it can be nothing without having to be it, or that it is a totality-detotalized—all these are one and the same thing.

⬿   ⬿   ⬿

But the meaning of the past, although strictly individualized, is totally dependent on this expectation which itself depends on an absolute nothingness; that is, on a free project which does not yet exist. My past therefore is a concrete and precise proposition which as such awaits ratification.

(15) Just as the geometrician is free to create a particular figure which pleases him but can not conceive of one which does not immediately enter into an infinity of relations with the infinity of other possible figures, so our free choice of ourselves by causing the upsurge of a certain evaluative order of our past, causes the appearance in the world of an infinity of relations of this past to the world and to the Other. And this infinity of relations is presented to us as *an infinity of conducts to be adopted* since it is in the future that we evaluate our past. We are *compelled* to adopt these conducts insofar as our past appears within the compass of our essential project. To will this project, in fact, is to will the past; and to will this past is to will to realize it by a thou-

sand secondary behaviors. Logically the requirements of the past are hypothetical imperatives: "If you wish to have such and such a past, act in such
and such a way." But as the first term is a concrete and categorical choice,
the imperative also is transformed into a categorical imperative.

(16) Freedom implies therefore the existence of an environment to be
changed: obstacles to be cleared, tools to be used. Of course it is freedom
which reveals them as obstacles, but by its free choice it can only interpret
the *meaning* of their being. It is necessary that they be simply there, wholly
brute, in order that there may be freedom. To be free is to-be-free-to-do,
and it is to-be-free-in-the-world. But if this is the case, then freedom by
recognizing itself as the freedom to change, recognizes and implicitly foresees in its original project the independent existence of the given on which
it is exercised. The internal negation reveals the in-itself as independent,
and it is this independence which constitutes in the in-itself its character
as a *thing*. But consequently what freedom posits by the simple upsurge of
its being is the fact that *it is as having to do with something other than itself.* To
do is precisely to change what has no need of something other than itself
in order to exist; it is to act on that which on principle is indifferent to the
action, that which can pursue its existence or its becoming without the
action. Without this indifference of exteriority on the part of the in-itself,
the very notion of *doing* would lose its meaning (as we have shown earlier
in connection with wish and decision), and consequently freedom itself
would collapse. Thus the very project of a freedom in general is a choice
which implies the anticipation and acceptance of some kind of resistance
somewhere. Not only does freedom constitute the compass within which
in-itselfs otherwise indifferent will be revealed as resistances, but
freedom's very project is in general to do in a resisting world by means of
a victory over the world's resistances.

FREEDOM AND SITUATION

(17) We are separated from things by nothing *except by our freedom*; it is
our freedom which is responsible for the fact that there are things with all
their indifference, their unpredictability, and their adversity, and for the

fact that we are inevitably separated from them; for it is on the ground of nihilation that they appear and that they are revealed as bound one to another. Thus the project of my freedom adds *nothing* to things: it causes *there to be* things; that is, precisely, realities provided with a coefficient of adversity and utilizable instrumentality. Freedom makes these things reveal themselves *in experience*—that is, raise themselves successively on the ground of the world in the course of a process of temporalization. Finally our freedom causes these things to manifest themselves as out of reach, independent, separated from me by the very nothingness which I secrete and which I am. It is because freedom is condemned to be free— *i.e.,* can not choose itself as freedom—that there are things; that is, a plenitude of contingency at the heart of which it is itself contingency. It is by the assumption of this contingency and by its surpassing that there can be at once a *choice* and an organization of things in *situation;* and it is the contingency of freedom and the contingency of the in-itself which are expressed *in situation* by the unpredictability and the adversity of the environment. Thus I am absolutely free and absolutely responsible for my situation. But I am never free except *in situation.*

Notes

1. A rupture introducing nothingness. [Ed.]
2. The *pour-soi,* the self-conscious activity characterizing human beings. [Ed.]
3. The *en-soi,* the stable unchanging reality we attribute to God, and to inanimate things. [Ed.]
4. Human reality, at times referring to individuals singly, and at times, collectively. [Ed.]

[Jean-Paul Sartre, "Being and Doing: Freedom," *Being and Nothingness,* part four, ch. 1, tr. Hazel Barnes (New York: Philosophical Library, 1956). (1) Pp. 439–41. (2) Pp. 443–44. (3) P. 449. (4) P. 453. (5) P. 461. (6) P. 472. (7) Pp. 480–81. (8) Pp. 484–85. (9) P. 486. (10) P. 487. (11) P. 494. (12) P. 495. (13) Pp. 495–96. (14) Pp. 501–502. (15) P. 503. (16) Pp. 506–507. (17) P. 509.]

(2b)

Freedom as doing what one wants to do

(2b1)
Thomas Hobbes
1588–1679

Leviathan

selections from pt. 2, ch. 1

Hobbes treats liberty, or freedom, within the context of the state. Defining liberty as the absence of opposition is the negative way of saying that liberty is the capability of doing what one wants to do (what one has a will to do). It is compatible with necessity, and opposed to constraint. In his view it is also compatible with the unlimited power of the sovereign who rules the state.

"LIBERTY AS THE ABSENCE OF OPPOSITION"

(1) Liberty, or freedom, signifieth, properly, the absence of opposition; by opposition, I mean external impediments of motion; and may be applied no less to irrational, and inanimate creatures, than to rational. For whatsoever is so tied, or environed, as it cannot move but within a certain space, which space is determined by the opposition of some external body, we say it hath not liberty to go further. And so of all living creatures, whilst they are imprisoned, or restrained, with walls, or chains; and of the water whilst it is kept in by banks, or vessels, that otherwise would spread itself into a larger space, we use to say, they are not at liberty to move in such manner, as without those external impediments they would. But when the impediment of motion, is in the constitution of the thing itself, we use not to say;

it wants the liberty; but the power to move; as when a stone lieth still, or a man is fastened to his bed by sickness.

And according to this proper, and generally received meaning of the word, a FREEMAN, *is he, that in those things, which by his strength and wit he is able to do, is not hindered to do what he has a will to*. But when the words *free*, and *liberty*, are applied to any thing but *bodies*, they are abused; for that which is not subject to motion, is not subject to impediment: and therefore, when it is said, for example, the way is free, no liberty of the way is signified, but of those that walk in it without stop. And when we say a gift is free, there is not meant any liberty of the gift, but of the giver, that was not bound by any law or covenant to give it. So when we *speak freely*, it is not the liberty of voice, or pronunciation, but of the man, whom no law hath obliged to speak otherwise than he did. Lastly, from the use of the word *free-will*, no liberty can be inferred of the will, desire, or inclination, but the liberty of the man; which consisteth in this, that he finds no stop, in doing what he has the will, desire, or inclination to do.

Fear and liberty are consistent; as when a man throweth his goods into the sea for *fear* the ship should sink, he doth it nevertheless very willingly, and may refuse to do it if he will: it is therefore the action of one that was *free*: so a man sometimes pays his debt, only for *fear* of imprisonment, which because nobody hindered him from detaining, was the action of a man at *liberty*. And generally all actions which men do in commonwealths, for *fear* of the law, are actions, which the doers had *liberty* to omit.

"LIBERTY AND NECESSITY CONSISTENT"

Liberty, and *necessity* are consistent: as in the water, that hath not only *liberty*, but a *necessity* of descending by the channel; so likewise in the actions which men voluntarily do: which, because they proceed from their will, proceed from *liberty*; and yet, because every act of man's will, and every desire, and inclination proceedeth from some cause, and that from another cause, in a continual chain, whose first link is in the hand of God the first of all causes, proceed from *necessity*. So that to him that could see the connexion of those causes, the *necessity* of all men's voluntary actions, would appear manifest. And therefore God, that seeth, and disposeth all things, seeth also that the *liberty* of man in doing what he will, is accompanied with the *necessity* of doing that which God will, and no more, nor less. For though men may do many things, which God does not command, nor is therefore author of them; yet they can have no passion, nor appetite to any thing, of which appetite God's will is not the cause. And did not his will assure the *necessity* of man's will, and consequently of all that on man's will dependeth, the *liberty* of men would be a contradiction, and impediment to the omnipotence and *liberty* of God. And this shall suffice, as to the matter in hand, of that natural *liberty*, which only is properly called *liberty*.

But as men, for the attaining of peace, and conservation of themselves thereby, have made an artificial man, which we call a commonwealth; so also have they made artificial chains, called *civil laws*, which they themselves, by mutual covenants, have fastened at one end, to the lips of that man, or assembly, to whom they have given the sovereign power; and at the other end to their own cars. These bonds, in their own nature but weak, may nevertheless be made to hold, by the danger, though not by the difficulty of breaking them.

In relation to these bonds only it is, that I am to speak now, of the *liberty* of *subjects*. For seeing there is no commonwealth in the world, wherein there be rules enough set down, for the regulating of all the actions, and words of men; as being a thing impossible: it followeth necessarily, that in all kinds of actions by the laws praetermitted, men have the liberty, of doing what their own reasons shall suggest, for the most profitable to themselves. For if we take liberty in the proper sense, for corporal liberty; that is to say, freedom from chains and prison; it were very absurd for men to clamor as they do, for the liberty they so manifestly enjoy. Again, if we take liberty, for an exemption from laws, it is no less absurd, for men to demand as they do, that liberty, by which all other men may be masters of their lives. And yet, as absurd as it is, this is it they demand; not knowing that the laws are of no power to protect them, without a sword in the hands of a man, or men, to cause those laws to be put in execution. The liberty of a subject, lieth therefore only in those things, which in regulating their actions, the sovereign hath praetermitted: such as is the liberty to buy, and sell, and otherwise contract with one another; to choose their own abode, their own diet, their own trade of life, and institute their children as they themselves think fit; and the like.

"LIBERTY AND UNLIMITED SOVEREIGN POWER"

Nevertheless we are not to understand, that by such liberty, the sovereign power of life and death, is either abolished, or limited. For it has been already shown, that nothing the sovereign representative can do to a subject, on what pretense soever, can properly be called injustice, or injury; because every subject is author of every act the sovereign doth; so that he never wanteth right to any thing, otherwise, than as he himself is the subject of God, and bound thereby to observe the laws of nature. And therefore it may, and doth often happen in commonwealths, that a subject may be put to death, by the command of the sovereign power; and yet neither do the other wrong: as when Jephtha caused his daughter to be sacrificed: in which, and the like cases, he that so dieth, had liberty to do the action, for which he is nevertheless, without injury put to death. And the same holdeth also in a sovereign prince, that putteth to death an innocent subject. For though the action be against the law of nature, as being contrary to equity, as was the killing of Uriah, by David; yet it was not an injury to Uriah, but to God. Not to Uriah, because the right to do what he pleased was given him by Uriah himself: and yet to God, because David was God's subject, and prohibited all iniquity by the law of nature: which distinction, David himself, when he repented the fact, evidently confirmed, saying, *To thee only have I sinned.* In the same manner, the people of Athens, when they banished the most potent of their commonwealth for ten years, thought they committed no injustice; and yet they never questioned what crime he had done; but what hurt he would do: nay they commanded the banishment of they knew not whom; and every citizen bringing his oystershell into the market place, written with the name of him he desired should be banished, without actually accusing him, sometimes banished an Aristides, for his reputation of justice; and sometimes a scurrilous jester, as Hyperbolus, to make a jest of it. And yet a mail cannot say, the sovereign people of Athens wanted right to banish them; or an Athenian the liberty to jest, or to be just.

The liberty, whereof there is so frequent and honorable mention, in the histories, and philosophy of the ancient Greeks, and Romans, and in the writings, and discourse of those that from them have received all their learning in the politics, is not the liberty of particular men; but the liberty of the commonwealth: which is the same with that which every man then should have, if there were no civil laws, nor commonwealth at all. And the effects of it also be the same. For as amongst masterless men, there is perpetual war, of every man against his neighbor; no inheritance, to transmit to the soil, nor to expect from the father; no propriety of goods, or lands; no security; but a full and absolute liberty in every particular man: so in states, and commonwealths not dependent on one another, every commonwealth, not every man, has all absolute liberty, to do what it shall judge, that is to say, what that man, or assembly that representeth it, shall judge most conducing to their benefit. But withal, they live in the condition of a perpetual war, and upon the confines of battle, with their frontiers armed, and cannons planted against their neighbors round about. The Athenians, and Romans were free; that is, free commonwealths: not that any particular men had the liberty to resist their own representative; but that their representative had the liberty to resist, or invade other people. There is written on the turrets of the city of Lucca in great characters at this day, the word LIBERTAS; yet no mail can thence infer, that a particular man has more liberty, or immunity from the service of the commonwealth there, than in Constantinople. Whether a commonwealth be monarchical, or popular, the freedom is still the same.

But it is an easy thing, for men to be deceived, by the specious name of liberty; and for want of judgment to distinguish, mistake that for their private inheritance, and birth-right, which is the right of the public only. And when the same error is confirmed by the authority of men in reputation for their writings on this subject, it is no wonder if it produce sedition, and change of government. In these western parts of the world, we are made to receive our opinions concerning the institution, and rights of commonwealths, from Aristotle, Cicero, and other men, Greeks and Romans, that living under popular states, derived those rights, not from the principles of nature, but transcribed them into their books, out of the practice of their own commonwealths, which were popular; as the grammarians describe the rules of language, out of the practice of the time; or the rules of poetry, out of the poems of Homer and Virgil. And because the Athenians were taught, to keep them from desire of changing their government, that they were freemen, and all that lived under monarchy were slaves; therefore Aristotle puts it down in his *Politics*, (*lib.* 6. *cap.* ii.) *In democracy,* LIB-

ERTY *is to be supposed: for it is commonly held, that no man is* FREE *in any other government.* And as Aristotle; so Cicero, and other writers have grounded their civil doctrine, on the opinions of the Romans, who were taught to hate monarchy, at first, by them that having deposed their sovereign, shared amongst them the sovereignty of Rome; and afterwards by their successors. And by reading of these Greek, and Latin authors, men from their childhood have gotten a habit, under a false show of liberty, of favoring tumults, and of licentious controlling the actions of their sovereigns, and again of controlling those controllers; with the effusion of so much blood, as I think I may truly say, there was never any thing so dearly bought, as these western parts have bought the learning of the Greek and Latin tongues.

"OBLIGATION AND THE TRUE LIBERTY OF THE SUBJECT"

To come now to the particulars of the true liberty of a subject; that is to say, what are the things, which though commanded by the sovereign, he may nevertheless, without injustice, refuse to do; we are to consider, what rights we pass away, when we make a commonwealth; or, which is all one, what liberty we deny ourselves, by owning all the actions, without exception, of the man, or assembly we make our sovereign. For in the act of our *submission,* consisteth both our *obligation,* and our *liberty*; which must therefore be inferred by arguments taken from thence; there being no obligation on any man, which ariseth not from some act of his own; for all men equally, are by nature free. And because such arguments, must either be drawn from the express .words, *I authorize all his actions,* or from the intention of him that submitteth himself to his power, which intention is to be understood by the end for which he so submitteth; the obligation, and liberty of the subject, is to be derived, either from those words, or others equivalent; or else from the end of the institution of sovereignty, namely, the peace of the subjects within themselves, and their defense against .a common enemy.

First therefore, seeing sovereignty by institution, is by covenant of every one to every one; and sovereignty by acquisition, by covenants of the vanquished to the victor, or child to the parent; it is manifest, that every subject has liberty in all those things, the right whereof cannot by covenant be transferred. I have shewn before in the 14th chapter, that covenants, not to defend a man's own body, are void. Therefore,

If the sovereign command a man, though justly condemned, to kill, wound, or maim himself; or not to resist those that assault him; or to abstain from the use of food, air, medicine, or any other thing, without which he cannot live; yet hath that man the liberty to disobey.

If a man be interrogated by the sovereign, or his authority, concerning a crime done by himself, he is not bound, without assurance of pardon, to confess it; because no man, as I have shown in the same chapter, can be obliged by covenant to accuse himself.

Again, the consent of a subject to sovereign power, is contained in these words, *I authorize, or take upon me, all his actions*; in which there is no restriction at all, of his own former natural liberty: for by allowing him to *kill me*, I am not bound to kill myself when he commands me. It is one thing to say, *kill me, or my fellow, if you please*; another thing to say, *I will kill myself, or my fellow*. It followeth therefore, that

No man is bound by the words themselves, either to kill himself, or any other man; and consequently, that the obligation a man may sometimes have, upon the command of the sovereign to execute any dangerous, or dishonorable office, dependeth not on the words of our submission; but on the intention, which is to be understood by the end thereof. When therefore our refusal to obey, frustrates the end for which the sovereignty was ordained; then there is no liberty to refuse: otherwise there is.

Upon this ground, a man that is commanded as a soldier to fight against the enemy, though his sovereign have right enough to punish his refusal with death, may nevertheless in many cases refuse, without injustice; as when he substituteth a sufficient soldier in his place: for in this case he deserteth not the service of the commonwealth. And there is allowance to be made for natural timorousness; not only to women, of whom no such dangerous duty is expected, but also to men of feminine courage. When armies fight, there is on one side, or both, a running away; yet when they do it not out of treachery, but fear, they are not esteemed to do it unjustly, but dishonorably. For the same reason, to avoid battle, is not injustice, but cowardice. But he that enrolleth himself a soldier, or taketh imprest money, taketh away the excuse of a timorous nature; and is obliged, not only to go to the battle, but also not to run from it, without his captain's leave. And when the defense of the commonwealth, requireth at once the help of all that are able to bear arms, every one is obliged; because otherwise the institution of the commonwealth, which they have not the purpose, or courage to preserve, was in vain.

To resist the sword of the commonwealth, in defense of another man, guilty, or innocent, no man hath liberty; because such liberty, takes away from the sovereign, the means of protecting us; and is therefore destructive of the very essence of government. But in case a great many men together, have already resisted the sovereign power unjustly, or committed some capital crime, for which every one of them expecteth death, whether have they not the liberty then to join together, and assist, and defend one another? Certainly they have: for they but defend their lives, which the guilty man may as well do, as the innocent. There was indeed injustice in the first breach of their duty; their bearing of arms subsequent to it, though it be to maintain what they have done, is no new unjust act. And if it be only to defend their persons, it is not unjust at all. But the offer of pardon taketh from them, to whom it is offered, the plea of self-defense, and maketh their perseverance in assisting, or defending the rest, unlawful.

As for other liberties, they depend on the silence of the law. In cases where the sovereign has prescribed no rule, there the subject hath the liberty to do, or forbear, according to his own discretion. And therefore such liberty is in some places more, and in some less; and in some times more, in other times less, according as they that have the sovereignty shall think most convenient. As for example, there was a time, when in England a man might enter into his own land, and dispossess such as wrongfully possessed it, by force. But in aftertimes, that liberty of forcible entry, was taken away by a statute made, by the king, in parliament. And in some places of the world, men have the liberty of many wives: in other places, such liberty is not allowed.

If a subject have a controversy with his sovereign, of debt, or of right of possession of lands or goods, or concerning any service required at his hands, or concerning any penalty, corporal, or pecuniary, grounded on a precedent law; he hath the same liberty to sue for his right, as if it were against a subject; and before such judges, as are appointed by the sovereign. For seeing the sovereign demandeth by force of a former law, and not by virtue of his power; he declareth thereby, that he requireth no more, than shall appear to be due by that law. The suit therefore is not contrary to the will of the sovereign; and consequently the subject bath the liberty to demand the hearing of his cause; and sentence, according to that law. But if he demand, or take any thing by pretense of his power; there lieth, in that case, no action of law; for all that is done by him in virtue of his power, is done by the authority of every subject, and consequently he that brings an action against the sovereign, brings it against himself.

If a monarch, or sovereign assembly, grant a liberty to all, or any of his subjects, which grant standing, he is disabled to provide for their safety, the grant is void; unless he directly renounce, or transfer the sovereignty to another. For in that he might openly, if it had been his win, and in plain terms, have renounced, or transferred it, and did not; it is to be understood it was not his will, but that the grant proceeded from ignorance of the repugnancy between such a liberty and the sovereign power; and therefore sovereignty is stiff retained; and consequently all those powers, which are necessary to the exercising thereof; such as are the power of war, and peace, of judicature, of appointing officers, and councillors, of levying money, and the rest named in the eighteenth chapter.

The obligation of subjects to the sovereign, is understood to last as long, and no longer, than the power lasteth, by which he is able to protect them. For the right men have by nature to protect themselves, when none else can protect them, can by no covenant be relinquished. The sovereignty is the soul of the commonwealth; which once departed from the body, the members do no more receive their motion from it. The end of obedience is protection; which, wheresoever a man seeth it, either in his own, or in another's sword, nature applieth his obedience to it, and his endeavor to maintain it. And though sovereignty, in the intention of them that make it, be immortal; yet is it in its own nature, not only subject to violent death, by foreign war; but also through the ignorance, and passions of men, it hath in it, from the very institution, many seeds of a natural mortality, by intestine discord.

If a subject be taken prisoner in war; or his person, or his means of life be within the guards of the enemy, and hath his life and corporal liberty given him, on condition to be subject to the victor, he hath liberty to accept the condition; and having accepted it, is the subject of him that took him; because he had no other way to preserve himself. The case is the same, if he be detained on the same terms, in a foreign country. But if a man be held in prison, or bonds, or is not trusted with the liberty of his body; he cannot be understood to be bound by covenant to subjection; and therefore may, if he can, make his escape by any means whatsoever.

If a monarch shall relinquish the sovereignty, both for himself, and his heirs; his subjects return to the absolute liberty of nature; because, though nature may declare who are his sons, and who are the nearest of his kin; yet it dependeth on his own will, as hath been said in the precedent chapter, who shall be his heir. If therefore he will have no heir, there is no sovereignty, nor subjection. The case is the same, if he die without known kindred, and without declaration of his heir. For then there can no heir be known, and consequently no subjection be due.

If the sovereign banish his subject; during the banishment, he is not subject. But he that is sent on a message, or hath leave to travel, is still sub-ject; but it is, by contract between sovereigns, not by virtue of the covenant of subjection. For whosoever entereth into another's dominion, is subject to all the laws thereof; unless he have a privilege by the amity of the sov-ereigns, or by special license.

If a monarch subdued by war, render himself subject to the victor; his subjects are delivered from their former obligation, and become obliged to the victor. But if he be held prisoner, or have not the liberty of his own body; he is not understood to have given away the right of sovereignty; and therefore his subjects are obliged to yield obedience to the magistrates for-merly placed, governing not in their own name, but in his. For, his right remaining, the question is only of the administration; that is to say, of the magistrates and officers; which, if he have not means to name, he is sup-posed to approve those, which he himself had formerly appointed.

[Thomas Hobbes, *Leviathan*, 1651, ed. N. Oakeshott (Oxford: Basil Black-well, spelling modernized, date not given). (1) Pt. 2, ch. 21, pp. 136–45.]

François Voltaire

1694–1778

The Ignorant Philosopher
ch. 13

As Voltaire puts it, freedom is the power to do what one wishes. As with Hobbes, it opposes constraint but not necessity.

"AM I FREE?"

(1) Let us not go beyond the circle of our existence, but persevere in examining ourselves as far as we are able. I remember that one day ... a reasoner would have induced me to reason. He asked me, if I was free? I answered, that I was not in prison; that I had the key of my chamber; that I was perfectly free. That is not what I ask you, he said to me; do you believe your will is at liberty to desire, or not to desire, that you should throw yourself out at the window? Do you think, with the angel of the school, that a free choice is an appetitive power, and that a free choice is lost by sin? I looked attentively at my man, and endeavored to see in his eyes whether he was out of his mind; and I answered him, that I understood nothing of his jargon.

However, the question concerning the liberty of man greatly interested me. I consulted the schoolmen, and, like them, I continued in darkness. I consulted Locke,[1] and I perceived some rays of light. I read Collins's[2] Treatise, which appeared to be the works of Locke perfected; and I have not read any thing since, which has given me a greater degree of knowledge. This is what has been conceived by my feeble reason, aided by these two great men; the only persons in my opinion, who, in writing on this subject, have understood themselves, and the only persons who have made themselves understood by others.

There is nothing without a cause. An effect without a cause is an absurdity. Whenever I wish or desire, it must be in consequence of my judgment, good or bad; this judgment is necessary, therefore my will is also necessary. Indeed, it would be very singular, that all nature, that all the planets, should obey eternal laws, and that there should be a little animal, five feet high, who, in defiance of these laws, could act as he pleased, at the mere direction of his own caprice. He must act by chance, and chance is nothing. We have invented the word to express the known effect of causes unknown.

My ideas necessarily enter my brain. How can my will, which depends on those ideas, be at the same time necessitated and absolutely free? I feel, on a thousand occasions, this will can effect nothing; as when a disorder overwhelms me, when passion transports me, when my judgment cannot comprehend the objects which are presented to me, etc. I ought therefore to suppose, that the laws of nature being always the same, my will is not more free in things which appear to me most indifferent, than in those wherein I find myself impelled by an invincible force.

To be truly free, is to have power. When I can do what I wish, I am at liberty: but I necessarily wish what I wish; otherwise I wish without reason, without cause, which is impossible. My liberty consists in walking when I am inclined to walk, and when I have not the gout.

My liberty consists in not doing a wicked action when my mind necessarily represents it as wicked, to subdue a passion, when my mind makes me perceive the danger of it, and when the horror of the action powerfully combats my desire. We may repress our passions; (as I have already signified No. IV.) but then we are not the more free in repressing our desires, than when we suffer ourselves to be led away by our inclinations: for, in the one case as well as in the other, we irresistibly follow our last idea, and this last idea is necessary. I therefore necessarily do what it dictates to me. It is strange that men should not be content with this measure of liberty; i.e., with the power they have received from nature, to do in many cases what they choose. The planets have not this power; we possess it; and our pride induces us sometimes to think, that we possess still more. We imagine, that we have the incomprehensible and absurd gift of wishing without reason, and without any other motive than that of wishing. See Number XXIX.

I cannot pardon Dr. Clarke[3] for having artfully combated these truths while he felt the force of them, and which could not be well accommodated to his systems. No, it is not to be allowed in such a philosopher to attack Collins in the manner of a sophist, to change the state of the question by reproaching Collins with calling man *a necessary agent*. Agent or patient what does it signify? Agent when he moves voluntarily; patient when he receives ideas. What effect has the name on the thing? Man is, in all things, a dependent being, as all nature is dependent; and he cannot be excepted from all other beings.

In Samuel Clarke, the preacher has stifled the philosopher. He distinguishes physical necessity from moral necessity. And what is moral necessity? It may appear probable to you that a queen of England, who is crowned, and has the holy oil poured on her head in a church, will not take off her royal robes to lay herself quite naked on the altar, although an adventure of a similar kind is related of a queen of Congo. You call that a moral necessity in a queen of our climate; but it is in fact a physical and eternal necessity, arising from the constitution of things. It is as certain that this queen will not commit such folly, as it is that she will one day die. Moral necessity is only a word; every thing which is done is absolutely necessary. There is no medium between necessity and chance; and you know there is no chance; therefore every thing that comes to pass is necessary.

To embarrass the thing further, a distinction has been imagined between necessity and constraint; but is constrain any thing but a degree of necessity which we perceive; or is necessity any thing but constraint that is unperceived? Archimedes is equally necessitated to continue in his room when shut in, and when so entirely occupied by a problem, as not to admit the idea of going out.

Ducunt volentem fata, nolentem trahunt.

The fates lead those who are willing, and drag those who are unwilling.

The poor ignorant philosopher who now thinks thus, has not always thought in the same manner, but he is at length compelled to yield.

NOTES

1. *Q.v.* John Locke (2a3, above). [Ed.]

2. Anthony Collins, 1676–1729; philosopher/theologian; friend and defender of John Locke. Notice that "Locke perfected" is a Second Definition doctrine, although the original Locke is First Definition. [Ed.]

3. Samuel Clarke, 1675–1729; philospher/theologian; friend and defender of Isaac Newton against Leibniz. The three thinkers mentioned in such quick succession by Voltaire are British. It is possible that thought crossed the English Channel more expeditiously during the period of the Enlightenment than earlier—or later. [Ed.]

[Voltaire, *The Ignorant Philosopher*, tr. D. Williams (London: printed for Fielding and Walker in Pater-Noster-Row, 1779). (1) Ch. 13, pp. 12–15.]

David Hume

1711–1776

"Of Liberty and Necessity,"

An Enquiry Concerning Human Understanding
sec. VIII, parts 1 and 2
The Philosophical Works
A Treatise of Human Nature
bk. II, part III, secs. 1 and 2

In two separate readings Hume argues that liberty should be viewed as opposing constraint rather than necessity, else it is the same as chance. Both sections were titled "Of Liberty and Necessity." We are constrained by society to operate within certain boundaries; and we are constrained by habit, working through constant conjunction, to believe in causality. Metaphysical necessity may underlie constant conjunction, but we have no idea what it would be. Hence, Hume's view is that liberty contrasts with constraint and is compatible with necessity both psychologically and, if we could get to it, and if there is such a thing, physical necessity as well.

FROM THE ENQUIRY

(1) By liberty...we can only mean *a power of acting or not acting, according to the determinations of the will;* that is, if we choose to remain at rest, we may; if we choose to move, we also may. Now this hypothetical liberty is

universally allowed to belong to every one, who is not a prisoner and in chains. Here then is no subject of dispute.

Whatever definition we may give of liberty, we should be careful to observe two requisite circumstances; *first*, that it be consistent with plain matter of fact; *secondly*, that it be consistent with itself. If we observe these circumstances, and render our definition intelligible, I am persuaded that all mankind will be found of one opinion with regard to it.

It is universally allowed, that nothing exists without a cause of its existence, and that chance, when strictly examined, is a mere negative word, and means not any real power, which has any where, a being in nature. But it is pretended, that some causes are necessary, some not necessary. Here then is the advantage of definitions. Let any one *define* a cause, without comprehending, as a part of the definition, a *necessary connexion* with its effect; and let him show distinctly the origin of the idea, expressed by the definition; and I shall readily give up the whole controversy. But if the foregoing explication of the matter be received, this must be absolutely impracticable. Had not objects a regular conjunction with each other, we should never have entertained any notion of cause and effect; and this regular conjunction produces that inference of the understanding, which is the only connexion, that we can have any comprehension of. Whoever attempts a definition of cause, exclusive of these circumstances, will be obliged, either to employ unintelligible terms, or such as are synonymous to the term, which he endeavors to define.[1] And if the definition above mentioned be admitted; liberty, when opposed to necessity, not to constraint, is the same thing with chance; which is universally allowed to have no existence.

(2) Necessity may be defined two ways, conformably to the two definitions of *cause*, of which it makes an essential part. It consists either in the constant conjunction of like objects, or in the inference of the understanding from one object to another. Now necessity, in both these senses, (which, indeed, are, at bottom, the same) has universally, though tacitly, in the schools, in the pulpit, and in common life, been allowed to belong to the will of man; and no one has ever pretended to deny, that we can draw inferences concerning human actions, and that those inferences are founded on the experienced union of like actions, with like motives, inclinations, and circumstances. The only particular, in which any one can

differ, is, that either, perhaps, he will refuse to give the name of necessity to this property of human actions: But as long as the meaning is understood, I hope the word can do no harm: Or that he will maintain it possible to discover something farther in the operations of matter. But this, it must be acknowledged, can be of no consequence to morality or religion, whatever it may be to natural philosophy or metaphysics.

FROM THE TREATISE

(3) Section 1. All those objects, of which we call the one *cause* and the other *effect*, considered in themselves, are as distinct and separate from each other, as any two things in nature, nor can we ever, by the most accurate survey of them, infer the existence of the one from that of the other. 'Tis only from experience and the observation of their constant union, that we are able to form this inference; and even after all, the inference is nothing but the effects of custom on the imagination. We must not here be content with saying, that the idea of cause and effect arises from objects constantly united; but must affirm, that 'tis the very same with the idea of these objects, and that the *necessary connexion* is not discovered by a conclusion of the understanding, but is merely a perception of the mind. Wherever, therefore, we observe the same union, and wherever the union operates in the same manner upon the belief and opinion, we have the idea of causes and necessity, tho' perhaps we may avoid those expressions. Motion in one body in all past instances, that have fallen under our observation, is followed upon impulse by motion in another. 'Tis impossible for the mind to penetrate farther. From this constant union it *forms* the idea of cause and effect, and by its influence *feels* the necessity. As there is the same constancy, and the same influence in what we call moral evidence, I ask no more. What remains can only be a dispute of words.

And indeed, when we consider how aptly *natural* and *moral* evidence cement together, and form only one chain of argument betwixt them, we shall make no scruple to allow, that they are of the same nature, and derived from the same principles. A prisoner, who has neither money nor interest, discovers the impossibility of his escape, as well from the obstinacy of the goaler, as from the walls and bars with which he is surrounded; and in all attempts for his freedom chooses rather to work upon the stone and iron of the one, than upon the inflexible nature of the other. The same prisoner, when conducted to the scaffold, foresees his death as certainly from the constancy and fidelity of his guards as from the operation of the ax or wheel. His mind runs along a certain train of ideas: The refusal of the soldiers to consent to his escape, the action of the executioner; the separation of the head and body; bleeding, convulsive motions, and death. Here is a connected chain of natural causes and voluntary actions; but the mind feels no difference betwixt them in passing from one link to another; nor is less certain of the future event than if it were connected with the present impressions of the memory and senses by a train of causes cemented together by what we are pleased to call a *physical necessity*. The same experienced union has the same effect on the mind, whether the united objects be motives, volitions and actions; or figure and motion. We may change the names of things; but their nature and their operation on the understanding never change.

I dare be positive no one will ever endeavor to refute these reasonings otherwise than by altering my definitions, and assigning a different meaning to the terms of *cause, and effect, and necessity, and liberty, and chance*. According to my definitions, necessity makes an essential part of causation; and consequently liberty, by removing necessity, removes also causes, and is the very same thing with chance. As chance is commonly thought to imply a contradiction, and is at least directly contrary to experience, there are always the same arguments against liberty or free-will. If any one alters the definitions, I cannot pretend to argue with him, 'till I know the meaning he assigns to these terms.

(4) Section 2. I believe we may assign the three following reasons for the prevalence of the doctrine of liberty, however absurd it may be in one sense, and unintelligible in any other. First, after we have performed any action; tho' we confess we were influenced by particular views and motives; 'tis difficult for us to persuade ourselves we were governed by necessity, and that 'twas utterly impossible for us to have acted otherwise; the idea of necessity seeming to imply something of force, and violence, and constraint, of which we are not sensible. Few are capable of distinguishing betwixt the liberty of *spontaneity*, as it is called in the schools, and the liberty of *indifference*; betwixt that which is opposed to violence, and that

which means a negation of necessity and causes. The first is even the most common sense of the word; and as 'tis only that species of liberty, which it concerns us to preserve, our thoughts have been principally turned toward it, and have almost universally confounded it with the other.

Secondly, there is a *false sensation or experience* even of the liberty of indifference; which is regarded as an argument for its real existence. The necessity of any action, whether of matter or of the mind, is not properly a quality in the agent, but in any thinking or intelligent being, who may consider the action, and consists in the determination of his thought to infer its existence from some preceding objects: As liberty or chance, on the other hand, is nothing but the want of that determination, and a certain looseness, which we feel in passing or not passing from the idea of one to that of the other. Now we may observe, that tho' in reflecting on human actions we seldom feel such a looseness or indifference, yet it very commonly happens, that in performing the actions themselves we are sensible of something like it: And as all related or resembling objects are readily taken for each other, this has been employed as a demonstrative or even an intuitive proof of human liberty. We feel that our actions are subject to our will on most occasions, and imagine we feel that the will itself is subject to nothing; because when by a denial of it we are provoked to try, we feel that it moves easily every way, and produces an image of itself even on that side, on which it did not settle. This image or faint motion, we persuade ourselves, could have been compleated into the thing itself; because, should that be denied, we find, upon a second trial, that it can. But these efforts are all in vain; and whatever capricious and irregular actions we may perform; as the desire of showing our liberty is the sole motive of our actions; we can never free ourselves from the bonds of necessity. We may imagine we feel a liberty within ourselves; but a spectator can commonly infer our actions from our motives and character; and even where he cannot, he concludes in general, that he might, were he perfectly acquainted with every circumstance of our situation and temper, and the most secret springs of our complexion and disposition. Now this is the very essence of necessity, according to the foregoing doctrine.

A third reason why the doctrine of liberty has generally been better received in the world, than its antagonist, proceeds from *religion*, which has been very unnecessarily interested in this question. There is no method of reasoning more common, and yet none more blameable, than in philosophical debates to endeavor to refute any hypothesis by a pretext of its dangerous consequences to religion and morality. When any opinion leads us into absurdities, 'tis certainly false; but 'tis not certain an opinion is false, because 'tis of dangerous consequence. Such topics, therefore, ought entirely to be foreborn, as serving nothing to the discovery of truth, but only to make the person of an antagonist odious. This I observe in general, without pretending to draw any advantage from it. I submit myself frankly to an examination of this kind, and dare venture to affirm, that the doctrine of necessity, according to my explication of it, is not only innocent, but even advantageous to religion and morality.

I define necessity two ways, conformable to the two definitions of *cause*, of which it makes an essential part. I place it either in the constant union and conjunction of like objects, or in the inference of the mind from the one to the other. Now necessity, in both these senses, has universally, tho' tacitly, in the schools, in the pulpit, and in common life, been allowed to belong to the will of man, and no one has ever pretended to deny, that we can draw inferences concerning human actions, and that those inferences are founded on the experienced union of like actions with like motives and circumstances. The only particular in which any one can differ from me, is either, that perhaps he will refuse to call this necessity. But as long as the meaning is understood, I hope the word can do no harm. Or that he will maintain there is something else in the operations of matter. Now whether it be so or not is of no consequence to religion, whatever it may be to natural philosophy. I may be mistaken in asserting, that we have no idea of any other connexion in the actions of body, and shall be glad to be farther instructed on that head: But sure I am, I ascribe nothing to the actions of the mind, but what must readily be allowed of. Let no one, therefore, put an invidious construction on my words, by saying simply, that I assert the necessity of human actions, and place them on the same footing with the operations of senseless matter. I do not ascribe to the will that unintelligible necessity, which is supposed to lie in matter. But I ascribe to matter, that intelligible quality, call it necessity or not, which the most rigorous orthodoxy does or must allow to belong to the will. I change, therefore, nothing in the received systems, with regard to the will, but only with regard to material objects.

Nay I shall go farther, and assert, that this kind of necessity is so essential to religion and morality, that without it there must ensue an absolute subversion of both, and that every other supposition is entirely destructive to all laws both *divine* and *human.* 'Tis indeed certain, that as all human laws are founded on rewards and punishments, 'tis supposed as a fundamental principle, that these motives have an influence on the mind, and both produce the good and prevent the evil actions. We may give to this influence what name we please; but as 'tis usually conjoined with the action, common sense requires it should be esteemed a cause, and be looked upon as an instance of that necessity, which I would establish.

This reasoning is equally solid, when applied to *divine* laws, so far as the deity is considered as a legislator, and is supposed to inflict punishment and bestow rewards with a design to produce obedience. But I also maintain, that even where he acts not in his magisterial capacity, but is regarded as the avenger of crimes merely on account of their odiousness and deformity, not only 'tis impossible, without the necessary connexion of cause and effect in human actions, that punishments could be inflicted compatible with justice and moral equity; but also that it could ever enter into the thoughts of any reasonable being to inflict them. The constant and universal object of hatred or anger is a person or creature endowed with thought and consciousness; and when any criminal or injurious actions excite that passion, 'tis only by their relation to the person or connexion with him. But according to the doctrine of liberty or chance, this connexion is reduced to nothing, nor are men more accountable for those actions, which are designed and premeditated, than for such as are the most casual and accidental. Actions are by their very nature temporary and perishing; and where they proceed not from some cause in the characters and disposition of the person, who performed them, they infix not themselves upon him, and can neither redound to his honor, if good, nor infamy, if evil. The action itself may be blameable; it may be contrary to all the rules of morality and religion: But the person is not responsible for it; and as it proceeded from nothing in him, that is durable or constant, and leaves nothing of that nature behind it, 'tis impossible he can, upon its account, become the object or punishment or vengeance. According to the hypothesis of liberty, therefore, a man is as pure and untainted, after having committed the most horrid crimes, as at the first moment of his birth, nor is his character any way concerned in his actions; since they are not derived from it, and the wickedness of the one can never be used as a proof of the depravity of the other. 'Tis only upon the principles of necessity, that a person acquires any merit or demerit from his actions, however the common opinion may incline to the contrary.

But so inconsistent are men with themselves, that though they often assert, that necessity utterly destroys all merit and demerit either towards mankind or superior powers, yet they continue still to reason upon these very principles or necessity in all their judgments concerning this matter. Men are not blamed for such evil actions as they perform ignorantly and casually, whatever may be their consequences. Why? but because the causes of these actions are only momentary, and terminate in them alone. Men are less blamed for such evil actions, as they perform hastily and unpremeditately, than for such as proceed from thought and deliberation. For what reason? but because a hasty temper, tho' a constant cause in the mind, operates only by intervals, and infects not the whole character. Again, repentance wipes off every crime, especially if attended with an evident reformation of life and manners. How is this to be accounted for? But by asserting that actions render a person criminal, merely as they are proofs of criminal passions or principles in the mind; and when by any alteration of these principles they cease to be just proofs, they likewise cease to be criminal. But according to the doctrine of *liberty* or *chance* they never were just proofs, and consequently never were criminal.

Here then I turn to my adversary, and desire him to free his own system from these odious consequences before he charge them upon others. Or if he rather chooses, that this question should be decided by fair arguments before philosophers, than by declamations before the people, let him return to what I have advanced to prove that liberty and chance are synonymous; and concerning the nature of moral evidence and the regularity of human actions. Upon a review of these reasonings, I cannot doubt of an entire victory....

NOTE

1. Thus, if a cause be defined, *that which produces any thing*; it is easy to observe, that *producing* is synonymous to *causing*. In like manner, if a cause be defined as *that*

by which anything exists; this is liable to the same objection. For what is meant by these words, *by which?* Had it been said, that a cause is *that* after which *anything constantly exists*; we should have understood the terms. For this is, indeed, all we know of the matter. And this constancy forms the very essence of necessity, nor have we any other idea of it.

[David Hume, "Of Liberty and Necessity," *An Enquiry Concerning Human Understanding*, sec. VIII, part I, *The Philosophical Works*, ed. T. H. Green and T. H. Grose, vol. 4 (Darmstadt, Ger: Scientia Verlag Aalen, 1992). (1) Pp. 78–79. (2) Part II, p. 79. (3) "Of Liberty and Necessity," *A Treatise of Human Nature*, 1739 (Oxford: Clarendon Press, 1888), bk. II, part III, sec. 1, pp. 405–407. (4) Sec. 2, pp. 407–12.]

(2b4)

Jonathan Edwards

1703–1758

selections from *Freedom of the Will*

Edwards' view fits the second definition of freedom (*q.v.* D), believing that we have the power to do what we will, although our wills are determined by God. He is concerned to show that this is what freedom is generally held to be.

THE MEANING OF FREEDOM.

(1) The plain and obvious meaning of the words "freedom" and "liberty," in common speech, is power, opportunity, or advantage, that anyone has, to do as he pleases. Or in other words, his being free from hindrance or impediment in the way of doing, or conducting in any respect, as he wills.[1] And the contrary to liberty, whatever name we call that by, is a person's being hindered or unable to conduct as he will, or being necessitated to do otherwise.

If this which I have mentioned be the meaning of the word "liberty," in the ordinary use of language; as I trust that none that has ever learned to talk, and is unprejudiced, will deny; then it will follow, that in propriety of speech, neither liberty, nor its contrary, can properly be ascribed to any being or thing, but that which has such a faculty, power or property, as is called "will." For that which is possessed of no such thing as will, can't have any power or opportunity of doing according to its will, nor be necessitated to act contrary to its will, nor be restrained from acting agreeably to it. And therefore to talk of liberty, or the contrary, as belonging to the very will itself, is not to speak good sense; if we judge of sense, and nonsense, by the original and proper signification of words. For the will itself is not an agent that has a will: the power of choosing, itself, has not a power of choosing. That which has the power of volition or choice is the man or the soul, and not the power of volition itself. And he that has the liberty of doing according to his will, is the agent or doer who is possessed of the will; and not the will which he is possessed of. We say with propriety, that a bird let loose has power and liberty to fly; but not that the bird's power of flying has a power and liberty of flying. To be free is the property of an agent, who is possessed of powers and faculties, as much as to be cunning, valiant, bountiful, or zealous. But these qualities are the properties of men or persons; and not the properties of properties.

There are two things that are contrary to this which is called liberty in common speech. One is *constraint*; the same is otherwise called force, compulsion, and coaction; which is a person's being necessitated to do a thing *contrary* to his will. The other is *restraint*; which is his being hindered, and not having power to do *according* to his will. But that which has no will, can't be the subject of these things.—I need say the less on this head, Mr. Locke having set the same thing forth, with so great clearness, in his *Essay on the Human Understanding.*[2]

But one thing more I would observe concerning what is vulgarly called liberty; namely, that power and opportunity for one to do and conduct as he will, or according to his choice, is all that is meant by it; without taking into the meaning of the word, anything of the cause or original of that choice; or at all considering how the person came to have such a volition; whether it was caused by some external motive, or internal habitual bias; whether it was determined by some internal antecedent volition, or whether it happened without a cause; whether it was necessarily connected with something foregoing, or not connected. Let the person come by his volition or choice how he will, yet, if he is able, and there is nothing in the way to hinder his pursuing and executing his will, the man is fully and perfectly free, according to the primary and common notion of freedom.

What has been said may be sufficient to shew what is meant by liberty, according to the common notions of mankind, and in the usual and primary acceptation of the word: but the word, as used by Arminians, Pelagians and others, who oppose the Calvinists, has an entirely different signification. These several things belong to their notion of liberty: 1. That it consists in a self-determining power in the will, or a certain sovereignty the will has over itself, and its own acts, whereby it determines its own volitions; so as not to be dependent in its determinations, on any cause without itself, nor determined by anything prior to its own acts. 2. Indifference belongs to liberty in their notion of it, or that the mind, previous to the act of volition be, *in equilibrio.* 3. Contingence is another thing that belongs and is essential to it; not in the common acceptation of the word, as that has been already explained, but as opposed to all necessity, or any fixed and certain connection with some previous ground or reason of its existence. They suppose the essence of liberty so much to consist in these things, that unless the will of man be free in this sense, he has no real freedom, how much soever he may be at liberty to act according to his will.

A moral agent is a being that is capable of those actions that have a moral quality, and which can properly be denominated good or evil in a moral sense, virtuous or vicious, commendable or faulty. To moral agency belongs a moral faculty, or sense of moral good and evil, or of such a thing as desert or worthiness of praise or blame, reward or punishment; and a capacity which an agent has of being influenced in his actions by moral inducements or motives, exhibited to the view of understanding and reason, to engage to a conduct agreeable to the moral faculty.

The sun is very excellent and beneficial in its action and influence on the earth, in warming it, and causing it to bring forth its fruits; but it is not a moral agent: its action, though good, is not virtuous or meritorious. Fire that breaks out in a city, and consumes great part of it, is very mischievous in its operation; but is not a moral agent: what it does is not faulty or sinful, or deserving of any punishment. The brute creatures are not moral agents: the actions of some of 'em are very profitable and pleasant; others are very hurtful: yet, seeing they have no moral faculty, or sense of desert, and don't act from choice guided by understanding, or with a capacity of reasoning and reflecting, but only from instinct, and are not capable of being influenced by moral inducements, their actions are not properly sinful or virtuous; nor are they properly the subjects of any such moral treatment for what they do, as moral agents are for their faults or good deeds.

CAUSALITY

(2) Before I enter on any argument on this subject, I would explain how I would be understood, when I use the word "cause" in this discourse: since, for want of a better word, I shall have occasion to use it in a sense which is more extensive, than that in which it is sometimes used.

≈   ≈   ≈

...I sometimes use the word "cause," in this inquiry, to signify any antecedent, either natural or moral, positive or negative, on which an event, either a thing, or the manner and circumstance of a thing, so depends, that it is the ground and reason, either in whole, or in part, why it is, rather than not; or why it is as it is, rather than otherwise; or, in other words, any antecedent with which a consequent event is so connected, that it truly belongs to the reason why the proposition which affirms that event, is true; whether it has any positive influence, or not. And in an agreeableness to this, I sometimes use the word "effect" for the consequence of another thing, which is perhaps rather an occasion than a cause, most properly speaking.

≈   ≈   ≈

Having thus explained what I mean by cause, I assert, that nothing ever comes to pass without a cause. What is self-existent must be from eternity, and must be unchangeable: but as to all things that *begin to be*, they are not self-existent, and therefore must have some foundation of their existence without themselves. That whatsoever begins to be, which before was not, must have a cause why it then begins to exist, seems to be the first dictate of the common and natural sense which God hath implanted in the minds of all mankind, and the main foundation of all our reasonings about the existence of things, past, present, or to come.

And this dictate of common sense equally respects substances and modes, or things and the manner and circumstances of things. Thus, if we see a body which has hitherto been at rest, start out of a state of rest, and begin to move, we do as naturally and necessarily suppose there is some cause or reason of this new mode of existence, as of the existence of a body itself which had hitherto not existed. And so if a body, which had hitherto moved in a certain direction, should suddenly change the direction of its motion; or if it should put off its old figure, and take a new one; or change its color: the beginning of these new modes is a new event, and the mind of mankind necessarily supposes that there is some cause or reason of them.

If this grand principle of common sense be taken away, all arguing from effects to causes ceaseth, and so all knowledge of any existence, besides what we have by the most direct and immediate intuition. Particularly all our proof of the being of God ceases: we argue his being from our own being, and the being of other things, which we are sensible once were not, but have begun to be; and from the being of the world, with all its constituent parts, and the manner of their existence; all which we see plainly are not necessary in their own nature, and so not self-existent, and therefore must have a cause. But if things, not in themselves necessary, may begin to be without a cause, all this arguing is vain.

❦   ❦   ❦

But if once this grand principle of common sense be given up, that what is not necessary in itself, must have a cause; and we begin to maintain, that things may come into existence, and begin to be, which heretofore have not been, of themselves, without any cause; all our means of ascending in our arguing from the creature to the Creator, and all our evidence of the being of God, is cut off at one blow. In this case, we can't prove that there is a God, either from the being of the world, and the creatures in it, or from the manner of their being, their order, beauty and use. For if things may come into existence without any cause at all, then they doubtless may without any cause answerable to the effect. Our minds do alike naturally suppose and determine both these things; namely, that what begins to be has a cause, and also that it has a cause proportionable and agreeable to the effect. The same principle which leads us to determine, that there cannot be anything coming to pass without a cause, leads us to determine that there cannot be more in the effect than in the cause.

Yea, if once, it should be allowed, that things may come to pass without a cause, we should not only have no proof of the being of God, but we should be without evidence of the existence of anything whatsoever, but our own immediately present ideas and consciousness. For we have no way to prove anything else, but by arguing from effects to causes: from the ideas now immediately in view, we argue other things not immediately in view: from sensations now excited in us, we infer the existence of things without us, as the causes of these sensations: and from the existence of these things, we argue other things, which they depend on, as effects on causes. We infer the past existence of ourselves, or anything else, by memory; only as we argue, that the ideas, which are now in our minds, are the consequences of past ideas and sensations. We immediately perceive nothing else but the ideas which are this moment extant in our minds. We perceive or know other things only by means of these, as necessarily connected with others, and dependent on them. But if things may be without causes, all this necessary connection and dependence is dissolved, and so all means of our knowledge is gone. If there be no absurdity or difficulty in supposing one thing to start out of nonexistence, into being, of itself without a cause; then there is no absurdity or difficulty in supposing the same of millions of millions. For nothing, or no difficulty multiplied, still is nothing, or no difficulty: nothing multiplied by nothing don't increase the sum.

And indeed, according to the hypothesis I am opposing, of the acts of the will coming to pass without a cause, it is the case in fact, that millions of millions of events are continually coming into existence contingently, without any cause or reason why they do so, all over the world, every day and hour, through all ages. So it is in a constant succession, in every moral agent. This contingency, this efficient Nothing, this effectual No-Cause, is always ready at hand, to produce this sort of effects, as long as the agent exists, and as often as he has occasion.

If it were so, that things only of one kind, viz. acts of the will, seemed to come to pass of themselves; but those of this sort in general came into being thus; and it were an event that was continual, and that happened in a course, wherever were capable subjects of such events; this very thing would demonstrate that there was some cause of them, which made such a difference between this event and others, and that they did not really happen contingently. For contingence is blind, and does not pick and choose for a particular sort of events. Nothing has no choice. This No-

Cause, which causes no existence, can't cause the existence which comes to pass, to be of one particular sort only, distinguished from all others. Thus, that only one sort of matter drops out of the heavens, even water, and that this comes so often, so constantly and plentifully, all over the world, in all ages, shows that there is some cause or reason of the failing of water out of the heavens; and that something besides mere contingence has a hand in the matter.

If we should suppose Nonentity to be about to bring forth; and things were coming into existence, without any cause or antecedent, on which the existence, or kind or manner of existence depends; or which could at all determine whether the things should be; stones, or stars, or beasts, or angels, or human bodies, or souls, or only some new motion or figure in natural bodies, or some new sensations in animals, or new ideas in the human understanding, or new volitions in the will; or anything else of all the infinite number of possibles; then certainly it would not be expected, although many millions of millions of things are coming into existence in this manner, all over the face of the earth, that they should all be only of one particular kind, and that it should be thus in all ages, and that this sort of existences should never fail to come to pass where there is room for them, or a subject capable of them, and that constantly, whenever there is occasion for them.

If any should imagine, there is something in the sort of event that renders it possible for it to come into existence without a cause; and should say, that the free acts of the will are existences of an exceeding different nature from other things; by reason of which they may come into existence without any previous ground or reason of it, though other things cannot; if they make this objection in good earnest, it would be an evidence of their strangely forgetting themselves: for they would be giving an account of some ground of the existence of a thing, when at the same time they would maintain there is no ground of its existence. Therefore I would observe, that the particular nature of existence, be it never so diverse from others, can lay no foundation for that thing's coming into existence without a cause; because to suppose this, would be to suppose the particular nature of existence to be a thing prior to the existence; and so a thing which makes way for existence, with such a circumstance, namely without a cause or reason of existence. But that which in any respect makes way for a thing's coming into being, or for any manner or circumstance of its first existence, must be prior to the existence. The distinguished nature of the effect, which is something belonging to the effect, can't have influence backward, to act before it is. The peculiar nature of that thing called volition, can do nothing, can have no influence, while it is not. And afterwards it is too late for its influence: for then the thing has made sure of existence already, without its help.

So that it is indeed as repugnant to reason, to suppose that an act of the will should come into existence without a cause, as to suppose the human soul, or an angel, or the globe of the earth, or the whole universe, should come into existence without a cause. And if once we allow, that such a sort of effect as a volition may come to pass without a cause, how do we know but that many other sorts of effects may do so too? 'Tis not the particular kind of effect that makes the absurdity of supposing it has being without a cause, but something which is common to all things that ever begin to be, viz. that they are not self-existent, or necessary in the nature of things.

(3) That every act of the will has some cause, and consequently (by what has been already proved) has a necessary connection with its cause, and so is necessary by a necessity of connection and consequence, is evident by this, that every act of the will whatsoever, is excited by some motive: which is manifest, because, if the will or mind, in willing and choosing after the manner that it does, is excited so to do by no motive or inducement, then it has no end which it proposes to itself, or pursues in so doing; it aims at nothing, and seeks nothing. And if it seeks nothing, then it don't go after anything, or exert any inclination or preference towards anything. Which brings the matter to a contradiction; because for the mind to will something, and for it to go after something by an act of preference and inclination, are the same thing.

But if every act of the will is excited by a motive, then that motive is the cause of the act of the will. If the acts of the will are excited by motives, then motives are the causes of their being excited; or, which is the same thing, the cause of their being put forth into act and existence. And if so, the existence of the acts of the will is properly the effect of their motives. Motives do nothing as motives or inducements, but by their influence; and so much as is done by their influence, is the effect of them. For that is the notion of an effect, something that is brought to pass by the influence of another thing.

And if volitions are properly the effects of their motives, then they are necessarily connected with their motives. Every effect and event being, as was proved before, necessarily connected with that which is the proper ground and reason of its existence. Thus it is manifest, that volition is necessary, and is not from any self-determining power in the will: the volition which is caused by previous motive and inducement, is not caused by the will exercising a sovereign power over itself, to determine, cause and excite volitions in itself. This is not consistent with the will's acting in a state of indifference and equilibrium, to determine itself to a preference; for the way in which motives operate, is by biasing the will, and giving it a certain inclination or preponderation one way.

GOD'S FOREKNOWLEDGE AND MORAL NECESSITY

(4) That the acts of the wills of moral agents are not contingent events, in that sense, as to be without all necessity, appears by God's certain foreknowledge of such events.

In handling this argument, I would in the first place prove, that God has a certain foreknowledge of the voluntary acts of moral agents; and secondly, show the consequence, or how it follows from hence, that the volitions of moral agents are not contingent, so as to be without necessity of connection and consequence.

First, I am to prove, that God has an absolute and certain foreknowledge of the free actions of moral agents.

One would think, it should be wholly needless to enter on such an argument with any that profess themselves Christians: but so it is; God's certain foreknowledge of the free acts of moral agents, is denied by some that pretend to believe the Scriptures to be the Word of God; and especially of late. I therefore shall consider the evidence of such a prescience in the most High, as fully as the designed limits of this essay will admit of; supposing myself herein to have to do with such as own the truth of the Bible.

Arg. I. My first argument shall be taken from God's prediction of such events. Here I would in the first place lay down these two things as axioms.

(a) If God don't foreknow, he can't foretell such events; that is, he can't peremptorily and certainly foretell them. If God has no more than an uncertain guess concerning events of this kind, then he can declare no more than an uncertain guess. Positively to foretell, is to profess to foreknow, or to declare positive foreknowledge.

(b) If God don't certainly foreknow the future volitions of moral agents, then neither can he certainly foreknow those events which are consequent and dependent on these volitions. The existence of the one depending on the existence of the other, the knowledge of the existence of the one depends on the knowledge of the existence of the other; and the one can't be more certain than the other.

Therefore, how many, how great, and how extensive soever the consequences of the volitions of moral agents may be; though they should extend to an alteration of the state of things through the universe, and should be continued in a series of successive events to all eternity, and should in the progress of things branch forth into an infinite number of series, each of them going on in an endless line or chain of events; God must be as ignorant of all these consequences, as he is of the volition whence they first take their rise: all these events, and the whole state of things depending on them, how important, extensive and vast soever, must be hid from him.

(5) 'Tis true, the common people and children, in their notion of a faulty act or deed of any person, do suppose that it is the person's *own act* and deed. But this is all that belongs to what they understand by a thing's being a person's *own deed* or action; even that it is something done by him of choice. That some exercise or motion should begin of itself, don't belong to their notion of an action, or doing. If so, it would belong to their notion of it, that it is something which is the cause of its own beginning: and that is as much as to say, that it is before it begins to be. Nor is their notion of an action some motion or exercise that begins accidentally, without any cause or reason; for that is contrary to one of the prime dictates of common sense, namely, that everything that begins to be, has some cause or reason why it is.

The common people, in their notion of a faulty or praiseworthy deed or work done by anyone, do suppose that the man does it in the exercise of *liberty*. But then their notion of liberty is only a person's having opportunity of doing as he pleases. They have no notion of liberty consisting in the will's first acting, and so causing its own acts; and determining, and so causing its own determinations; or choosing, and so causing its own choice. Such a notion of liberty is what none have, but those that have darkened their own minds with confused metaphysical speculation, and abstruse and ambiguous terms. If a man is not restrained from acting as his will determines, or constrained to act otherwise; then he has liberty, according to common notions of liberty, without taking into the idea that grand contradiction of all the determinations of a man's free will being the effects of the determinations of his free will. Nor have men commonly any notion of freedom consisting in indifference. For if so, then it would be agreeable to their notion, that the greater indifference men act with, the more freedom they act with; whereas the reverse is true. He that in acting, proceeds with the fullest inclination, does what he does with the greatest freedom, according to common sense. And so far is it from being agreeable to common sense, that such liberty as consists in indifference is requisite to praise or blame, that on the contrary, the dictate of every man's natural sense through the world is, that the further he is from being indifferent in his acting good or evil, and the more he does either with full and strong inclination, the more is he esteemed or abhorred, commended or condemned.

If it were inconsistent with the common sense of mankind, that men should be either to be blamed or commended in any volitions they have or fail of, in case of moral necessity or impossibility; then it would surely also be agreeable to the same sense and reason of mankind, that the nearer the case approaches to such a moral necessity or impossibility, either through a strong antecedent moral propensity on the one hand, or a great antecedent opposition and difficulty on the other, the nearer does it approach to a being neither blamable nor commendable; so that acts exerted with such preceding propensity would be worthy of proportionably less praise; and when omitted, the act being attended with such difficulty, the omission would be worthy of the less blame. It is so, as was observed before, with natural necessity and impossibility, propensity and difficulty: as 'tis a plain dictate of the sense of all mankind, that natural necessity and impossibility takes away *all* blame and praise; and therefore, that the nearer the approach is to these through previous propensity or difficulty, so praise and blame are proportionably *diminished*. And if it were as much a dictate of common sense, that moral necessity of doing, or impossibility of avoiding, takes away *all* praise and blame, as that natural necessity or impossibility does this; then, by a perfect parity of reason, it would be as much the dictate of common sense, that an *approach* to moral necessity of doing, or impossibility of avoiding, *diminishes* praise and blame, as that an approach to natural necessity and impossibility does so. 'Tis equally the voice of common sense, that persons are *excusable in part*, in neglecting things difficult against their wills, as that they are *excusable wholly* in neglecting things impossible against their wills. And if it made no difference, whether the impossibility were natural and against the will, or moral, lying in the will, with regard to excusableness; so neither would it make any difference, whether the difficulty, or approach to necessity be natural against the will, or moral, lying in the propensity of the will.

But 'tis apparent, that the reverse of these things is true. If there be an approach to a moral necessity in a man's exertion of good acts of will, they being the exercise of a strong propensity to good, and a very powerful love to virtue; 'tis so far from being the dictate of common sense, that he is less virtuous, and the less to be esteemed, loved and praised; that 'tis agreeable to the natural notions of all mankind that he is so much the better man, worthy of greater respect, and higher commendation. And the stronger the inclination is, and the nearer it approaches to necessity in that respect, or to impossibility of neglecting the virtuous act, or of doing a vicious one; still the more virtuous, and worthy of higher commendation. And on the other hand, if a man exerts evil acts of mind; as for instance, acts of pride or malice, from a rooted and strong habit or principle of haughtiness and maliciousness, and a violent propensity of heart to such acts; according to the natural sense of all men, he is so far from being the less hateful and blamable on that account, that he is so much the more worthy to be detested and condemned by all that observe him.

Moreover, 'tis manifest that it is no part of the notion which mankind commonly have of a blamable or praiseworthy act of the will, that it is an act which is not determined by an antecedent bias or motive, but by the sovereign power of the will itself; because if so, the greater hand such causes have in determining any acts of the will, so much the less virtuous or vicious would they be accounted; and the less hand, the more virtuous or vicious. Whereas the reverse is true: men don't think a good act to be the less praiseworthy, for the agent's being much determined in it by a good inclination or a good motive; but the more. And if good inclination or motive has but little influence in determining the agent, they don't think his act so much the more virtuous, but the less. And so concerning evil acts, which are determined by evil motives or inclinations.

Yea, if it be supposed that good or evil dispositions are implanted in the hearts of men by nature itself (which, it is certain, is vulgarly supposed in innumerable cases) yet it is not commonly supposed that men are worthy of no praise or dispraise for such dispositions; although what is natural is undoubtedly necessary, nature being prior to all acts of the will whatsoever. Thus for instance, if a man appears to be of a very haughty or malicious disposition, and is supposed to be so by his natural temper, 'tis no vulgar notion, no dictate of the common sense and apprehension of men, that such dispositions are no vices or moral evils, or that such persons are not worthy of disesteem, odium and dishonor; or that the proud or malicious acts which flow from such natural dispositions, are worthy of no resentment. Yea, such vile natural dispositions, and the strength of 'em, will commonly be mentioned rather as an aggravation of the wicked acts that come from such a fountain, than an extenuation of 'em. Its being natural for men to act thus, is often observed by men in the height of their indignation: they will say, "'Tis his very nature: he is of a vile natural temper; 'tis as natural to him to act so, as it is to breathe; he can't help serving the devil," etc. But it is not thus with regard to hurtful mischievous things that any are the subjects or occasions of by *natural necessity*, against their inclinations. In such a case, the necessity, by the common voice of mankind, will be spoken of as a full excuse. Thus 'tis very plain, that common sense makes a vast difference between these two kinds of necessity, as to the judgment it makes of their influence on the moral quality and desert of men's actions.

≈ ≈ ≈

Some seem to disdain the distinction that we make between *natural* and *moral* necessity, as though it were altogether impertinent in this controversy: "That which is necessary (say they) is necessary; it is that which must be, and can't be prevented. And that which is impossible, is impossible, and can't be done: and therefore none can be to blame for not doing it." And such comparisons are made use of, as the commanding of a man to walk who has lost his legs, and condemning and punishing him for not obeying; inviting and calling upon a man, who is shut up in a strong prison, to come forth, etc. But in these things Arminians[3] are very unreasonable. Let common sense determine whether there be not a great difference between those two cases; the one, that of a man who has offended his prince, and is cast into prison; and after he has lain there a while, the king comes to him, calls him to come forth to him; and tells him that if he will do so, and will fall down before him, and humbly beg his pardon, he shall be forgiven, and set at liberty, and also be greatly enriched, and advanced to honor: the prisoner heartily repents of the folly and wickedness of his offense against his prince, is thoroughly disposed to abase himself, and accept of the king's offer; but is confined by strong walls, with gates of brass, and bars of iron. The other case is, that of a man who is of a very unreasonable spirit, of a haughty, ungrateful, willful disposition; and moreover, has been brought up in traitorous principles; and has his heart possessed with an extreme and inveterate enmity to his lawful sovereign; and for his rebellion is cast into prison, and lies long there, loaden with heavy chains, and in miserable circumstances. At length the compassionate prince comes to the prison, orders his chains to be knocked off, and his prison doors to be set wide open; calls to him, and tells him, if he will come forth to him, and fall down before him, acknowledge that lie has treated him unworthily, and ask his forgiveness; he shall be forgiven, set at liberty, and set in a place of great dignity and profit in his court. But he is so stout and stomachful, and full of haughty malignity, that he can't be willing to accept the offer: his rooted strong pride and malice have perfect power over him, and as it were bind him, by binding his heart: the opposition of his heart has the mastery over him, having an influence on his mind far superior to the king's grace and condescension, and to all his kind offers and promises. Now, is it agreeable to common sense, to assert and stand to it, that there is no difference between these two cases, as to any worthiness of blame in the prisoners; because, forsooth, there is a necessity in both, and the required act in each case is impossible? 'Tis true, a man's evil dispositions may be as strong and immovable as the bars of a castle. But who can't see, that when a man, in the latter case, is said to be "unable" to obey the command, the expression is used improperly, and not in the sense it has originally and in common speech? And that it may properly be said to be in the rebel's power to come out of prison, seeing he can easily do it if he pleases; though by reason of his vile temper of heart which is fixed and rooted, 'tis impossible that it should please him?

Upon the whole, I presume there is no person of good understanding, who impartially considers the things which have been observed, but will allow that 'tis not evident from the dictates of the common sense, or natural notions of mankind, that moral necessity is inconsistent with praise and blame. And therefore, if the Arminians would prove any such inconsistency, it must be by some philosophical and metaphysical arguments, and not common sense.

NOTES

1. I say not only "doing," but "conducting"; because a voluntary forbearing to do, sitting still, keeping silence, etc., are instances of persons' conduct, about which liberty is exercised; though they are not properly called "doing."

2. [Locke, *Essay*, Bk. II, ch. 21, nos. 14–21; I, 319–24. See above, Intro., Pt. 4, no. 1.]

3. Those who believe in the view of freedom dismissed at the start of (5), essentially, the first definition which he believed to be a product of "confused metaphysical speculation." [Ed.]

[Jonathan Edwards, *Freedom of the Will*, 1754 (New Haven: Yale University Press, 1957). (1) Pp. 163–65. (2) Pp. 180–85. (3) Pp. 225–26. (4) Pp. 239–40. (5) Pp. 358–633.]

(2c)

Freedom as acting in terms of one's inner or real or essential nature

(2c1)

Epictetus

60–138

"Of Freedom"

ch. 1 of bk. IV of Epictetus, *Epictetus, The Discourses*

Freedom as complete independence is related to the judgment of one's inner reason.

(1) He is free who lives as he wills, who is subject neither to compulsion, nor hindrance, nor force, whose choices are unhampered, whose desires attain their end, whose aversions do not fall into what they would avoid. Who, then, wishes to live in error?—No one.—Who wishes to live deceived, impetuous, unjust, unrestrained, peevish, abject?—No one.—Therefore, there is no bad man who lives as he wills, and accordingly no bad man is free. And who wishes to live in grief, fear, envy, pity, desiring things and failing to get them, avoiding things and falling into them?—No one at all.—Do we find, then, any bad man free from grief or fear, not falling into what he would avoid, nor failing to achieve what he desires?—No one.—Then we find no bad man free, either.

(2) Consider now, in the case of the animals, how we employ the concept of freedom. Men shut up tame lions in a cage, and bring them up, and feed them, and some take them around with them. And yet who will call such a lion free? Is it not true that the more softly the lion lives the more slavishly he lives? And what lion, were he to get sense and reason, would care to be one of these lions? Why, yes, and the birds yonder, when they are

caught and brought up in cages, what do they suffer in their efforts to escape? And some of them starve to death rather than endure such a life, while even such as live, barely do so, and suffer and pine away, and if ever they find any opening, make their escape. Such is their desire for physical freedom, and a life of independence and freedom from restraint. And what is wrong with you here in your cage? "What a question! My nature is to fly where I please, to live in the open air, to sing when I please. You rob me of all this, and then ask, 'What is wrong with you?'"

That is why we shall call free only those animals which do not submit to captivity, but escape by dying as soon as they are captured. So also Diogenes says somewhere: "The one sure way to secure freedom is to die cheerfully"; and to the Persian king he writes: "You cannot enslave the Athenian State any more than you can enslave the fish."

(3) For what is it that every man is seeking? To live securely, to be happy, to do everything as he wishes to do, not to be hindered, not to be subject to compulsion. When, therefore, he becomes a friend of Caesar, has he been relieved of hindrance, relieved of compulsion, does he live securely, does he live serenely? From whom shall we inquire? What better witness have we than this very man who has become Caesar's friend? Come into the midst and tell us. When did you sleep more peacefully, now or before you became Caesar's friend? Immediately the answer comes: "Stop, I implore you by the gods, and do not jest at my lot; you don't know what I suffer, miserable man that I am; no sleep visits me, but first one person comes in and then another and reports that Caesar is already awake, and is already coming out; then troubles, then worries!" Come, when did you dine more pleasantly, now or formerly? Listen to him and to what he has to say on this topic. If he is not invited, he is hurt, and if he is invited, he dines like a slave at a master's table, all the time careful not to say or do something foolish. And what do you suppose he is afraid of? That he be scourged like a slave? How can he expect to get off as well as that? But as befits so great a man, a friend of Caesar, he is afraid he will lose his head. When did you take your bath in greater peace? And when did you take your exercise at greater leisure? In a word, which life would you rather live, your present life or the old one? I can take oath that no one is so insensate or so incurable as not to lament his misfortunes the more he is a friend of Caesar.

When, therefore, neither those who are styled kings live as they will, nor the friends of these kings, what free men are left?—Seek and you will find. For nature has given you resources to find the truth. But if you are unable of yourself, by employing these resources alone, to find the next step, listen to those who have already made the search. What do they say? Does freedom seem to you to be a good?—Yes, the greatest.—Is it possible, then, for a man who has this greatest good to be unhappy, or to fare ill?— No.—When, therefore, you see men unhappy, miserable, grieving, declare confidently that they are not free.—I do so declare.—Very well, then, we have now got away from buying and selling[1] and arrangements of that kind in the acquisition of property. For if you are right in agreeing to these propositions, whether it be the Great King[2] who is unhappy, or a little king, whether it be a man of consular rank, or one who has been a consul twice, he could not be free.—Granted.

Answer me, then, this further question: Does freedom seem to you to be a great and noble thing, and precious?—Of course.—Is it possible, then, for a man who achieves a thing so great and precious and noble, to be of abject spirit?—It is not.—When, therefore, you see one man cringing before another, or flattering him contrary to his own opinion, say confidently of this man also that he is not free; and that not merely if he be doing so for the sake of a paltry meal, but even if it be for a governorship or a consulship. Call rather those who do these things for certain small ends slaves on a small scale, and the others, as they deserve, slaves on a grand scale—This also I grant.—And does freedom seem to you to be something independent and self-governing?—Of course.—When, therefore, it is in another's power to put hindrances in a man's way and subject him to compulsion, say confidently that this man is not free. And please don't look at his grandfathers and great-grandfathers, or look for a deed of sale or purchase, but if you hear him say "Master," in the center of his being and with deep emotion, call him a slave, even if twelve fasces[3] precede him; and if you hear him say, "Alas! What I must suffer!" call him a slave; and, in short, if you see him wailing, complaining, in misery, call him a slave in a *toga praetexta*.[4] However, if he does none of these things, do not call him free yet, but find out what his judgements are, whether they are in any respect subject to compulsion, to hindrance, to unhappiness; and if you find him to be that kind of a person, call him a slave on holiday at the Saturnalia;[5] say that his master is out of town; later on he will return, and then you will learn what the fellow suffers.—Who will return?—Anyone who has control over the things which some man desires, to get these for him or to take them away.—Have we, then, so many masters?—Yes, so many. For even before these personal masters we have masters in the form of circumstances, and these are many. Hence, it needs must follow that those too who have authority over some one of these circumstances are our masters. Why, look you, no one is afraid of Caesar himself, but he is afraid of death, exile, loss of property, prison, disfranchisement. Nor does anyone love Caesar himself, unless in some way Caesar is a person of great merit; but we love wealth, a tribuneship, a praetorship, a consulship. When we love and hate and fear these things, it needs must be that those who control them are masters over us. That is why we even worship those persons as gods; for we consider that what has power to confer the greatest advantage is divine. And then we lay down the wrong minor premiss: "This man has power to confer the greatest advantage." It needs must be that the conclusion from these premisses is wrong too.[6]

What, then, is it which makes a man free from hindrance and his own master? For wealth does not do it, nor a consulship, nor a province, nor a kingdom, but something else has to be found. What, therefore, is it which makes a man free from hindrance and restraint in writing?—The knowledge of how to write.—And what in playing on the harp?—The knowledge of how to play on the harp.—So also in living, it is the knowledge of how to live. Now you have already heard this, as a general principle, but consider it also in its particular applications. Is it possible for the man who is aiming at some one of these things which are under the control of others to be free from hindrance?—No.—Is it possible for him to be free from restraint?—No.—Therefore, it is not possible for him to be free, either. Consider then : Have we nothing which is under our own exclusive control, or is everything in that state; or are some things, under our control and others under the control of others?—How do you mean?—When you want your body to be whole, is the matter under your control, or not?—It is not.—And when you want it to be well?—Nor that, either.—And to live or to die?—Nor that, either.—Therefore.—Therefore, your body is not your own possession, it is subject to everyone who is stronger than you are.—Granted.—And your farm, is it under your control to have it when you want, and as long as you want, and in the condition that you want?—No.—And your paltry slaves?—No.—And your clothes?—No.—And your paltry house?—No.—And your horses?—None of these things.—And if you wish by all means your children to live, or your wife, or your brother, or your friends, is the matter under your control?—No, nor that, either.

Have you, then, nothing subject to your authority, which is under your control and yours only, or do you have something of that sort?—I do not know.—Look, then, at the matter this way, and consider it. No one can make you assent to what is false, can he?—No one.—Well, then, in the region of assent you are free from hindrance and restraint.—Granted.—Come, can anyone force you to choose something that you do not want?—He can; for when he threatens me with death or bonds, he compels me to choose.—If, however, you despise death and bonds do you pay any further heed to him?—No.—Is it, then, an act of your own to despise death, or is it not your own act?—It is mine.—So it is your own act to choose, or is it not?— Granted that it is mine.—And to refuse something? This also is yours.—Yes, but suppose I choose to go for a walk and the other person hinders me?—What part of you will he hinder? Surely not your assent?—No; but my poor body.—Yes, as he would a stone.—Granted that, but I do not proceed to take my walk.—But who told you, "It is your own act to take a walk unhindered." As for me, I told you that the only unhindered thing was the desire; but where there is a use of the body and its cooperation, you have heard long ago that nothing is your own.—Granted that also.—Can anyone force you to desire what you do not want?—No one.—Or to purpose or plan, or, in a word, to deal with the impressions that come to you?—No, nor that, either; but he will hinder me, when I set my desire upon something, from achieving what I desire.—If you desire something which is your own and not subject to hindrance, how will he hinder you?—Not at all.—Who, then, tells you that the man who sets his desire upon what is not his own is free from hindrance?

Shall I not, then, set my desire on health?—No, not at all, nor on anything else which is not your own. For that which is not in your power to acquire or to keep is none of yours. Keep far away from it not merely your hands, but above all your desire; otherwise, you have delivered yourself into slavery, you have bowed your neck to the burden, if you admire anything that is not your own, if you conceive a violent passion for anything that is in subjection to another and mortal.—Is not my hand my own?—It is a part of you, but by nature it is clay, subject to hindrance and compulsion, a slave to everything that is stronger than you are. And why do I name you the hand? You ought to treat your whole body like a poor loaded-down donkey, as long as it is possible, as long as it is allowed; and if it be commandeered and a soldier lay hold of it, let it go, do not resist nor grumble. If you do, you will get a beating and lose your little donkey just the same. But when this is the way in which you should act as regards the body, consider what is left for you to do about all the other things that are provided for the sake of the body. Since the body is a little donkey, the other things become little bridles for a little donkey, little pack-saddles, little shoes, and barley, and fodder. Let them go too, get rid of them more quickly and cheerfully than of the little donkey itself.

Once prepared and trained in this fashion to distinguish what is not your own from what is your own possession, the things which are subject to hindrance from those which are free from it, to regard these latter as your concern, and the former as no concern of yours, diligently to keep your desire fixed on the latter, and your aversion directed toward the former, then have you any longer anyone to fear?—No one.—Of course; what is there to be fearful about? About the things that are your own, wherein is the true nature of good and evil for you? And who has authority over these? Who can take them away, who can hinder them, any more than one can hinder God? But shall you be fearful about your body and your property? About the things that are not your own? About the things that are nothing to you? And what else have you been studying, from the very outset, but how to discriminate between what is your own and what is not your own, what is under your control and what is not under your control, what is subject to hindrance and what is free from it? For what purpose did you go to the philosophers? That you might no less than before be unfortunate and miserable? You will not, then, in that case, be free from fear and perturbation. And what has pain to do with you? For fear of things anticipated becomes pain when these things are present. And what will you any longer passionately seek? For you possess a harmonious and regulated desire for the things that are within the sphere of the moral purpose, as being excellent, and as being within your reach; and you desire nothing outside the sphere of the moral purpose, so as to give place to that other element of unreason, which pushes you along and is impetuous beyond all measure.

Now when you face things in this fashion, what man can inspire fear in you any longer? For what has one human being about him that is calculated to inspire fear in another human being, in either his appearance, or conversation, or intercourse in general, any more than one horse, or dog, or bee inspires fear in another horse, or dog, or bee? Nay, it is *things* that inspire man with fear; and when one person is able to secure them for another, or to take them away, then he becomes capable of inspiring fear.

How, then, is a citadel destroyed? Not by iron, nor by fire, but by judgements. For if we capture the citadel in the city, have we captured the citadel of fever also, have we captured that of pretty wenches also, in a word, the acropolis within us, and have we cast out the tyrants within us, whom we have lording it over each of us every day, sometimes the same tyrants, and sometimes others? But here is where we must begin, and it is from this side that we must seize the acropolis and cast out the tyrants; we must yield up the paltry body, its members, the faculties, property, reputation, offices, honors, children, brothers, friends—count all these things as alien to us. And if the tyrants be thrown out of the spot, why should I any longer raze the fortifications of the citadel, on my own account, at least? For what harm does it do me by standing? Why should I go on and throw out the tyrant's bodyguard? For where do I feel them? Their rods, their spears, and their swords they are directing against others. But I have never been hindered in the exercise of my will, nor have I ever been subjected to compulsion against my will. And how is this possible? I have submitted my freedom of choice unto God. He wills that I shall have fever; it is my will too. He wills that I should choose something; it is my will too. He wills that I should desire something; it is my will too. He wills that I should get something; it is my wish too. He does not will it; I do not wish it. Therefore, it is my will to die; therefore, it is my will to be tortured on the rack. Who can hinder me any longer against my own views, or put compulsion upon me? That is no more possible in my case than it would be with Zeus.

This is the way also with the more cautious among travellers....

...he reflects and comes to the thought that, if he attach himself to God, he will pass through the world in safety.

How do you mean "attach himself"?—Why, so that whatever God

wills, he also wills, and whatever God does not will, this he also does not will.—How, then, can this be done?—Why, how else than by observing the choices of God and His governance? What has He given me for my own and subject to my authority, and what has He left for Himself? Everything within the sphere of the moral purpose He has given me, subjected them to my control, unhampered and unhindered. My body that is made of clay, how could He make that unhindered? Accordingly He has made it subject to the revolution of the universe—my property, my furniture, my house, my children, my wife. Why, then, shall I strive against God? Why shall I will what is not in the province of the will, to keep under all circumstances what has not been given me outright? But how should I keep them? In accordance with the terms upon which they have been given, and for as long as they can be given. But He who gave also takes away. Why, then, shall I resist? I do not say that I shall be a fool for trying to use force upon one who is stronger than I am, but before that I shall be wicked. For where did I get these things when I came into the world? My father gave them to me. And who gave them to him? Who has made the sun, who the fruits, who the seasons, who the union and fellowship of men one with another?

And so, when you have received everything, and your very self, from Another, do you yet complain and blame the Giver, if He take something away from you? Who are you, and for what purpose have you come? Did not He bring you into the world? Did not He show you the light? Did not He give you fellow-workers? Did not He give you senses also and reason? And as what did He bring you into the world? Was it not as a mortal being? Was it not as one destined to live upon earth with a little portion of paltry flesh, and for a little while to be a spectator of His governance, and to join with Him in His pageant and holiday? Are you not willing, then, for so long as has been given you, to be a spectator of His pageant and His festival, and then when He leads you forth, to go, after you have made obeisance and returned thanks for what you have heard and seen? " No," you say, " but I wanted to go on with the holiday." Yes, and so do the initiates in the mysteries want to go on with the initiation, and no doubt the spectators at Olympia want to see still other athletes; but the festival has come to an end; leave, depart as a grateful and reverent spectator departs; make room for others; yet others must be born, even as you were born, and once born they must have land, and houses, and provisions. But if the first-comers do not move along, what is left for those who follow after? Why are you insatiate? Why never satisfied? Why do you crowd the world?

(4) This is what you ought to practice from morning till evening. Begin with the most trifling things, the ones most exposed to injury, like a pot, or a cup, and then advance to a tunic, a paltry dog, a mere horse, a bit of land; thence to yourself, your body, and its members, your children, wife, brothers. Look about on every side and cast these things away from you. Purify your judgements, for fear lest something of what is not your own may be fastened to them, or grown together with them, and may give you pain when it is torn loose. And every day while you are training your-self, as you do in the gymnasium, do not say that you are "pursuing phi-losophy" (indeed an arrogant phrase!), but that you are a slave presenting your emancipator in court, for this is the true freedom.

(5) Come, now, and let us review the points on which we have reached agreement. The unhampered man, who finds things ready to hand as he wants them, is free. But the man who can be hampered, or subjected to com-pulsion, or hindered, or thrown into something against his will, is a slave. And who is unhampered? The man who fixes his aim on nothing that is not his own. And what are the things which are not our own? All that are not under our control, either to have, or not to have, or to have of a certain quality, or under certain conditions. Therefore, the body is not our own, its members are not our own, property is not our own. If, then, you conceive a strong passion for some one of these things, as though it were your imme-diate possession, you will be punished as he should be who fixes his aim upon what is not his own. This is the road which leads to freedom, this is the only surcease of slavery, to be able to say at any time with your whole heart,

> Lead thou me on, O Zeus, and Destiny,
> To that goal long ago to me assigned.[7]

(6) For freedom is not acquired by satisfying yourself with what you desire, but by destroying your desire. And that you may learn the truth of all this, as you have toiled for those other things, so also transfer your toil to these; keep vigils for the sake of acquiring a judgement which will make

you free, devote yourself to a philosopher instead of to a rich old man, be seen about *his* doors; it will be no disgrace to be so seen, you will not retire thence empty and without profit, if you approach him in the right fashion. Anyway, try it at least; there is no disgrace in making the attempt.

Notes

1. The reference is to the ordinary method of acquiring slaves, since relatively few were ever bred.

2. That is, of Persia.

3. The number for a consul.

4. The robe worn by high officials at Rome. Cf. 1. 2, 18.

5. When slaves had special liberties.

6. The major premiss is: "What has power to confer the greatest advantage is divine"; the minor premiss, as in the text; from which follows the conclusion: "Therefore, this man is divine," which is wrong because of the false minor premiss.

7. From the *Hymn* of Cleanthes.

[Epictetus, selected passages from "Of Freedom," ch. 1 of bk. IV of *Epictetus, the Discourses,* tr. W. A. Oldfather, vol. II (Cambridge: Harvard Univ. Press, 1928). (1) Pp. 245–46. (2) Pp. 251–53. (3) Pp. 257–81. (4) P. 283. (5) P. 289. (6) P. 305.]

(2c2)
Baruch (Benedict) Spinoza
1632–1677

selections from *Ethics*
Necessity and the Divine Nature

Necessity, perfection, and blessedness interpenetrate in freedom, and God is the supreme exemplar.

DEFINITION *VII*

(1) VII. That thing is called free, which exists solely by the necessity of its own nature, and of which the action is determined by itself alone. On the other hand, that thing is necessary, or rather constrained, which is determined by something external to itself to a fixed and definite method of existence or action.

NECESSITY AND THE DIVINE NATURE

(2) *Prop. XVI. From the necessity of the divine nature must follow an infinite number of things in infinite ways—that is, all things which can fall within the sphere of infinite intellect.*

Proof.—This proposition will be clear to everyone, who remembers that from the given definition of any thing the intellect infers several properties, which really necessarily follow therefrom (that is, from the actual essence of the thing defined); and it infers more properties in proportion as the definition of the thing expresses more reality, that is, in proportion as the essence of the thing defined involves more reality. Now, as the divine nature has absolutely infinite attributes (by Def. vi.), of which each expresses infinite essence after its kind, it follows that from the necessity of its nature an infinite number of things (that is, everything which can fall within the sphere of an infinite intellect) must necessarily follow. *Q.E.D.*

Corollary I.—Hence it follows, that God is the efficient cause of all that can fall within the sphere of an infinite intellect.

Corollary II.—It also follows that God is a cause in himself, and not through an accident of his nature.

Corollary III.—It follows, thirdly, that God is the absolutely first cause.

Prop. XVII. God acts solely by the laws of his own nature, and is not constrained by anyone.

Proof.—We have just shown (in Prop. xvi.), that solely from the necessity of the divine nature, or, what is the same thing, solely from the laws of his nature, an infinite number of things absolutely follow in an infinite number of ways; and we proved (in Prop. xv.), that without God nothing can be nor be conceived; but that all things are in God. Wherefore nothing can exist outside himself, whereby he can be conditioned or constrained to act. Wherefore God acts solely by the laws of his own nature, and is not constrained by anyone. *Q.E.D.*

Corollary I.—It follows: 1. That there can be no cause which, either extrinsically or intrinsically, besides the perfection of his own nature, moves God to act.

Corollary II.—It follows: 2. That God is the sole free cause. For God alone exists by the sole necessity of his nature (by Prop. xi. and Prop. xiv., Coroll. i.), and acts by the sole necessity of his nature, wherefore God is (by Def. vii.) the sole free cause. *Q.E.D.*

Note.—Others think that God is a free cause, because he can, as they think, bring it about, that those things which we have said follow from his nature—that is, which are in his power, should not come to pass, or should not be produced by him. But this is the same as if they said, that God could bring it about, that it should not follow from the nature of a triangle, that its three interior angles should not be equal to two right angles; or that from a given cause no effect should follow, which is absurd.

Moreover, I will show below, without the aid of this proposition, that neither intellect nor will appertain to God's nature. I know that there are many who think that they can show, that supreme intellect and free will do appertain to God's nature; for they say they know of nothing more perfect, which they can attribute to God, than that which is the highest perfection in ourselves. Further, although they conceive God as actually supremely intelligent, they yet do not believe, that he can bring into existence everything which he actually understands, for they think that they would thus destroy God's power. If, they contend, God had created everything which is in his intellect, he would not be able to create anything more, and this, they think, would clash with God's omnipotence; therefore, they prefer to assert that God is indifferent to all things, and that he creates nothing except that which he has decided, by some absolute exercise of will, to create. However, I think I have shown sufficiently clearly (by Prop. xvi.), that from God's supreme power, or infinite nature, an infinite number of things—that is, all things have necessarily flowed forth in an infinite number of ways, or always follow from the same necessity; in the same way as from the nature of a triangle it follows from eternity and for eternity, that its three interior angles are equal to two right angles. Wherefore the omnipotence of God has been displayed from all eternity, and will for all eternity remain in the same state of activity. This manner of treating the question attributes to God an omnipotence, in my opinion, far more perfect. For, otherwise, we are compelled to confess that God understands an infinite number of creatable things, which he will never be able to create, for, if he created all that he understands, he would, according to this showing, exhaust his omnipotence, and render himself imperfect. Wherefore, in order to establish that God is perfect, we should be reduced to establishing at the same time, that he cannot bring to pass everything over which his power extends; this seems to be a hypothesis most absurd, and most repugnant to God's omnipotence.

MENTAL DECISION AND BODILY STATE THE SAME THING

(3) ... many believe, that we are only free in respect to objects which we moderately desire, because our desire for such can easily be controlled

by the thought of something else frequently remembered, but that we are by no means free in respect to what we seek with violent emotion, for our desire cannot then be allayed with the remembrance of anything else. However, unless such persons had proved by experience that we do many things which we afterwards repent of, and again that we often, when assailed by contrary emotions, see the better and follow the worse, there would be nothing to prevent their believing that we are free in all things. Thus an infant believes that of its own free will it desires milk, an angry, child believes that it freely desires vengeance, a timid child believes that it freely desires to run away; further, a drunken man believes that he utters from the free decision of his mind words which, when he is sober, he would willingly have withheld: thus, too, a delirious man, a garrulous woman, a child, and others of like complexion, believe that they speak from the free decision of their mind, when they are in reality unable to restrain their impulse to talk. Experience teaches us no less clearly than reason, that men believe themselves to be free, simply because they are conscious of their actions, and unconscious of the causes whereby those actions are determined; and, further, it is plain that the dictates of the mind are but another name for the appetites, and therefore vary according to the varying state of the body. Everyone shapes his actions according to his emotion, those who are assailed by conflicting emotions know not what they wish; those who are not attacked by any emotion are readily swayed this way or that. All these considerations clearly show that a mental decision and a bodily appetite, or determined state, are simultaneous, or rather are one and the same thing, which we call decision, when it is regarded under and explained through the attribute of thought, and a conditioned state, when it is regarded under the attribute of extension, and deduced from the laws of motion and rest. This will appear yet more plainly in the sequel. For the present I wish to call attention to another point, namely, that we cannot act by the decision of the mind, unless we have a remembrance of having done so. For instance, we cannot say a word without remembering that we have done so. Again, it is not within the free power of the mind to remember or forget a thing at will. Therefore the freedom of the mind must in any case be limited to the power of uttering or not uttering something which it remembers. But when we dream that we speak, we believe that we speak from a free decision of the mind, yet we do not speak, or, if we do, it is by a spontaneous motion of the body. Again, we dream that we are concealing something, and we seem to act from the same decision of the mind as that, whereby we keep silence when awake concerning something we know. Lastly, we dream that from the free decision of our mind we do something, which we should not dare to do when awake.

Now I should like to know whether there be in the mind two sorts of decisions, one sort illusive, and the other sort free ? If our folly does not carry us so far as this, we must necessarily admit, that the decision of the mind, which is believed to be free, is not distinguishable from the imagination or memory, and is nothing more than the affirmation, which an idea, by virtue of being an idea, necessarily involves (II. xlix.). Wherefore these decisions of the mind arise in the mind by the same necessity, as the ideas of things actually existing. Therefore those who believe, that they speak or keep silence or act in any way from the free decision of their mind, do but dream with their eyes open.

A FREE MAN THINKS OF NOTHING LESS THAN DEATH.

(4) *Prop. LXVII. A free man thinks of death least of all things; and his wisdom is a meditation not of death but of life.*

Proof.—A free man is one who lives under the guidance of reason, who is not led by fear (IV. 1xiii.), but who directly desires that which is good (IV. lxiii. Coroll.), in other words (IV. xxiv.), who strives to act, to live, and to preserve his being on the basis of seeking his own true advantage; wherefore such an one thinks of nothing less than of death, but his wisdom is a meditation of life. *Q.E.D.*

Prop. LXVIII. If men were born free, they would, so long as they remained free, form no conception of good and evil.

Proof.—I call free him who is led solely by reason; he, therefore, who is born free, and who remains free, has only adequate ideas; therefore (IV. lxiv. Coroll.) he has no conception of evil, or consequently (good and evil being correlative) of good. *Q.E.D.*

Note.—It is evident, from IV. iv., that the hypothesis of this Proposition is false and inconceivable, except in so far as we look solely to the nature of man, or rather to God; not in so far as the latter is infinite, but only in so far as he is the cause of man's existence.

This, and other matters which we have already proved, seem to have been signified by Moses in the history of the first man. For in that narrative no other power of God is conceived, save that whereby he created man, that is the power wherewith he provided solely for man's advantage; it is stated that God forbade man, being free, to eat of the tree of the knowledge of good and evil, and that, as soon as man should have eaten of it, he would straightway fear death rather than desire to live. Further, it is written that when man had found a wife, who was in entire harmony with his nature, he knew that there could be nothing in nature which could be more useful to him; but that after he believed the beasts to be like himself, he straightway began to imitate their emotions (III. xxvii.), and to lose his freedom; this freedom was afterwards recovered by the patriarchs, led by the spirit of Christ; that is, by the idea of God, whereon alone it depends, that man may be free, and desire for others the good which he desires for himself, as we have shown above (IV. xxxvii.).

Prop. LXIX. The virtue of a free man is seen to be as great, when it declines dangers, as when it overcomes them.

Proof.—Emotion can only be checked or removed by an emotion contrary to itself, and possessing more power in restraining emotion (IV. vii.). But blind daring and fear are emotions, which can be conceived as equally great (IV. v. and iii.): hence, no less virtue or firmness is required in checking daring than in checking fear (III. lix. note); in other words (Def. of the Emotions, xl. and xli.), the free man shows as much virtue, when he declines dangers, as when he strives to overcome them. *Q.E.D.*

Corollary.—The free man is as courageous in timely retreat as in combat; or, a free man shows equal courage or presence of mind, whether he elect to give battle or to retreat.

Note.—What courage (*animositas*) is, and what I mean thereby, I explained in III. lix. note. By danger I mean everything, which can give rise to any evil, such as pain, hatred, discord, etc.

Prop. LXX. The free man, who lives among the ignorant, strives, as far as he can, to avoid receiving favors from them.

Proof.—Everyone judges what is good according to his disposition (III. xxxix. note); wherefore an ignorant man, who has conferred a benefit on another, puts his own estimate upon it, and, if it appears to be estimated less highly by the receiver, will feel pain (III. xlii.). But the freeman only desires to join other men to him in friendship (IV. xxxvii.), not repaying their benefits with others reckoned as of like value, but guiding himself and others by the free decision of reason, and doing only such things as he knows to be of primary importance. Therefore the free man, lest he should become hateful to the ignorant, or follow their desires rather than reason, will endeavor, as far as he can, to avoid receiving their favors.

Note.—I say, *as far as he can*. For though men be ignorant, yet are they men, and in cases of necessity could afford us human aid, the most excellent of all things: therefore it is often necessary to accept favors from them, and consequently to repay such favors in kind; we must, therefore, exercise caution in declining favors, lest we should have the appearance of despising those who bestow them, or of being, from avaricious motives, unwilling to requite them, and so give ground for offence by the very fact of striving to avoid it. Thus, in declining favors, we must look to the requirements of utility and courtesy.

Prop. LXXI. Only free men are thoroughly grateful one to another.

Proof.—Only free men are thoroughly useful one to another, and associated among themselves by the closest necessity of friendship (IV. xxxv. and Coroll. i.), only such men endeavor, with mutual zeal of love, to confer benefits on each other (IV. xxxvii.), and, therefore, only they are thoroughly grateful one to another. *Q.E.D.*

Note.—The goodwill, which men who are led by blind desire have for one another, is generally a bargaining or enticement, rather than pure goodwill. Moreover, ingratitude is not an emotion. Yet it is base, inasmuch as it generally shows, that a man is affected by excessive hatred, anger, pride, avarice, etc. He who, by reason of his folly, knows not how to return benefits, is not ungrateful, much less he who is not gained over by the gifts of a courtesan to serve her lust, or by a thief to conceal his thefts, or by any similar persons. Contrariwise, such an one shows a constant mind, inasmuch as he cannot by any gifts be corrupted, to his own or the general hurt.

Prop. LXXII. The free man never acts fraudulently, but always in good faith.

Proof.—If it be asked: What should a man's conduct be in a case where he could by breaking faith free himself from the danger of present death? Would not his plan of self-preservation completely persuade him to deceive ? This may be answered by pointing out that, if reason persuaded him to act thus, it would persuade all men to act in a similar manner, in which case reason would persuade men not to agree in good faith to unite their forces, or to have laws in common, that is, not to have any general laws, which is absurd.

Prop. LXXIII. The man, who is guided by reason, is more free in a State, where he lives under a general system of law, than in solitude, where he is independent.

Proof.—The man, who is guided by reason, does not obey through fear (IV. lxiii.): but, in so far as he endeavors to preserve his being according to the dictates of reason, that is (IV. lxvi. note), in so far as he endeavors to live in freedom, he desires to order his life according to the general good (IV. xxxvii.), and, consequently (as we showed in IV. xxxvii. note ii.), to live according to the laws of his country. Therefore the free man, in order to enjoy greater freedom, desires to possess the general rights of citizenship. *Q.E.D.*

"OF THE POWER OF THE UNDERSTANDING, OR OF HUMAN FREEDOM"

(5) At length I pass to the remaining portion of my Ethics, which is concerned with the way leading to freedom. I shall therefore treat therein of the power of the reason, showing how far the reason can control the emotions, and what is the nature of Mental Freedom or Blessedness; we shall then be able to see, how much more powerful the wise man is than the ignorant.

Prop. XL. In proportion as each thing possesses more of perfection, so is it more active, and less passive; and, vice versa, in proportion as it is more active, so is it more perfect.

Proof.—In proportion as each thing is more perfect, it possesses more of reality (II. Def. vi.), and, consequently (III. iii. and note), it is to that extent more active and less passive. This demonstration may be reversed, and thus prove that, in proportion as a thing is more active, so is it more perfect. *Q.E.D.*

Corollary.—Hence it follows that the part of the mind which endures, be it great or small, is more perfect than the rest. For the eternal part of the mind (V. xxiii. xxix.) is the understanding, through which alone we are said to act (III. iii.); the part which we have shown to perish is the imagination (V. xxi.), through which only we are said to be passive (III. iii. and general Def. of the Emotions); therefore, the former, be it great or small, is more perfect than the latter. *Q.E.D.*

Note.—Such are the doctrines which I had purposed to set forth concerning the mind, in so far as it is regarded without relation to the body; whence, as also from I. xxi. and other places, it is plain that our mind, in so far as it understands, is an eternal mode of thinking, which is determined by another eternal mode of thinking, and this other by a third, and so on to infinity; so that all taken together at once constitute the eternal and infinite intellect of God.

Prop. XLI. Even if we did not know that our mind is eternal, we should still consider as of primary importance piety and religion, and generally all things which, in Part IV, we showed to be attributable to courage and highmindedness.

Proof.—The first and only foundation of virtue, or the rule of right living is (IV. xxii. Coroll. and xxiv.) seeking one's own true interest. Now, while we determined what reason prescribes as useful, we took no account of the mind's eternity, which has only become known to us in this Fifth Part. Although we were ignorant at that time that the mind is eternal, we nevertheless stated that the qualities attributable to courage and highmindedness are of primary importance. Therefore, even if we were still ignorant of this doctrine, we should yet put the aforesaid precepts of reason in the first place. *Q.E.D.*

Note.—The general belief of the multitude seems to be different. Most people seem to believe that they are free, in so far as they may obey their lusts, and that they cede their rights, in so far as they are bound to live according to the commandments of the divine law. They therefore believe that piety, religion, and, generally, all things attributable to firmness of mind, are burdens, which, after death, they hope to lay aside, and to receive the reward for their bondage, that is, for their piety and religion; it is not only by this hope, but also, and chiefly, by the fear of being horribly punished after death, that they are induced to live according to the divine commandments, so far as their feeble and infirm spirit will carry them.

If men had not this hope and this fear, but believed that the mind perishes with the body, and that no hope of prolonged life remains for the wretches who are broken down with the burden of piety, they would return to their own inclinations, controlling everything in accordance with their lusts, and desiring to obey fortune rather than themselves. Such a course appears to me not less absurd than if a man, because he does not believe that he can by wholesome food sustain his body for ever, should wish to cram himself with poisons and deadly fare; or if, because he sees that the mind is not eternal or immortal, he should prefer to be out of his mind altogether, and to live without the use of reason; these ideas are so absurd as to be scarcely worth refuting.

Prop. XLII. Blessedness is not the reward of virtue, but virtue itself; neither do we rejoice therein, because we control our lusts, but, contrariwise, because we rejoice therein, we are able to control our lusts.

Proof.—Blessedness consists in love towards God (V. xxxvi. and note), which love springs from the third kind of knowledge (V. xxxii. Coroll.) ; therefore this love (III. iii. lix.) must be referred to the mind, in so far as the latter is active; therefore (IV. Def. viii.) it is virtue itself. This was our first point. Again, in proportion as the mind rejoices more in this divine love or blessedness, so does it the more understand (V. xxxii.); that is (V. iii. Coroll.), so much the more power has it over the emotions, and (V. xxxviii.) so much the less is it subject to those emotions which are evil; therefore, in proportion as the mind rejoices in this divine love or blessedness, so has it the power of controlling lusts. And, since human power in controlling the emotions consists solely in the understanding, it follows that no one rejoices in blessedness, because he has controlled his lusts, but, contrariwise, his power of controlling his lusts arises from this blessedness itself. *Q.E.D.*

Note.—I have thus completed all I wished to set forth touching the mind's power over the emotions and the mind's freedom. Whence it appears, how potent is the wise man, and how much he surpasses the ignorant man, who is driven only by his lusts. For the ignorant man is not only distracted in various ways by external causes without ever gaining the true acquiescence of his spirit, but moreover lives, as it were unwitting of himself, and of God, and of things, and as soon as he ceases to suffer, ceases also to be.

Whereas the wise man, in so far as he is regarded as such, is scarcely at all disturbed in spirit, but, being conscious of himself, and of God, and of things, by a certain eternal necessity, never ceases to be, but always possesses true acquiescence of his spirit.

If the way which I have pointed out as leading to this result seems exceedingly hard, it may nevertheless be discovered. Needs must it be hard, since it is so seldom found. How would it be possible, if salvation wore ready to our hand, and could without great labor be found, that it should be by almost all men neglected? But all things excellent are as difficult as they are rare.

[Spinoza, Selections from *Ethics*, tr. R. H. M. Elwes (New York: Dover Publications, Inc., 1951). (1) Part I, p. 46. (2) Pp. 59–61. (3) Part III, prop. 1, pp. 133–35. (4) Part IV, props. LXVII–LXXll, pp. 232–35. (5) Part V, p. 244; props. XL–XLII, pp. 268–71.]

(2c3)

G. W. F. Hegel

1770–1831

The Phenomenology of Mind

Hegel's approach to freedom turns on analysis of what it is to have an independent consciousness. Given his approach, combining philosophy with cultural analysis, the independent consciousness takes many forms on the way to its home in the Absolute. With respect to lordship and bondage it is the bondsman who has what freedom there is in this relationship, because he, not the lord, finally possesses the independent consciousness.

"LORDSHIP AND BONDAGE"

(1) ... what is done by the bondsman is properly an action on the part of the master. The latter exists only for himself, that is his essential nature; he is the negative power without qualification, a power to which the thing is naught. And he is thus the absolutely essential act in this situation, while the bondsman is not so, he is an unessential activity. But for recognition proper there is needed the moment that what the master does to the other he should also do to himself, and what the bondsman does to himself, he should do to the other also. On that account a form of recognition has arisen that is one sided and unequal.

In all this, the unessential consciousness is, for the master, the object which embodies the truth of his certainty of himself. But it is evident that this object does not correspond to its notion; for, just where the master has effectively achieved lordship, he really finds that something has come about quite different from an independent consciousness. It is not an independent, but rather a dependent consciousness that he has achieved. He is thus not assured of self-existence as his truth; he finds that his truth is rather the unessential consciousness, and the fortuitous unessential action of that consciousness.

The truth of the independent consciousness is accordingly the consciousness of the bondsman. This doubtless appears in the first instance outside itself, and not as the truth of self-consciousness. But just as lordship showed its essential nature to be the reverse of what it wants to be, so, too, bondage will, when completed, pass into the opposite of what it immediately is: being a consciousness repressed within itself, it will enter into itself, and change round into real and true independence.

We have seen what bondage is only in relation to lordship. But it is a self-consciousness, and we have now to consider what it is, in this regard, in and for itself. In the first instance, the master is taken to be the essential reality for the state of bondage; hence, for it, the truth is the independent consciousness existing for itself, although this truth is not taken yet as inherent in bondage itself. Still, it does in fact contain within itself this truth of pure negativity and self-existence, because it has experienced this reality within it. For this consciousness was not in peril and fear for this element or that, nor for this or that moment of time, it was afraid for its entire being; it felt the fear of death, the sovereign master. It has been in that experience melted to its inmost soul, has trembled throughout its every fibre, and all that was fixed and steadfast has quaked within it. This complete perturbation of its entire substance, this absolute dissolution of all its stability into fluent continuity, is, however, the simple, ultimate nature of self-consciousness, absolute negativity, pure self-referent existence, which consequently is involved in this type of consciousness. This moment of pure self-existence is moreover a fact for it; for in the master it finds this as its object. Further, this bondsman's consciousness is not only this total dissolution in a general way; in serving and toiling the bondsman actually carries this out. By serving he cancels in every particular aspect his dependence on and attachment to natural existence, and by his work removes this existence away.

The feeling of absolute power, however, realized both in general and in the particular form of service, is only dissolution implicitly; and albeit the fear of the lord is the beginning of wisdom, consciousness is not therein aware of being self-existent. Through work and labor, however, this consciousness of the bondsman comes to itself. In the moment which corresponds to desire in the case of the master's consciousness, the aspect of the non-essential relation to the thing seemed to fall to the lot of the servant, since the thing there retained its independence. Desire has reserved to itself the pure negating of the object and thereby unalloyed feeling of self. This satisfaction, however, just for that reason is itself only a state of evanescence, for it lacks objectivity or subsistence. Labor, on the other hand, is desire restrained and checked, evanescence delayed and postponed; in other words, labor shapes and fashions the thing. The negative relation to the object passes into the *form* of the object, into something that is permanent and remains; because it is just for the laborer that the object has independence. This negative mediating agency, this activity giving shape and form, is at the same time the individual existence, the pure self-existence of that consciousness, which now in the work it does is externalized and passes into the condition of permanence. The consciousness that toils and serves accordingly attains by this means the direct apprehension of that independent being as its self.

But again, shaping or forming the object has not only the positive significance that the bondsman becomes thereby aware of himself as factually and objectively self-existent; this type of consciousness has also a negative import, in contrast with its first moment, the element of fear. For in shaping the thing it only becomes aware of its own proper negativity, its existence on its own account, as an object, through the fact that it cancels the actual form confronting it. But this objective negative element is precisely the alien, external reality, before which it trembled. Now, however, it destroys this extraneous alien negative, affirms and sets itself up as a negative in the element of permanence, and thereby becomes for itself a self-existent being. In the master, the bondsman feels self-existence to be something external, an objective fact; in fear self-existence is present within himself; in fashioning the thing, self-existence comes to be felt explicitly as his own proper being, and he attains the consciousness that he himself exists in its own right and on its own account (*an und für sich*). By the fact that the form is objectified, it does not become something other than the consciousness moulding the thing through work; for just that form is his pure self-existence, which therein becomes truly realized. Thus precisely in labor where there seemed to be merely some outsider's mind and ideas involved, the bondsman becomes aware, through this rediscovery of himself by himself, of having and being a "mind of his own."

For this reflexion of self into self the two moments, fear and service in general, as also that of formative activity, are necessary: and at the same time both must exist in a universal manner. Without the discipline of service and obedience, fear remains formal and does not spread over the whole known reality of existence. Without the formative activity shaping the thing, fear remains inward and mute, and consciousness does not become objective for itself. Should consciousness shape and form the thing without the initial state of absolute fear, then it has a merely vain and futile "mind of its own"; for its form or negativity is not negativity *per se*, and hence its formative activity cannot furnish the consciousness of itself as essentially real. If it has endured not absolute fear, but merely some slight anxiety, the negative reality has remained external to it, its substance has not been through and through infected thereby. Since the entire content of its natural consciousness has not tottered and shaken, it is still inherently a determinate mode of being; having a "mind of its own" (*der eigene Sinn*) is simply stubbornness (*Eigensinn*), a type of freedom which does not get beyond the attitude of bondage. As little as the pure form can become its essential nature, so little is that form, considered as extending over particulars, a universal formative activity, an absolute notion; it is rather a piece of cleverness which has mastery within a certain range, but not over the universal power nor over the entire objective reality.

STOIC FREEDOM
(THE FREEDOM OF SELF-CONSCIOUSNESS)

(2) Independent self-consciousness partly finds its essential reality in the bare abstraction of Ego. On the other hand, when this abstract ego develops further and forms distinctions of its own, this differentiation does not become an objective inherently real content for that self-consciousness.

Hence this self-consciousness does not become an ego which truly differentiates itself in its abstract simplicity, or one which remains identical with itself in this absolute differentiation. The repressed and subordinated type of consciousness, on the other hand, becomes, in the formative activity of work, an object to itself, in the sense that the form, given to the thing when shaped and moulded, is his object; he sees in the master, at the same time, self-existence as a real mode of consciousness. But the subservient consciousness as such finds these two moments fall apart—the moment of itself as independent object, and the moment of this object as a mode of consciousness, and so its own proper reality. Since, however, the form and the self-existence are for us, or objectively in themselves, one and the same, and since in the notion of independent consciousness the inherent reality is consciousness, the phase of inherent existence (*Ansichsein*) or thinghood, which received its shape and form through labor, is no other substance than consciousness. In this way, we have a new attitude or mode of consciousness brought about: a type of consciousness which takes on the form of infinitude, or one whose essence consists in unimpeded movement of consciousness. It is one which *thinks* or is free self-consciousness. For thinking does not mean being an abstract ego, but an ego which has at the same time the significance of inherently existing in itself; it means being object to itself or relating itself to objective reality in such a way that this connotes the self-existence of that consciousness for which it is an object. The object does not for thinking proceed by way of presentations or figures, but of notions, conceptions, i.e., of a differentiated reality or essence, which, being an immediate content of consciousness, is nothing distinct from it. What is presented, shaped and constructed, and existent as such, has the form of being something other than consciousness. A notion, however, is at the same time an existent, and this distinction, so far as it falls in consciousness itself, is its determinate content. But in that this content is, at the same time, a conceptually constituted, a comprehended (*begriffener*) content, consciousness remains immediately aware within itself of its unity with this determinate existent so distinguished; not as in the case of a presentation, where consciousness from the first has to take special note that this is its idea; on the contrary, the notion is for me *eo ipso* and at once *my* notion. In thinking I am free, because I am not in an other, but remain simply and solely in touch with myself; and the object which for me is my essential reality, is in undivided unity my self-existence; and my procedure in dealing with notions is a process within myself.

It is essential, however, in this determination of the above attitude of self-consciousness to keep hold of the fact that this attitude is thinking consciousness in general, that its object is immediate unity of the self's implicit, inherent existence, and of its existence explicitly for self. The self-same consciousness which repels itself from itself, becomes aware of being an element existing in itself. But to itself it is this element to begin with only as universal reality in general, and not as this essential reality appears when developed in all the manifold details it contains, when the process of its being brings out all its fullness of content.

This freedom of self-consciousness, as is well known, has been called *Stoicism*, in so far as it has appeared as a phenomenon conscious of itself in the course of the history of man's spirit. Its principle is that consciousness is essentially that which thinks, is a thinking reality, and that anything is really essential for consciousness, or is true and good, only when consciousness in dealing with it adopts the attitude of a thinking being.

SKEPTICAL FREEDOM
(INDEPENDENCE FOUND IN NEGATING THE WORLD)

(3) In Skepticism, on the other hand, this negative process is a moment of self-consciousness, which does not simply find its truth and its reality vanish, without selfconsciousness knowing how, but rather which in the certainty of its own freedom, itself makes this other, so claiming to be real, vanish. Self-consciousness here not only makes the objective as such to disappear before the negations of Skepticism but also its own function in relation to the object, where the object is held to be objective and made good— i.e., its function of perceiving as also its process of securing what is in danger of being lost, viz. sophistry and *its* self-constituted and self-established truth. By means of this self-conscious negation, self-consciousness procures for itself the certainty of its own freedom, brings about the experience of that freedom, and thereby raises it into the truth. What vanishes is what is determinate, the difference which, no matter what its nature or whence it comes, sets up to be fixed and unchangeable. The difference has

nothing permanent in it, and must vanish before thought because to be differentiated just means not to have being in itself, but to have its essential nature solely in an other. Thinking, however, is the insight into this character of what is differentiated; it is the negative function in its simple, ultimate form.

Skeptical self-consciousness thus discovers, in the flux and alternation of all that would stand secure in its presence, its own freedom, as given by and received from its own self. It is aware of being this ἀταραξία[1] of self-thinking thought, the unalterable and genuine certainty of its self. This certainty does not arise as a result out of something extraneous and foreign which stowed away inside itself its whole complex development; a result which would thus leave behind the process by which it came to be. Rather, consciousness itself is thoroughgoing dialectical restlessness, this mêlée of presentations derived from sense and thought, whose differences collapse into oneness, and whose identity is similarly again resolved and dissolved—for this identity is itself determinateness as contrasted with non-identity. This consciousness, however, as a matter of fact, instead of being a selfsame consciousness, is here neither more nor less than an absolutely fortuitous embroglio, the giddy whirl of a perpetually self-creating disorder. This is what it takes itself to be; for itself maintains and produces this self-impelling confusion. Hence it even confesses the fact; it owns to being an entirely fortuitous *individual* consciousness—a consciousness which is empirical, which is directed upon what admittedly has no reality for it, which obeys what, in its regard, has no essential being, which realizes and does what it knows to have no truth. But while it passes in this manner for an individual, isolated, contingent, in fact animal life, and a lost self-consciousness, it also, on the contrary, again turns itself into universal self-sameness; for it is the negativity of all singleness and all difference. From this self-identity, or rather within its very self, it falls back once more into that contingency and confusion, for this very self-directed process of negation has to do solely with what is single and individual, and is occupied with what is fortuitous. This form of consciousness is, therefore, the aimless fickleness and instability of going to and fro, hither and thither, from one extreme of self-same self-consciousness, to the other contingent, confused and confusing consciousness. It does not itself bring these two thoughts of itself together. It finds its freedom, at one time, in the form of elevation above all the whirling complexity and all the contingency of mere existence, and again, at another time, likewise confesses to falling back upon what is unessential, and to being taken up with that.

"ABSOLUTE FREEDOM AND TERROR"

Following skeptical freedom, Hegel discusses the "unhappy con-sciousness" (unhappy because divided); consciousness shaped by reason, by pleasure, by sentiment (the Romantic movement), by ethics, and by spirit. One form of spirit is spirit in the form of absolute freedom, which he titles "Absolute Freedom and Terror" (thinking of terror in the French Revolution). Writing of the nega-tion in this form of freedom, Hegel says:

(4) ... its negation is negation with a filling and a content—either honor and wealth, which it gains in the place of the self that it has alienated from itself; or the language of esprit and insight, which the distraught conscious-ness acquires; or, again, the negation is the heaven of belief or the principle of utility belonging to the stage of enlightenment. All these determinate elements disappear with the disaster and ruin that overtake the self in the state of absolute freedom;[2] its negation is meaningless death, sheer horror of the negative which has nothing positive in it, nothing that gives a filling.

ABSOLUTE KNOWLEDGE OR SPIRIT

Finally, our freedom is the reflection in us, in what we are and do, of absolute knowledge or spirit. In these final pages the process of achieving this standpoint moves through time, space, nature, and history, to end in Absolute Spirit.

(5) With absolute knowledge, then, Spirit has wound up the process of its embodiment, so far as the assumption of those various shapes or modes is affected with the insurmountable distinction which consciousness implies

[i.e., the distinction of consciousness from its object or content]. Spirit has attained the pure element of its existence, the notion. The content is, in view of the freedom of its own existence, the self that empties (external-izes) itself; in other words, that content is the *immediate* unity of self-knowl-edge. The pure process of thus externalizing itself constitutes—when we consider this process in its content—the *necessity* of this content. The diver-sity of content is, *qua* determinate, due to relation, and is not inherent; and its restless activity consists in cancelling and superseding itself, or is nega-tivity. Thus the necessity or diversity, like its free existence, is the self too; and in this self-form, in which existence is immediately thought, the con-tent is a notion. Seeing, then, that Spirit has attained the notion, it unfolds its existence and develops its processes in this ether of its life and is *(Philo-sophical) Science.*[3] The moments of its process are set forth therein no longer as determinate modes or shapes of consciousness, but—since the distinc-tion, which consciousness implies, has reverted to and has become a dis-tinction within the self—as determinate notions, and as the organic self-explaining and self-constituted process of these notions. While in the *Phe-nomenology of Mind* each moment is the distinction of knowledge and truth, and is the process in which that distinction is cancelled and transcended, Absolute Knowledge does not contain this distinction and supersession of distinction. Rather, since each moment has the form of the notion, it unites the objective form of truth and the knowing self in an immediate unity. Each individual moment does not appear as the process of passing back and forward from consciousness or figurative (imaginative) thought to self-con-sciousness and conversely: on the contrary, the pure shape liberated from the condition of being an appearance in mere consciousness,—the pure notion with its further development,—depends solely on its pure charac-teristic nature. Conversely, again, there corresponds to every abstract moment of Absolute Knowledge a mode in which mind as a whole makes its appearance. As the mind that actually exists is not richer than it,[4] so, too, mind in its actual content is not poorer. To know the pure notions of knowl-edge in the form in which they are modes or shapes of consciousness—this constitutes the aspect of their reality, according to which their essential ele-ment, the notion, appearing there in its simple mediating activity as thinking, breaks up and separates the moments of this mediation and exhibits them to itself in accordance with their immanent opposition.

Absolute Knowledge contains within itself this necessity of relinquishing itself from the form of the pure notion, and necessarily involves the transition of the notion into consciousness. For Spirit that knows itself is, just for the reason that it grasps its own notion, immediate identity with itself; and this, in the distinction that it implies, is the certainty of what is immediate or is sense-consciousness—the beginning from which we started. This process of releasing itself from the form of its self is the highest freedom and security of its knowledge of itself.

All the same, this relinquishment (externalization) of self is still incomplete. This process expresses the relation of the certainty of its self to the object, an object which, just by being in a relation, has not yet attained its full freedom. Knowledge is aware not only of itself, but also of the negative of itself, or its limit. Knowing its limit means knowing how to sacrifice itself. This sacrifice is the self-abandonment, in which Spirit sets forth, in the form of free fortuitous happening, its process of becoming Spirit, intuitively apprehending outside it its pure self as Time, and likewise its existence as Space. This last form into which Spirit passes, *Nature*, is its living immediate process of development. Nature—Spirit divested of self (externalized)—is, in its actual existence, nothing but this eternal process of abandoning its (Nature's) own independent subsistence, and the movement which reinstates Subject.

The other aspect, however, in which Spirit comes into being, *History*, is the process of becoming in terms of knowledge, a conscious self-mediating process—Spirit externalized and emptied into Time. But this form of abandonment is, similarly, the emptying of itself by itself; the negative is negative of itself. This way of becoming presents a slow procession and succession of spiritual shapes (*Geistern*), a gallery of pictures, each of which is endowed with the entire wealth of Spirit, and moves so slowly just for the reason that the self has to permeate and assimilate all this wealth of its substance. Since its accomplishment consists in Spirit knowing what it is, in fully comprehending its substance, this knowledge means its concentrating itself on itself (*Insichgehen*), a state in which Spirit leaves its external existence behind and gives its embodiment over to Recollection (*Erinnerung*). In thus concentrating itself on itself, Spirit is engulfed in the night of its own self consciousness; its vanished existence is, however, conserved therein; and this superseded existence—the previous state, but born anew from the womb of knowledge—is the new stage of existence, a new world, and a new embodiment or mode of Spirit. Here it has to begin all over again at its immediacy,[5] as freshly as before, and thence rise once more to the measure of its stature, as if, for it, all that preceded were lost, and as if it had learned nothing from the experience of the spirits that preceded. But recollection (*Erinnerung*) has conserved that experience, and is the inner being, and, in fact, the higher form of the substance. While, then, this phase of Spirit begins all over again its formative development, apparently starting solely from itself, yet at the same time it commences at a higher level. The realm of spirits developed in this way, and assuming definite shape in existence, constitutes a succession, where one detaches and sets loose the other, and each takes over from its predecessor the empire of the spiritual world. The goal of the process is the revelation of the depth of spiritual life, and this is the Absolute Notion. This revelation consequently means superseding its "depth," is its "extension" or *spatial* embodiment, the negation of this inwardly self-centered (*insichseiend*) ego—a negativity which is its self-relinquishment, its externalization, or its substance: and this revelation is also its *temporal* embodiment, in that this externalization in its very nature relinquishes (externalizes) itself, and so exists at once in its spatial "extension" as well as in its "depth" or the self. The goal, which is Absolute Knowledge or Spirit knowing itself as Spirit, finds its pathway in the recollection of spiritual forms (*Geister*) as they are in themselves and as they accomplish the organization of their spiritual kingdom. Their conservation, looked at from the side of their free existence appearing in, the form of contingency, is *History*; looked at from the side of their intellectually comprehended organization, it is the *Science* of the ways in which knowledge appears.[6] Both together, or History (intellectually) comprehended (*begriffen*), form at once the recollection and the Golgotha of Absolute Spirit, the reality, the truth, the certainty of its throne, without which it were lifeless, solitary, and alone. Only

> The chalice of this realm of spirits
> Foams forth to God His own Infinitude.[7]

NOTES

1. From the Greek 'not' and 'disturbed', hence, 'serenity', a Greek ideal sanctioned in the movements of Skeptical and Epicurean philosophy. [Ed.]

2. In the sense of abstract autonomy.

3. *I.e.*, Absolute or completely coherent Knowledge.

4. Absolute Knowledge.

5. *Cp.* Aristotle, *Metaph.*, 1071*b*, "Movement can neither come into being, nor cease to be; nor can time come into being, or cease to be."

6. "Phenomenology."

7. Adaptation of Schiller's *Die Freundschaft* ad fin.

[G. W. F. Hegel, *The Phenomenology of Mind*, 1807, tr. and notes, J. B. Baillie (Harper Torch Book. New York: Harper and Row, 1967). (1) Pp. 236–40. (2) Pp. 242–44. (3) Pp. 248–49. (4) P. 608. (5) Pp. 804–808.]

(2c4)
Friedrich Nietzsche
1844–1900

selections from *Ecce Homo*; *Beyond Good and Evil*; *Human, All Too Human*; *Thus Spoke Zarathustra*; and *The Dawn of Day*

Although strongly third definition, as seen in the first passage set forth below, Nietzsche also believes that the individuality of the "free spirit" is inevitably nonconformist (*q.v.* 4–6 below). While there is also the suggestion of first definition choice (*q.v.* 8 and 9), he also claims determinism and eternal return (*q.v.* 10–17). The determinism may well be incompatible with his third and first definition passages.

"How One Becomes What One Is"

(1) At this point I can no longer evade a direct answer to the question, *how one becomes what one is*. And here I touch upon the master stroke of the art of self-preservation—*selfishness*.... If we assume that one's life-task—the determination and the fate of one's life-task—appreciably surpasses the average measure, nothing would be more dangerous than to come face to face with one's self by the side of this life-task. The fact that one becomes what one is, presupposes that one has not the remotest suspicion of what one is. From this standpoint a unique meaning and value is given to even the blunders of one's life, the temporary deviations and aberrations, the hesitations, the timidities, the earnestness wasted upon tasks remote from the central one. In these matters there is opportunity for great wisdom, perhaps

- Our purpose is to become what we are
↑ if we try to know ourselves too soon, then we are something different
↑ we must make wrong choices to become wise
∴ wrong choices becoming right (mistakes)

Know thyself

even the highest wisdom; in circumstances, where *nosce teipsum*[1] would be the
passport to ruin, the forgetting of one's self, the misunderstanding, the belit-
tling, the narrowing and the mediocratizing of one's self, amount to reason
itself. In moral terms: to love one's neighbor and to live for others and for
other things *may* be the means of protection for the maintenance of the most
rigorous egoism. This is the exceptional case in which I, contrary to my
custom and conviction, take the side of the "selfless" tendencies, for here
they are engaged in the service of selfishness and self-discipline. The whole
surface of consciousness—for consciousness *is* a surface—must be kept free
of any of the great imperatives. Beware even of every striking word, of
every striking gesture! They all lead to the dangerous possibility that the
instinct may "understand itself" too soon. Meanwhile the organizing "idea,"
destined to mastery, continues to grow in the depths—it begins to command, it leads you slowly back from your deviations and aberrations, it
makes ready individual qualities and capacities, which will some day make
themselves felt as indispensable to the whole of your task—gradually it cul-
tivates all the serviceable faculties before it ever whispers a word concerning
the dominant task, the "goal," the "purpose," and the "meaning." Viewed
from this angle, my life is simply amazing. For the task of *transvaluing values*,
more abilities were necessary perhaps than could ever be found combined
in one individual; and above all, opposed abilities which must yet not be
mutually inimical and destructive. An order of rank among capacities; distance; the art of separating without creating hostility; to confuse nothing; to
reconcile nothing;—to be tremendously various and yet to be the reverse of
chaos—all this was the first condition, the long secret work and artistry of
my instinct. Its superior guardianship manifested itself so powerfully that at
no time did I have any intimation of what was growing within me—until
suddenly all my capacities were ripe, and one day burst forth in full perfection. I can recall no instance of my ever having exerted myself, there is no
evidence of *struggle* in my life; I am the reverse of a heroic nature. To "will"
something, to "strive" after something, to have a "purpose" or a "desire" in
my mind—I know none of these things from experience. At this very
moment I look out upon my future—a *broad* future!—as upon a calm sea: no
longing disturbs its serenity. I have not the slightest wish that anything
should be different than it is: I myself do not wish to be different.... I have
always been this way. I have never had a desire.

for he selfless is to keep from knowing oneself too soon.

honesty to own / & own - premature

vain

- He has followed every instinct making good & bad choices but accepting it all.
- you won wish for it
- let life lead you

(2) ...the commanding something, which the people call "spirit," wants to be master over itself and its surroundings and to feel its mastery: it has the will from multiplicity to simplicity—a will that would tie together, harness, be master, and that really is masterly. Its needs and capacities are thus the same as those the physiologists find in everything that lives, grows, and reproduces. The power of the spirit to appropriate what is foreign manifests itself in a strong tendency to assimilate the new to the old, to simplify the manifold....

THE FREE SPIRIT DEVELOPING

(3) ...from the desert of these years of temptation and experiment, it is still a long road to that tremendous overflowing certainty and health which may not dispense even with wickedness, as a means and fish-hook of knowledge, to that *mature* freedom of spirit which is equally self-mastery and discipline of the heart and permits access to many and contradictory modes of thought—to that inner spaciousness and indulgence of super-abundance which excludes the danger that the spirit may even on its own road perhaps lose itself and become infatuated and remain seated intoxicated in some corner or other, to that superfluity of formative, curative, moulding and restorative forces which is precisely the sign of *great* health, that superfluity which grants to the free spirit the dangerous privilege of living *experimentally* and of being allowed to offer itself to adventure: the master's privilege of the free spirit! In between there may lie long years of convalescence, years full of variegated, painfully magical transformations ruled and led along by a tenacious *will to health* which often ventures to clothe and disguise itself as health already achieved. There is a midway condition which a man of such a destiny will not be able to recall without emotion: it is characterized by a pale, subtle happiness of light and sunshine, a feeling of bird-like freedom, bird-like altitude, bird-like exuberance, and a third thing in which curiosity is united with a tender contempt. A 'free-spirit'—this cool expression does one good in every condition, it is almost warming. One lives no longer in the fetters of love and hatred, without yes, without no, near or far as one wishes, preferably slipping away, evading, fluttering off, gone again, again flying aloft; one is spoiled, as

everyone is who has at some time seen a tremendous number of things *beneath* him—and one becomes the opposite of those who concern themselves with things which have nothing to do with them. Indeed, the free spirit henceforth has to do only with things—and how many things!—with which he is no longer *concerned.* . . .

A step further in convalescence: and the free spirit again draws near to life—slowly, to be sure, almost reluctantly, almost mistrustfully. It again grows warmer around him, yellower, as it were; feeling and feeling for others acquire depth, warm breezes of all kind blow across him. It seems to him as if his eyes are only now open to what is *close at hand*. He is astonished and sits silent: where *had* he been? These close and closest things: how changed they seem! what bloom and magic they have acquired! He looks back gratefully—grateful to his wandering, to his hardness and self-alienation, to his viewing of far distances and bird-like flights in cold heights. What a good thing he had not always stayed 'at home,' stayed 'under his own roof' like a delicate apathetic loafer! He had been *beside* himself: no doubt of that. Only now does he see himself—and what surprises he experiences as he does so! What unprecedented shudders! What happiness even in the weariness, the old sickness, the relapses of the convalescent! How he loves to sit sadly still, to spin out patience, to lie in the sun! Who understands as he does the happiness that comes in winter, the spots of sunlight on the wall! They are the most grateful animals in the world, also the most modest, these convalescents and lizards again half turned towards life:—there are some among them who allow no day to pass without hanging a little song of praise on the hem of its departing robe. And, to speak seriously: to become sick in the manner of these free spirits, to remain sick for a long time and then, slowly, slowly, to become healthy, by which I mean 'healthier', is a fundamental *cure* for all pessimism (the cancerous sore and inveterate vice, as is well known, of old idealists and inveterate liars). There is wisdom, practical wisdom, in for a long time prescribing even health for oneself only in small doses.

At that time it may finally happen that, under the sudden illumination of a still stressful, still changeable health, the free, ever freer spirit begins to unveil the riddle of that great liberation which had until then waited dark, questionable, almost untouchable in his memory. If he has for long hardly dared to ask himself: 'why so apart? so alone? renouncing everything

What once controlled you, you can through understanding and experience, you are able to control

to see things from many points of view is to see the good + bad in all things you realize your path

I once reverenced? renouncing reverence itself? why this hardness, this suspiciousness, this hatred for your own virtues?'—now he dares to ask it aloud and hears in reply something like an answer. 'You shall become master over yourself, master also over your virtues. Formerly *they* were your masters; but they must be only your instruments beside other instruments. You shall get control over your For and Against and learn how to display first one and then the other in accordance with your higher goal. You shall learn to grasp the sense of perspective in every value judgement—the displacement, distortion and merely apparent teleology of horizons and whatever else pertains to perspectivism; also the quantum of stupidity that resides in antitheses of values and the whole intellectual loss which every For, every Against costs us. You shall learn to grasp the *necessary* injustice in every For and Against, injustice as inseparable from life, life itself as *conditioned* by the sense of perspective and its injustice. You shall above all see with your own eyes where injustice is always at its greatest: where life has developed at its smallest, narrowest, neediest, most incipient and yet cannot avoid taking *itself* as the goal and measure of things and for the sake of its own preservation secretly and meanly and ceaselessly crumbling away and calling into question the higher, greater, richer—you shall see with your own eyes the problem of *order of rank*, and how power and right and spaciousness of perspective grow into the heights together. You shall—enough: from now on the free spirit *knows* what 'you shall' he has obeyed, and he also knows what he now *can*, what only now he—*may* do....

This is how the free spirit elucidates to himself that enigma of liberation, and inasmuch as he generalizes his own case ends by adjudicating on what he has experienced thus. 'What has happened to me,' he says to himself, 'must happen to everyone in whom a task wants to become incarnate and "come into the world."' The secret force and necessity of this task will rule among and in the individual facets of his destiny like an unconscious pregnancy—long before he has caught sight of this task itself or knows its name. Our vocation commands and disposes of us even when we do not yet know it; it is the future that regulates our today. Given it is *the problem of order of rank* of which we may say it is *our* problem, we free spirits: it is only now, at the midday of our life, that we understand what preparations, bypaths, experiments, temptations, disguises the problem had need of

before it was *allowed* to rise up before us, and how we first had to experience the most manifold and contradictory states of joy and distress in soul
and body, as adventurers and circumnavigators of that inner world called
'man,' as surveyors and gaugers of that 'higher' and 'one upon the other'
that is likewise called 'man'—penetrating everywhere, almost without fear,
disdaining nothing, losing nothing, asking everything, cleansing everything
of what is chance and accident in it and as it were thoroughly sifting it—
until at last we had the right to say, we free spirits: 'Here—a *new* problem!
Here a long ladder upon whose rungs we ourselves have sat and climbed—
which we ourselves have at some time *been*! Here a higher, a deeper, a
beneath-us, a tremendous long ordering, an order of rank, which we see:
here—*our* problem!'— *problem of hindsight*

(4) *Free spirit a relative concept.*—He is called a free spirit who thinks — *not*
differently from what, on the basis of his origin, environment, his class and *confined*
profession, or on the basis of the dominant views of the age, would have *to the*
been expected of him. He is the exception, the fettered spirits are the rule; *popular*
the latter reproach him that his free principles either originate in a desire *or common*
to shock and offend or eventuate in free actions, that is to say in actions *way of*
incompatible with sound morals. Occasionally it is also said that this or that *thinking*
free principle is to be attributed to perversity and mental overexcitation;
but this is merely the voice of malice, which does not believe what it says
but desires only to wound: for the superior quality and sharpness of his
intellect is usually written on the face of the free spirit in characters clear
enough even for the fettered spirit to read. But the two other derivations of
free spiritedness are honestly meant; and many free spirits do in fact come
to be what they are in one or other of these ways. But the principles they
arrive at along these paths could nonetheless be truer and more reliable
than those favored by the fettered spirits. In the case of the knowledge of
truth the point is whether or not one *possesses* it, not from what motives one
sought it or along what paths one found it. If the free spirits are right, the
fettered spirits are wrong, regardless of whether the former have arrived at
the truth by way of immorality or the latter have hitherto cleaved to
untruth out of morality.—In any event, however, what characterizes the
free spirit is not that his opinions are the more correct but that he has liberated himself from tradition, whether the outcome has been successful or

Free — go against the grain in order to find true-knowledge
fettered — follow certain morality think whatever done one
tells them is true because they say it is so — Blind faith

a failure. As a rule, though, he will nonetheless have truth on his side, or at least the spirit of inquiry after truth: he demands reasons, the rest demand faith.

those who have not touched a certain high but are on the far path.

(5) *Free-ranging spirits.*—Which of us would dare to call himself a free spirit if he would not wish to pay homage in his own way to those men to whom this name has been applied as an *insult* by taking on to his own shoulders some of this burden of public disapprobation and revilement? What, however, we may call ourselves in all seriousness (and without being in any way defiant) is 'free-ranging spirits', because we feel the tug towards freedom as the strongest drive of our spirit and, in antithesis to the fettered and firm-rooted intellects, see our ideal almost in a spiritual nomadism— to employ a modest and almost contemptuous expression.

"THE FREE SPIRIT, ENEMY OF FETTERS"

(6) But the free spirit, the enemy of fetters, the nonadorer who dwells in the woods, is as hateful to the people as a wolf to dogs. To hound him out of his lair—that is what the people have ever called "a sense of decency"; and against him the people still set their fiercest dogs.

"Truth is there: after all, the people are there! Let those who seek beware!"—these words have echoed through the ages. You wanted to prove your people right in their reverence: that is what you called "will to truth," you famous wise men. And your hearts ever said to themselves: "From among the people I came, and from there too the voice of God came to me." As the people's advocates you have always been stiff-necked and clever like asses.

And many who were powerful and wanted to get along smoothly with the people harnessed in front of their horses a little ass, a famous wise man.

And now I should wish, you famous wise men, that you would at long last throw off the lion's skin completely. The skin of the beast of prey, mottled, and the mane of those who search, seek, and conquer.

Oh, to make me believe in your "truthfulness" you would first have to break your revering will.

Truthful I call him who goes into godless deserts, having broken his revering heart. In the yellow sands, burned by the sun, he squints thirstily at the islands abounding in wells, where living things rest under dark trees. Yet his thirst does not persuade him to become like these, dwelling in comfort; for where there are oases there are also idols.

Hungry, violent, lonely, godless: thus the lion-will wants itself. Free from the happiness of slaves, redeemed from gods and adorations, fearless and fear-inspiring, great and lonely: such is the will of the truthful.

It was ever in the desert that the truthful have dwelt, the free spirits, as masters of the desert; but in the cities dwell the well-fed, famous wise men—the beasts of burden. For, as asses, they always pull the people's cart.

⚘ ⚘ ⚘

Spirit is the life that itself cuts into life: with its own agony it increases its own knowledge.

"FREE FOR WHAT?"

(7) Free *from* what? As if that mattered to Zarathustra! But your eyes should tell me brightly: free *for* what?

"WHAT WE ARE FREE TO DO"

(8) We can act as the gardeners of our impulses, and—which few people know—we may cultivate the seeds of anger, pity, vanity, or excessive brooding, and make these things fecund and productive, just as we can train a beautiful plant to grow along trellis-work. We may do this with the good or bad taste of a gardener, and as it were, in the French, English, Dutch, or Chinese style. We may let nature take its own course, only trimming and embellishing a little here and there; and finally, without any knowledge or consideration, we may even allow the plants to spring up in accordance with their own natural growth and limitations, and fight out their battle among themselves,—nay, we can even take delight in such chaos, though we may possibly have a hard time with it! All this is at our option: but how many know that it is? Do not the majority of people

believe in themselves as complete and perfect facts? and have not the great philosophers set their seal on this prejudice through their doctrine of the unchangeability of character?

(9) *Overcoming of the passions.*—The man who has overcome his passions has entered into possession of the most fertile ground; like the colonist who has mastered the forests and swamps. To *sow* the seeds of good spiritual works in the soil of the subdued passions is then the immediate urgent task. The overcoming itself is only a *means*, not a goal; if it is not so viewed, all kinds of weeds and devilish nonsense will quickly spring up in this rich soil now unoccupied, and soon there will be more rank confusion than there ever was before. *once we know ourselves and gain control we must use it for good*

THE ACCEPTANCE OF NECESSITY

(10) Where all time seemed to me a happy mockery of moments, where necessity was freedom itself playing happily with the sting of freedom.

it may seem that our will is free, but everything we do is necessary -is not free. If we were free we would know our future + we do not.

(11) *By the waterfall.*—At the sight of a waterfall we think we see in the countless curvings, twistings and breakings of the waves capriciousness and freedom of will; but everything here is necessary, every motion mathematically calculable. So it is too in the case of human actions; if one were all-knowing, one would be able to calculate every individual action, likewise every advance in knowledge, every error, every piece of wickedness. The actor himself, to be sure, is fixed in the illusion of free will; if for one moment the wheel of the world were to stand still, and there were an all-knowing, calculating intelligence there to make use of this pause, it could narrate the future of every creature to the remotest ages and describe every track along which this wheel had yet to roll. The actor's deception regarding himself, the assumption of free-will, is itself part of the mechanism it would have to compute.

(12) Thus: belief in freedom of will is a primary error committed by everything organic, as old as the impulse to the logical itself; belief in

unconditioned substances and in identical things is likewise a primary, ancient error committed by everything organic. Insofar, however, as all metaphysics has had principally to do with substance and freedom of will, one may designate it the science that treats of the fundamental errors of mankind—but does so as though they were fundamental truths.

(13) *Where the theory of freedom of will originated.*—Over one man *necessity* stands in the shape of his passions, over another as the habit of hearing and obeying, over a third as a logical conscience, over a fourth as caprice and a mischievous pleasure in escapades. These four will, however, seek the *freedom* of their will precisely where each of them is most firmly fettered: it is as if the silkworm sought the freedom of its will in spinning. How does this happen? Evidently because each considers himself most free where his *feeling of living* is greatest; thus, as we have said, in passion, in duty, in knowledge, in mischievousness respectively. That through which the individual human being is strong, wherein he feels himself animated, he involuntarily thinks must also always be the element of his freedom: he accounts dependence and dullness, independence and the feeling of living as necessarily coupled.—Here an experience in the social-political domain has been falsely transferred to the farthest metaphysical domain: in the former the strong man is also the free man; the lively feeling of joy and sorrow, high hope, boldness in desire, powerfulness in hatred is the property of the rulers and the independent, while the subjected man, the slave, lives dull and oppressed.—The theory of freedom of will is an invention of *ruling* classes.

Feeling no new chains.—So long as we do not *feel* that we are dependent on anything we regard ourselves as independent: a false conclusion that demonstrates how proud and lusting for power man is. For he here assumes that as soon as he experiences dependence he must under all circumstances notice and recognize it, under the presupposition that he is *accustomed* to living in independence and if, exceptionally, he lost it, he would at once perceive a sensation antithetical to the one he is accustomed to.—But what if the opposite were true: that he is *always* living in manifold dependence but regards himself *as free* when, out of long habituation, he *no longer perceives* the weight of the chains? It is only from *new* chains that he now suffers:—'freedom of will' really means nothing more than feeling no new chains.

*we cannot do more than we are already
allowed - accept limitations
+ know it*

we are limited beings

(14) *On the Domain of Freedom.*—We can *think* many more things than we
can do and experience—i.e., our faculty of thinking is superficial and is satisfied with what lies on the surface, it does not even perceive this surface. If
our intellect were strictly developed in proportion to our power, and our
exercise of this power, the primary principle of our thinking would be that
we can understand only that which we are able to do—if, indeed, there is
any understanding at all. The thirsty man is without water, but the creations
of his imagination continually bring the image of water to his sight, as if
nothing could be more easily procured. The superficial and easily satisfied
character of the intellect cannot understand real need, and thus feels itself
superior. It is proud of being able to do more, to run faster, and to reach the
goal almost within the twinkling of an eye: and in this way the domain of
thought, when contrasted with the domain of action, volition, and experience, appears to be the domain of liberty, while, as I have already stated, it
is nothing but the domain of superficiality and self-sufficiency.

we tend to see ourselves as unlimited when we only able to run faster there

is no such thing, but we believe this out of pride

(15) …it is because man *regards* himself as free, not because he is free,
that he feels remorse and pangs of conscience.—This feeling is, moreover,
something one can disaccustom oneself to, and many people do not feel it
at all in respect of actions which evoke it in others. It is a very changeable
thing, tied to the evolution of morality and culture and perhaps present in
only a relatively brief span of world history.—No one is accountable for
his deeds, no one for his nature; to judge is the same thing as to be unjust.
This also applies when the individual judges himself. The proposition is as
clear as daylight, and yet here everyone prefers to retreat back into the
shadows and untruth: from fear of the consequences.

It is not easy to realize that we have no control over own actions

*if we accept this then we will be free
- we feel a need to judge others a ourselves - pointless*

ETERNAL RETURN

(16) "Behold," I continued, "this moment! From this gateway,
Moment, a long, eternal lane leads *backward*: behind us lies an eternity.
Must not whatever *can* walk have walked on this lane before? Must not
whatever *can* happen have happened, have been done, have passed by
before? And if everything has been there before—what do you think,
dwarf, of this moment? Must not this gateway too have been there before?

Past was our path

*Past is unchangeable + so is future
our future is our path*

And are not all things knotted together so firmly that this moment draws after it *all* that is to come? Therefore—itself too? For whatever *can* walk—in this long lane out *there* too, it *must* walk once more.

"And this slow spider, which crawls in the moonlight, and this moonlight itself, and I and you in the gateway, whispering together, whispering of eternal things—must not all of us have been there before? And return and walk in that other lane, out there, before us, in this long dreadful lane—must we not eternally return?"

Thus I spoke, more and more softly; for I was afraid of my own thoughts and the thoughts behind my thoughts. Then suddenly I heard a dog howl nearby. Had I ever heard a dog howl like this? My thoughts raced back. Yes, when I was a child, in the most distant childhood: then I heard a dog howl like this. *he is now mature*

(17) *Mohammedan fatalism.*—Mohammedan fatalism embodies the fundamental error of setting man and fate over against one another as two separate things: man, it says, can resist fate and seek to frustrate it, but in the end it always carries off the victory; so that the most reasonable thing to do is to resign oneself or to live just as one pleases. In reality every man is himself a piece of fate; when he thinks to resist fate in the way suggested, it is precisely fate that is here fulfilling itself; the struggle is imaginary, but so is the proposed resignation to fate; all these imaginings are enclosed within fate.—The fear most people feel in face of the theory of the unfreedom of the will is fear in face of Mohammedan fatalism: they think that man will stand before the future feeble, resigned and with hands clasped because he is incapable of effecting any change in it: or that he will give free rein to all his impulses and caprices because these too cannot make any worse what has already been determined. The follies of mankind are just as much a piece of fate as are its acts of intelligence: that fear in face of a belief in fate is also fate. You yourself, poor fearful man, are the implacable *moira* enthroned even above the gods that governs all that happens; you are the blessing or the curse and in any event the fetters in which the strongest lies captive; in you the whole future of the world of man is predetermined: it is of no use for you to shudder when you look upon yourself.

Man and fate are one; there is no defiance of fate or resignation to fate. If you defy or resign that is your fate. In accepting this there is strength. We all have an equal place in fate. In this we all affect the world no greater, no lesser.

NOTE

　1. "Know thyself." [Ed.]

[Friedrich Nietzsche, (1) *Ecce Homo*, tr. C. Fadiman (New York: Modern Library, a division of Random House, 1927), pp. 43–46. (2) *Beyond Good and Evil*, tr. W. Kaufmann, sec. 230, *The Portable Nietzsche* (New York: Viking Press, 1968), p. 446. (3) *Human, All Too Human*, tr. R. J. Hollingdale (Cambridge: Cambridge Univ. Press, 1986), pp. 8–10. (4) *Ibid.*, p. 108. (5) *Ibid.*, p. 263. (6) *Thus Spoke Zarathustra, The Portable Nietzsche, op. cit.*, pp. 214–16. (7) *Ibid.*, p. 175. (8) *The Dawn of Day*, tr., J. M. Kennedy (New York: Russell and Russell, Inc., 1964), pp. 388–89. (9) *Human, All Too Human, op. cit.*, p. 323. (10) *Thus Spoke Zarathustra, op. cit.*, p. 309. (11) *Human, All Too Human, op. cit.*, p. 57. (12) *Ibid.*, p. 22. (13) *Ibid.*, pp. 305–306. (14) *Dawn of Day, op. cit.*, pp. 130–31. (15) *Human, All Too Human, op. cit.*, p. 35. (16) *Thus Spoke Zarathustra, op. cit.*, pp. 270–71. (17) *Human, All Too Human, op. cit.*, p. 325.]

(2c5)

B. F. Skinner

1904–1990

Reflections on Behaviorism and Society

As an Operationist, Skinner (*q.v.* D) extended the thrust of Watsonian behaviorism, arguing throughout his career that all human behavior is controlled. The feeling of being free is derived from what he called operant behavior with positive reinforcement. We are quite clear about the control in negative reinforcement (punishment). But positive reinforcement appears not to have an immediately antecedent event which can serve as cause. The immediately antecedent event is presumed, then, to be an objectified will, or choice. The will is objectified from such locutions as "He *will* go in spite of the danger." But the inner mechanism for all of us is really the Skinner box, devised for predicting the behavior of white rats. The presumption of the box is that output is the sum of all the inputs. If this is so in the case of humans, and Skinner believed it was, there is no need for an inner will or inner self. The Skinner box opposes the notion of self-determination where self is something other than the inputs.

The feeling of being free is the feeling that we are doing what we want to do, *i.e.*, what we are *pleased* to do, thus our second definition of freedom. That is the definition to which Skinner is closest. The subtlety of positive reinforcement lies in the apparent absence of external control. The control is pictured, if at all, as persuasion. It concerns changing minds rather than constraining behavior, a disguised control operating in education, psychotherapy, and religion. Finally, one is most pleased when developing one's genetic endowment. Such development appears to relate Skinner to the third definition of freedom, development of the inner nature which he denies. His *Walden II* imagined a functioning society whose controls shaped the community toward such development.

In the following selection Skinner makes a good-natured effort to correct the misinterpretations he believes his view has suffered. He repeats, at the end, that through positive reinforcement one's sense of freedom is enhanced.

"FREEDOM AND DIGNITY REVISITED"

(1) In a famous passage in *Notes from the Underground* Dostoevski insisted that man will never admit that his behavior can be predicted and controlled. He will "create destruction and chaos to gain his point. And if all this could in turn be analyzed and prevented by predicting that it would occur, then man would deliberately go mad to prove his point." Dostoevski was himself making a prediction, of course, and it had the curious effect of cutting off this last avenue of escape, since henceforth even deliberately going mad could be said to have been predicted.

My critics have, nevertheless, seemed bent on proving that he was right. Many of them have shown a taste for destruction and chaos, some of it not far short of madness. They have resorted to highly emotional terms, and a kind of hysterical blindness seems to have prevented some of them from reading what I actually wrote. An author who has been so widely misunderstood will naturally value Dostoevski's explanation.

My argument was surely simple enough. I was not discussing a philosophical entity called freedom but rather the behavior of those who struggle to be free. It is part of the human genetic endowment that when a person acts in such a way as to reduce "aversive" (e.g., potentially dangerous) stimuli, he is more likely to do so again. Thus, when other people attempt to control him through a threat of punishment, he learns to escape from them or attack them in order to weaken them. When he succeeds, he feels free, and the struggle ceases. But is he really free? To say with John Stuart Mill, that "liberty consists in doing what one desires" is to neglect the determiners of desires. There are certain kinds of control under which people feel perfectly free. The point has been made before, but I was offering some further evidence recently acquired in the experimental analysis of operant conditioning.

Such an interpretation is not metaphysics: it is a matter of identifying certain processes in an important field of human behavior. It does not—it cannot—lead to the suppression of any freedom we have ever enjoyed. On the contrary, it suggests that, there are ways in which we could all feel freer than ever before. For example, in spite of our supposed love of freedom, most of our practices in government, education, psychotherapy, and industry are still heavily punitive. People behave in given ways to avoid the consequences of not doing so. Perhaps this means simply that the struggle for freedom has not yet been finished, but I have argued that the continuing use of punishment is, on the contrary, an unwanted by-product of that struggle. We refuse to accept nonpunitive practices because they make it too clear that control is being exerted. When we punish bad behavior, we can give the individual credit for behaving well, but if we arrange conditions under which he "desires" to behave well, the conditions must get the credit.

I neglected to point out that under punitive practices we even justify behaving badly. Fortunately, this has now been done for me by the film "A Clockwork Orange." Writing in the *New York Review*, Christopher Ricks argues that aversion therapy takes the protagonist Alex "beyond freedom and dignity," and he quotes Anthony Burgess (author of the novel) in defense of the film. "What my, and Kubrick's [director of the film] parable tries to state is that it is preferable to have a world of violence undertaken in full awareness—violence chosen as an act of will—than a world conditioned to be good or harmless." Ricks says that I am one of the few who would contest that statement. I hope there are far more than a few. The film misrepresents the issue because the "therapy" that makes Alex good is brutally conspicuous while the conditioning that lies behind his "acts of will undertaken in full awareness" is easily missed.

The struggle for freedom has not reduced or eliminated control; it has merely corrected it. But what is good control, and who is to exert it? Either my answers to these questions have been unforgivably obscure or many of my critics have not reached the last chapters of my book. The question Who will control? is not to be answered with a proper name or by describing a kind of person (e.g., a benevolent dictator) or his qualifications (e.g., a behavioral engineer). To do so is to make the mistake of looking at the person rather than at the environment which determines his behavior. The struggle for freedom has moved slowly, and alas erratically, toward a culture in which controlling power is less and less likely to fall into the hands of individuals or groups who use it tyrannically. We have tried to construct such a culture by exerting countercontrol over those who misuse power. Countercontrol is certainly effective, but it leads at best to a kind of uneasy equilibrium. The next step can be taken only through the explicit design of a culture which goes beyond the immediate interests of controller and countercontroller.

Design for what? There is only one answer: the survival of the culture and of mankind. Survival is a difficult value (compared, say, with life, liberty, or the pursuit of happiness) because it is hard to predict the conditions a culture must meet, and we are only beginning to understand how to produce the behavior needed to meet them. Moreover, we are likely to reject survival as a value because it suggests competition with other cultures, as in social Darwinism, in which aggressive behavior is aggrandized. But other contingencies of survival are important, and the value of cooperative, supportive behavior can easily be demonstrated.

Must individual freedoms be "sacrificed" for the sake of the culture? Most of my critics contend that I am saying so, but the answer depends on how people are induced to work for the good of their culture. If they do so under a threat of punishment, then freedom (from such a threat) is sacrificed, but if they are induced to do so through positive reinforcement, their sense of freedom is enhanced. Young Chinese wear plain clothing, live in crowded quarters, eat simple diets, observe a rather puritanical sexual code and work long hours—all for the greater glory of China. Are they sacrificing freedom? They are if they are under aversive control, if they behave as they do because they will be denounced by their fellows when they behave otherwise. But if Mao succeeded in making signs of progress toward a greater China positively reinforcing, then it is possible that they feel freer, and happier, than most young Americans.

Misunderstanding no doubt arises from the word "control." Dostoevski used the metaphor of a piano key: strike it and it responds with a given tone. The metaphor was appropriate to the early reflexology of Dostoevski's time, which Pavlov's conditioned reflexes did little to change. But in operant conditioning a stimulus merely alters the likelihood that a response will be emitted. Good examples are to be found in verbal behavior. A verbal response is very different from the knee-jerk elicited by a tap on the patellar tendon. What a speaker says is determined in part by the current listener, in part by the recent verbal stimuli he has heard or seen, in part by a nonverbal setting, and in large part of course by his history as listener and speaker. These variables can be sorted out by identifying well-established behavioral processes.

[B. F. Skinner, *Reflections on Behaviorism and Society* (Englewood Cliffs, N.J.: Prentice-Hall, Inc., 1978). (1) Pp. 195–98.]

(2c6)
Daisetz T. Suzuki
1870–1966

selections from *The Essentials of Zen Buddhism*

The sole Eastern compendium of readings on freedom in our set is that of Zen Buddhism (*q.v.* D) as interpreted by Suzuki (*q.v.* D). Since it is not Suzuki's style to present his position by way of the Western essay on a set topic, it has been necessary to assemble numerous passages. The view is that of the third definition of freedom. Freedom depends upon self-knowledge. This self-knowledge and *satori* (*q.v.* D) are identical.

THE ILLUSION OF THE INTELLECT

(1) One of the illusions which the intellect sets before itself is that it is free, that it can choose. By cutting up a seamless piece of cloth called life into several parts, the intellect tries to examine them, thinking that they can be pieced together and then the original reproduced. This dividing and piecing together it claims to be its privilege, its enjoyment of freedom. But nothing is more ruinous than this to the proper status of intellection in the scheme of human life. For the intellect is not free by nature; its power to divide is really the power to kill itself. The intellect gains its freedom only when this killing of itself is accomplished. The choice of alternatives is not freedom in its real sense; to be free one must not be hampered in any possible way or in any possible sense; freedom means absolute independence.

184

Now for the intellect, analysis, with its counterpart synthesis, is its life; but this analyzing and synthesizing means self-limitation, because the work requires something to work upon as well as someone who works. Intellection is putting one thing against another, which is opposition, and opposition is self-restriction, giving up independence and freedom. Whatever freedom the intellect may enjoy in choosing one thing out of many, it is a limited freedom and not an absolute one. And if it is not an absolute one, the spirit can never feel rested and happy with itself. It is the Buddhist logic of self-identity that can give to the spirit what it desires by transcending dualism and all its consequent issues.

It is thus most decidedly not the intellect or reason which makes us free from the bondage of karma consciousness. All that the intellect does toward spiritual liberation is that it foreshadows, however faintly, the image of freedom, whereby the heart is somehow encouraged, though it cannot yet clearly see the way to its own liberation. I have said here "encouraged," but it may be better to say that the heart is all the more depressed: it sees something ahead and is yet utterly unable to locate it exactly. This feeling on the part of the Unconscious is reflected in the intellect, which will now exert all its powers in solving the problem of "thinking the Unthinkable."

(2) We are supposedly living in the same world, but who can tell the thing we popularly call a stone lying before this window is the same thing to all of us? According to the way we look at it, to some the stone ceases to be a stone, while to others it forever remains a worthless specimen of a geological product. And this initial divergence of views calls forth an endless series of divergencies later in our moral and spiritual lives. Just a little twisting, as it were, in our modes of thinking, and yet what a world of difference will grow up eventually between one another! So with Zen, satori is this twisting, or rather screwing, not in the wrong way, but in a deeper and fuller sense, and the result is the revelation of a world of entirely new values.

Again, you and I sip a cup of tea. The act is apparently alike, but who can tell what a wide gap there is subjectively between you and me? In your drinking there may be no Zen, while mine is brimfull of it. The reason is, the one moves in the logical circle and the other is out of it; that is to say, in one case rigid rules of intellection so called are asserting themselves, and the actor even when acting is unable to unfetter himself from these intellectual bonds; while in the other case the subject has struck a new path and is not at all conscious of the duality of his act; in him life is not split into object and subject or into acting and acted. The drinking at the moment to him means the whole fact, the whole world. Zen lives and is therefore free, whereas our "ordinary" life is in bondage; satori is the first step to freedom.

SATORI

(3) Ordinarily, we go out of ourselves to seek a place of ultimate rest. We walk on and on until we reach God, who is at the head of a long, tedious series of bifurcations and unifications.

Zen takes the opposite course and steps backward, as it were, to reach the undifferentiated continuum itself. It looks backward to a point before the world with all its dichotomies has yet made its debut. This means that Zen wants us to face a world into which time and space have not yet put their cleaving wedges. What kind of experience is this? Our experience has always been conditioned by logic, by time, and by space. Experience will be utterly impossible if it is not so conditioned. To refer to experience free from such conditions is nonsensical, one may say. Perhaps it is, so long as we uphold time and space as real and not conceptually projected. But even when these basic conditions of experience are denied, Zen talks of a certain kind of experience. If this be really the case, Zen experience must be said to take place in the timelessness of the Absolute Present.

(4) When satori obtains in the Absolute Present, all these questions solve themselves. The mind or consciousness, serially divided and developed in time, always escapes our prehension, is never "attainable" as to its reality. It is only when our unconscious consciousness, or what might be called super-consciousness, comes to itself, is awakened to itself, that our eyes open to the timelessness of the present in which and from which divisible time unfolds itself and reveals its true nature.

(5) The great discovery we owe Buddhism, and especially Zen, is that it has opened for us the way to see into the suchness of things, which is to have an insight into "the originally pure in essence and form which is the

ocean of transcendental *prajna*[1]-knowledge," as Gensha[2] says in one of his sermons. "The originally pure" is "a stillness which abides in the present."

(6) When poetically or figuratively expressed, satori is "the opening of the mind-flower," or "the removing of the bar," or "the brightening up of the mind-works."

All these tend to mean the clearing up of a passage which has been somehow blocked, preventing the free, unobstructed operation of a machine or a full display of the inner works. With the removal of the obstruction, a new vista opens before one, boundless in expanse and reaching the end of time. As life thus feels quite free in its activity, which was not the case before the awakening, it now enjoys itself to the fullest extent of its possibilities, to attain which is the object of Zen discipline. This is often taken to be equivalent to "vacuity of interest and poverty of purpose." But according to the Zen masters the doctrine of nonachievement concerns itself with the subjective attitude of mind which goes beyond the limitations of thought. It does not deny ethical ideals, nor does it transcend them; it is simply an inner state of consciousness without reference to its objective consequences.

As to the opening of satori, all that Zen can do is to indicate the way and leave the rest all to one's own experience; that is to say, following up the indication and arriving at the goal—this is to be done by oneself and without another's help. With all that the master can do, he is helpless to make the disciple take hold of the thing unless the latter is inwardly fully prepared for it.

ZEN

(7) Zen is not all negation, leaving the mind all blank as if it were pure nothing; for that would be intellectual suicide. There is in Zen something self-assertive, which, however, being free and absolute, knows no limitations and refuses to be handled in abstraction. Zen is a live fact, it is not like an inorganic rock or like an empty space. To come into contact with this living fact, nay, to take hold of it in every phase of life, is the aim of all Zen discipline.

(8) Zen wants absolute freedom, even from God. "No abiding place" means that; "Cleanse your mouth even when you utter the word 'Buddha'" amounts to the same thing. It is not that Zen wants to be morbidly unholy and godless, but that it knows the incompleteness of a name.

(9) We must remember, however, that we live in affirmation and not in negation, for life is affirmation itself; and this affirmation must not be the one accompanied or conditioned by a negation, such an affirmation is relative and not at all absolute. With such an affirmation life loses its creative originality and turns into a mechanical process grinding forth nothing but soulless flesh and bones. To be free, life must be an absolute affirmation. It must transcend all possible conditions, limitations, and antitheses that hinder its free activity. When Shuzan held forth his stick of bamboo, what he wanted his disciples to understand was to have them realize this form of absolute affirmation. Any answer is satisfactory if it flows out of one's inmost being, for such is always an absolute affirmation. Therefore, Zen does not mean a mere escape from intellectual imprisonment, which sometimes ends in sheer wantonness. There is something in Zen that frees us from conditions and at the same time gives us a certain firm foothold, which, however, is not a foothold in a relative sense. The Zen master endeavors to take away all footholds from the disciple which he has ever had since his first appearance on earth, and then to supply him with one that is really no foothold. If the stick of bamboo is not to the purpose, anything that comes handy will be made use of. Nihilism is not Zen, for this bamboo stick or anything else cannot be done away with as words and logic can. This is the point we must not overlook in the study of Zen.

(10) Evidently, Zen is the most irrational, inconceivable thing in the world. And this is why Zen is not subject to logical analysis or to intellectual treatment. It is to be directly and personally experienced by each of us in his inner being. Just as two stainless mirrors reflect each other, the fact and our own spirits must stand facing each other with no intervening agents. When this is done we are able to seize upon the living, pulsating fact itself.

Freedom is an empty word until this happens. The first object was to escape the bondage in which all finite beings find themselves, but if we do not cut asunder the very chain of ignorance that binds us hands and feet, where shall we look for deliverance? And this chain of ignorance is wrought of nothing else but the intellect and sensuous infatuation, which cling tightly to every thought we may have, to every feeling we may entertain. They are hard to get rid of, they are like wet clothes as is aptly expressed by the Zen masters. "We are born free and equal." Whatever this may mean socially or politically, Zen maintains that it is absolutely true in the spiritual domain, and that all the fetters and manacles we seem to be carrying about us are put on later through ignorance of the true condition of existence. All the treatments, sometimes literary and sometimes physical, which are liberally and kind-heartedly given by the masters to inquiring souls, are intended to regain the original state of freedom. And this is never really realized until we once personally experience it through our own efforts, independent of any ideational representation. The ultimate standpoint of Zen is that we have been led astray through ignorance to find a split in our own being, that there was from the very beginning no need for a struggle between the finite and the infinite, that the peace we seek so eagerly has been here all the time.

THE PARADOX OF THE INFINITE

(11) In an infinite series of finite numbers, 0 (zero) is at the ever-diminishing end, while ∞ (infinity) is at the ever-increasing end. Insofar as finite numbers are concerned, they cannot reach an end in either direction, either 0 or ∞, unless they perform a leap. But practically or logically speaking, a leap is another human thought symbol ingeniously devised. For how can there be an infinite leap? A leap is a finite conception. No infinities can be made to limit themselves, for when they do they are no longer infinities; both 0 and ∞ are unattainable. In a series of finite numbers, moving in either direction—negatively or positively, retrogressively or progressively—all that we can envisage and calculate and handle in any utilizable way is limited to the finite numbers. But such handling can never take place without having an unattainable at either end. Finite numbers are possible only within this equation: $0 = \infty$.

We now come to the paradox: the world we live in is a relative, finite world, limited in every way, and I say this world is possible only when it is placed within the infinite. In a world of infinity, then, the highest is the lowest, the limited is the unlimited, 2 is 3, 3 is 4, an idiot is a saint. "I" am "thou" and "thou" art "I," "I am walking and I am riding on a water buffalo," "I, empty-handed, hold a spade," "a cloud of dust rises in a well," "the surging ocean is as smoothly leveled as the mirror," "Buddha has never entered parinirvāna,"[3] "we are still listening to Buddha giving his sermon on Mount Vulture." Zen literature is a storehouse of such paradoxes. But since our limited world is inhabited by logicians, positivists, and philosophers of various hues, they would most decidedly not concur with my views.

To reach this world of infinity or Self or God, Zen insists we abandon our restless pursuit after logic, intellection, or ratiocination of any form—even if temporarily—and plunge ourselves deep into the bottomless abyss of primary "feeling," the eternally unquenchable yearning for "the unknown," or "the truth that will make us free" from the bondage of all forms of limitation and finitude.

(12) Now, the practical questions are: How is it possible for the human mind to conceive zero, infinity, endless continuity, uninterrupted stretches of time and space, or, according to Simone Weil, "a reality beyond the world"? How can the self, cut up and limited, ever come to conceive and even to realize the Self, unlimited, uncut, and infinite? Where do we get the concept of Self if our senses and intellect fail to see anything unlimited or infinite in their existential and experiential world? How do we or can we transcend "the absurdities of paradox and the insoluble contradictions" in which we are so helplessly involved? But somehow transcend we must, for otherwise there will be no peace of mind, no security, no freedom, for which we so desperately long.

RUBBISH IN THE MIND

(13) The mind is ordinarily chock full with all kinds of intellectual nonsense and passional rubbish. They are of course useful in their own ways in our daily life. There is no denying that. But it is chiefly because of these accumulations that we are made miserable and groan under the feeling of bondage. Each time we want to make a movement, they fetter us, they choke us, and cast a heavy veil over our spiritual horizon. We feel as if we are constantly living

under restraint. We long for naturalness and freedom, yet we do not seem to attain them. The Zen masters know this, for they too have gone through the same experiences. They want to have us rid ourselves of these wearisome burdens which we really do not have to carry in order to live a life of truth and enlightenment. Thus they utter a few words and demonstrate with action that, when rightly comprehended, will deliver us from the oppression and tyranny of these intellectual accumulations. But the comprehension does not come to us so easily. Being so long accustomed to the oppression, the mental inertia becomes hard to remove. In fact it has gone down deep into the roots of our own being, and the whole structure of personality is often to be overturned. The process of reconstruction is stained with tears and blood. But the height the great masters have climbed cannot otherwise be reached; the truth of Zen can never be attained unless it is attacked with the full force of one's being. The passage is strewn with thistles and brambles, and the climb is slippery in the extreme. It is no pastime but the most serious task in life; no idlers will ever dare attempt it. It is indeed a moral anvil on which your character is tempered. To the question, "What is Zen?" a master gave this answer, "Boiling oil over a blazing fire." This scorching experience we have to go through before Zen smiles on us and says, "Welcome home."

ON SEEING INTO OUR OWN NATURE

(14) The priest-scholar, Inshū, was greatly struck by the statement of Enō,[4] so conclusive and authoritative. Finding out very soon who this Enō was, Inshū asked him to enlighten him on the teaching of the master of Yellow Plum Mountain. The gist of Enō's reply was as follows:

"My master had no special instruction to give; he simply insisted upon the need of our seeing into our own Nature through our own efforts; he had nothing to do with meditation, or with deliverance. For whatever can be named leads to dualism, and Buddhism is not dualistic. To take hold of this nonduality of truth is the aim of Zen. The Buddha-nature of which we are all in possession, and the seeing into which constitutes Zen, is indivisible into such oppositions as good and evil, eternal and temporal, material and spiritual. To see dualism in life is due to confusion of thought; the wise, the enlightened, see into the reality of things unhampered by erroneous ideas."

(15) The messenger, however, wished to be instructed in the doctrine of Zen, that he might convey it to his august master at Court. Said Enō in the main as follows:

"It is a mistake to think that sitting quietly in contemplation is essential to deliverance. The truth of Zen opens by itself from within and it has nothing to do with the practice of *dhyāna*."[5]

(16) To meditate a man has to fix his thought on something, for instance, on the oneness of God, or His infinite love, or on the impermanence of things. But this is the very thing Zen desires to avoid. If there is anything Zen strongly emphasizes, it is the attainment of freedom, that is, freedom from all unnatural encumbrances. Meditation is something artificially put on; it does not belong to the native activity of the mind. Upon what do the fowl of the air meditate? Upon what do the fish in the water meditate? They fly; they swim. Is not that enough? Who wants to fix his mind on the unity of God and man? or on the nothingness of this life? Who wants to be arrested in the daily manifestations of his life-activity by such meditations as the goodness of a divine being or the everlasting fire of hell?

We may say that Christianity is monotheistic, and the Vedanta pantheistic; but we cannot make a similar assertion about Zen. Zen is neither monotheistic nor pantheistic; Zen defies all such designations. Hence there is no object in Zen upon which to fix the thought. Zen is a wafting cloud in the sky. No screw fastens it, no string holds it; it moves as it lists. No amount of meditation will keep Zen in one place. Meditation is not Zen. Neither pantheism nor monotheism provides Zen with its subjects of concentration. If Zen were monotheistic, it might tell its followers to meditate on the oneness of things where all differences and inequalities, enveloped in the all-illuminating brightness of the divine light, are obliterated. If Zen were pantheistic it would tell us that every meanest flower in the field reflects the glory of God. But what Zen says is: "After all things are reduced to oneness, where would that One be reduced?" Zen wants to have one's mind free and unobstructed; even the idea of oneness or allness is a stumbling block and a strangling snare which threatens the original freedom of the spirit.

Zen, therefore, does not ask us to concentrate our thought on the idea that a dog is God, or that three pounds of flax are divine. When Zen does this, it commits itself to a definite system of philosophy, and there is no more Zen. Zen just feels fire warm and ice cold, because when it freezes we shiver and welcome fire. The feeling is all in all as Faust declares; all our theorization fails to touch reality. But "the feeling" here must be understood in its deepest sense or in its purest form. Even if we say that "This is the feeling" Zen is no more there. Zen defies all concept-making. That is why Zen is difficult to grasp.

Whatever meditation Zen may propose, then, will be to take things as they are, to consider snow white and the raven black. When we speak of meditation we in most cases understand its abstract character; that is, meditation is known to be the concentration of the mind on some highly generalized proposition, which is, in the nature of things, not always closely and directly connected with the concrete affairs of life. Zen perceives or feels, and does not abstract nor meditate. Zen penetrates and is finally lost in the immersion. Meditation, on the other hand, is outspokenly dualistic and consequently inevitably superficial.

(17) The basic idea of Zen is to come in touch with the inner workings of our being, and to do this in the most direct way possible, without resorting to anything external or superadded. Therefore, anything that has the semblance of an external authority is rejected by Zen. Absolute faith is placed in a man's own inner being. For whatever authority there is in Zen, all comes from within. This is true in the strictest sense of the word. Even the reasoning faculty is not considered final or absolute. On the contrary, it hinders the mind from coming into the directest communication with itself. The intellect accomplishes its mission when it works as an intermediary, and Zen has nothing to do with an intermediary except when it desires to communicate itself to others. For this reason, all the scriptures are merely tentative and provisory, there is in them no finality. The central fact of life as it is lived, is what Zen aims to grasp, and this in the most direct and most vital manner. Zen professes itself to be the spirit of Buddhism, but in fact it is the spirit of all religions and philosophies. When Zen is thoroughly understood, absolute peace of mind is attained, and a man lives as he ought to live. What more may we hope?

(18) Zen in its essence is the art of seeing into the nature of one's own being, and it points the way from bondage to freedom. By making us drink

right from the fountain of life, it liberates us from all the yokes under which we finite beings are usually suffering in this world. We can say that Zen liberates all the energies properly and naturally stored in each of us, which are in ordinary circumstances cramped and distorted so that they find no adequate channel for activity.

This body of ours is something like an electric battery in which a mysterious power latently lies. When this power is not properly brought into operation, it either grows moldy and withers away or is warped and expresses itself abnormally. It is the object of Zen, therefore, to save us from going mad or being crippled. This is what I mean by freedom, giving free play to all the creative and benevolent impulses inherently lying in our hearts. Generally, we are blind to the fact that we are in possession of all the necessary faculties to make us happy and loving toward one another. All the struggles we see around us come from this ignorance. Zen, therefore, wants us to open a "third eye," as Buddhists call it, to the hitherto undreamed-of region shut away from us through our own ignorance. When the cloud of ignorance disappears, the infinity of the heavens is manifested, where we see for the first time into the nature of our own being. We then know the signification of life, it is no longer blind striving, nor is it a mere display of brutal forces.

(19) As to "seeing into one's own Nature," if this means a state of consciousness where there is neither the seeing subject nor the object seen, it cannot be anything else but a state of pure emptiness, which has no significance whatever for our everyday life, which is full of frustrations and expectations and vexations. This is true as far as our dualistic thinking is concerned. But we must remember that Zen deals with the most fundamental and most concrete experience lying at the basis of our daily living. Being an individual experience and not the conclusion of logical reasoning, it is neither abstract nor empty. On the contrary, it is most concrete, and filled with possibilities.

(20) "If you want to see what is the nature of your being, free your mind from thought of relativity and you will see by yourself how serene it is and yet how full of life it is."[6]

THE SELF

(21) We are too ego-centered. The ego shell in which we live is the hardest thing to outgrow. We seem to carry it all the time from childhood up to the time we die. We are, however, given chances to break through this shell, and the first and greatest of them is when we reach adolescence. This is the first time the ego comes to recognize the "other," or the awakening of sexual love. An ego, entire and undivided, now begins to feel a split in itself. Love hitherto dormant lifts its head and causes a great commotion. For the love now stirred demands at once the assertion and the annihilation of the ego. Love makes the ego lose itself in the object it loves, and yet at the same time it wants to have the object as its own. This is a contradiction, and a struggle that is a tragedy of life. This elemental feeling must be one of the divine agencies whereby man is urged to advance in his upward walk. God gives tragedies to perfect man. The greatest bulk of literature ever produced in this world is but the harping on the same string of love, and we never seem to grow weary of it. But this is not what we are concerned with here. I want to emphasize that through the awakening of love we get a glimpse into the infinity of things, and that this glimpse urges youth to Romanticism or to Rationalism according to his temperament and environment and education.

When the ego shell is broken and the "other" is taken into its own body, we can say that the ego has denied itself or that the ego has taken its first steps toward the infinite. Religiously, here ensues an intense struggle between the finite and the infinite, between the intellect and a higher power, or, more plainly, between the flesh and the spirit.

(22) Zen tells us: "Find your Self and you will be free and safe." But men today do not know what the Self is, and they are liable to take their egoistic small self for it. They attempt to make this small one assume the role and function of the big one.

(23) The Self according to Zen is a storehouse of creative possibilities where we find all stored: miracles and mysteries, natural and supernatural, ordinary and extraordinary, Almighty God and a good God, wolves and

lambs, briars and roses. Everything that comes out of the storehouse of infinite creativity is eternally fresh. Even our "earthly" life is not a series of humdrumnesses, it is full of wonders and viabilities. When we are awakened to this truth, we are no more "helpless puppets in a deterministic universe," because the truth makes us see that necessity is freedom and freedom is necessity in the eternally creative and ever-freshening Self.

(24) We hear and talk a great deal, particularly the psychologists, about spontaneity and about being spontaneous. But what they are talking about is a childlike spontaneity, an animal spontaneity, which is by no means the spontaneity and freedom of an adult human being. The truly human freedom and spontaneity must have long transcended this childish state of mind. It is true that there is spontaneity, a kind of freedom, in early life. But that is not the freedom of the really matured man! As long as he is unable to give up his childish freedom, he will need the help of a psychologist; but he can never expect to be free and spontaneous if he does not go through years, perhaps many decades, of self-discipline, at the end of which he will have reached the status of a fully matured manhood.

(25) When they are told to be spontaneous and uninhibited, they imagine they have recovered the original abode of security, and act self-assertively, indeed most arrogantly. Where there is no Self, spontaneity is licentiousness and licentiousness is sheer thraldom. To be spontaneous one must be in touch with the fount of creativity whose essential quality is to be itself, in its "isness." Without this experience, how can there be freedom, autarchy, unobstructedness? As to security, it is no problem at all. When one knows what the Self really is, one is emancipated from all sorts of bondage and is free. When one is free, what insecurity is there to feel? The main thing is to take hold of the Self, which is, as Zen people would say, seeing into one's own nature or *kokoro*.

"KARMA"

(26) We are now in a position to say something about karma. Human suffering is due to our being bound in karma, for all of us, as soon as we

are born, carry a heavy burden of past karma, which is, therefore, part of our very existence. In Japan the term is connected with bad deeds, and evil people are spoken of as bearing the karma of the past. But the original meaning of the term is "action," and human acts are valued as good, bad, or indifferent. In this sense, human beings are the only beings which have karma. All others move in accordance with the laws of their being, but it is human beings alone that can design and calculate and are conscious of themselves and of their doings. We humans are the sole self-conscious animals, or, as Pascal says, "thinking reeds." From thinking, from thinking consciously, we develop the faculty of seeing, designing, and planning beforehand, which demonstrates that we are free, and not always bound by the "inevitable laws" of Nature. Karma, therefore, which is the ethical valuation of our acts, is found only in human beings, and in fact as soon as we enter the world our karma is attached to us.

Not only are we wrapped up in our karma but we know the fact that we are so wrapped up. It may be better to say that we are karma, karma is ourself; moreover, we are all conscious of this fact, and yet this very fact of our being aware of the karma bondage is the spiritual privilege of humanity. For this privilege, implying freedom, means our being able to transcend karma. But we must remember that with freedom and transcendence there comes responsibility as well as struggle; and the struggle as an outcome of freedom means suffering. The value of human life indeed lies in this capability for suffering; where there is no suffering resulting from our consciousness of karmic bondage there is no power of attaining spiritual experience, and thereby reaching the field of nondistinction. Unless we definitely make up our minds to suffer we cannot enjoy the special spiritual privilege granted to us human beings. We must make full use of it, and, accepting the karma bondage as far as it extends, resolutely face all forms of suffering and thereby qualify ourselves for transcending them.

With the problem of karma we again encounter a contradiction, this more serious because it involves life itself; it is the contradiction of life and death. As long as we remain in the domain of intellection we may put it aside for a while as not concerning us very vitally. But when the question concerns life in its most fundamental sense, we cannot dispose of it lightly. If karma is human life itself, and there is no way to be free from it except by being deprived of life, which means self-destruction, how can there be any kind of emancipation? And without emancipation there is no spiritual life. We cannot be eternally suffering, however be the present fate of humanity. Just to be conscious of karma means no more than throwing ourselves into hell-fire. God would not visit upon us this form of punishment, however bad we may be. Is there not, after all, something in our recognition of karma which will lift us from it? But this is obviously a case of self-contradiction. We find ourselves plunged headlong into an ever-rotating whirlpool of human destiny.

The karma contradiction, as long as it is a contradiction, must be solved in the same way as its intellectual counterpart. The intellectual contradiction was solved when we entered the realm of nondistinction; so the karma contradiction is to be solved by entering the realm of no-karma. Where is this? It is where we became conscious of karma as underlying all human activities. This consciousness points to the way of liberation. The human privilege of self-judgment or self-appraisement is also the key to self-deliverance. Just because we are conscious of ourselves and know how to evaluate our deeds, we are permitted to have a glimpse into a realm where no such human judgment avails, that is, where karma is merged into no-karma and no-karma into karma.

NOTES

1. *Q.v.* D. ("transcendental wisdom," "existential intuition"). [Ed.]

2. Also known as Hsüan-sha; variously reported as living in the ninth, or the thirteenth century. [Ed.]

3. "Complete nirvana" entered upon death. [Ed.]

4. *Q.v.* D., Zen (2–3), alternately named Hung-jen, sixth patriarch of Zen in China. [Ed.]

5. *Q.v.* D. ("meditation"). [Ed.]

6. Enō, *q.v.* fn. 4. [Ed.]

[Daisetz T. Suzuki, *The Essentials of Zen Buddhism*, ed. Bernard Phillips (New York: E. P. Dutton and Co., 1962; reprint, Greenwood Press, Westport, Conn., 1973). (1) P. 407. (2) P. 161. (3) P. 211. (4) P. 210. (5) P. 213. (6) P. 155. (7) P. 34. (8) P. 159. (9) P. 51. (10) P. 335. (11) P. 379. (12) P. 380. (13) P. 339. (14) P. 136. (15) P. 137. (16) Pp. 11–12. (17) P. 15. (18) P. 327. (19) P. 212. (20) P. 137. (21) P. 330. (22) P. 376. (23) P. 376. (24) Pp. 60–61. (25) P. 377. (26) Pp. 402–403.]

Freedom as doing what one ought to do, i.e., as doing what is good

(2d1)
St. Augustine
354–430

"On the Free Will," from *The City of God*
selections from bk. IV and bk. V

The first reading contains Augustine's argument that divine foreknowledge is not incompatible with human freedom. The second reading expresses Augustine's view that "...the decision of the will is truly free only when it is not a slave to faults and sins."

"ON THE FOREKNOWLEDGE OF GOD AND THE FREE WILL OF MAN, AGAINST CICERO'S DEFINITION OF THEM"

(1) Cicero, in undertaking to refute the Stoics, considers himself helpless against them unless he can do away with divination. This he attempts to do by denying that there is any knowledge of the future. He argues with might and main that there is no such foreknowledge, either in man or in God, and that there is no way of predicting events. By this course he both denies the foreknowledge of God and essays to overthrow all prophecy, using futile arguments even when the truth of prophecy is clearer than daylight. He sets up as targets for criticism certain oracles that can easily be refuted, but does not prove his case, even against them. However, when it comes to disposing of the guesswork of the astrologers, his speech wins the day, for their statements are really such that they destroy and refute each other.

But we can much better put up with those who maintain even that destiny lies in the stars than with the man who strikes out all foreknowledge of the future. For it is a conspicuous act of madness both to agree that God exists and to deny his foreknowledge of the future. Since Cicero too was aware of this, he even hazarded the statement referred to in Scripture: "The fool hath said in his heart, There is no God," but this not in his own person, for he saw how unpopular and offensive it would be. That was his reason for putting the argument against the Stoics on this point into the mouth of Cotta, in his work *On the Nature of the Gods.* He also chose rather to deliver his verdict for Lucilius Balbus, to whom he assigned the defence of the Stoics, rather than for Cotta, who argued that there is no divine being.[1] But in the work *On Divination* he speaks in his own person and openly attacks belief in the foreknowledge of the future. The whole argument seems designed to avoid admitting the existence of fate and thereby sacrificing free will. For he thinks that if he grants that future events can be foreseen, then he will find it quite impossible to deny the existence of fate as a corollary.

But whatever may be the course of the involved debates and disputes of the philosophers, we Christians not only declare our belief in the existence of the supreme and true God, but also declare that he has a will, supreme power and foreknowledge. Nor do we fear that our acts of free will will not be acts of free will if it is granted that he whose foreknowledge cannot be mistaken foreknows that we will so act. Cicero had this fear and so rejected foreknowledge. The Stoics had it, and so they said that not everything happens by necessity, although they maintained that everything is brought about by fate.

What is it, then, that Cicero found so dangerous in the belief in foreknowledge of the future, that he strove to undermine it by his outrageous attack? Evidently the argument that, if all future events are foreknown, they will take place in the order in which their occurrence was foreknown, and if they are to take place in this order, then the order is determined for a foreknowing God. If the order of events is determined, the order of causes is determined, for nothing can happen that is not preceded by some efficient cause. But if there is a determined order of causes by which everything that happens happens, then all things that happen happen by fate. If this is the case, there is nothing really in our power, and the will really has no free choice. And if we grant this, says Cicero,[2] the whole basis of human life is overthrown: it is in vain that laws are made, that men employ reprimands and praise, denunciation and exhortation, and there is no justice in a system of rewards for the good and punishment for the bad. So in order to escape these consequences, so disgraceful and absurd and pernicious for humanity, Cicero chooses to reject foreknowledge of the future. He reduces a god-fearing soul to the dilemma of choosing one of two alternatives: either there is something governed by our will, or there is foreknowledge of the future. He thinks that it is impossible for both to exist at once, and that any support of one proposition is a denial of the other. If we choose foreknowledge of the future, freedom of the will is destroyed, and if we choose freedom of the will, foreknowledge of the future is excluded. And so, being a great and learned man, much concerned and thoroughly informed about human welfare, of these alternatives he chose free will, and in order to uphold it he denied foreknowledge of the future. Thus in his desire to make men free he made them irreligious.

But the God-fearing mind chooses both freedom and foreknowledge. It accepts both and supports both with religious loyalty. How so? asks Cicero. For if there is foreknowledge of the future, the whole series of consequences must follow, until the conclusion is reached that nothing is in our power. And again, if there is anything in our power, by reversing the steps of the argument we reach the conclusion that there is no foreknowledge of the future. All the steps are retraced in this way: If freedom of the will exists, all things do not come to pass by fate; if all things do not come to pass by fate, there is no fixed order for all causes; if there is no fixed order of causes, neither is there an order of things fixed for a foreknowing God, for things cannot happen except as their efficient causes come first. If there is no order of things fixed for a foreknowing God, then things do not all come to pass as he knew beforehand that they would come, and if all things do not come to pass as he knew beforehand, then, Cicero says, the foreknowledge of all things does not exist in God's mind.

As against these rash assertions, blasphemous and irreligious as they are, we Christians declare both that God knows all things before they happen, and that it is by our own free will that we act, whenever we feel and know that a thing is done by us of our own volition. But we do not say that all things come to pass by fate. No indeed, we say that nothing comes to pass by fate. For the word fate is commonly used of the position of the stars at the moment of conception or birth, and we have shown that the word means nothing, but is the frivolous assertion of an unreality. Moreover, as for the order of causes in which the will of God is all powerful, we neither deny it nor do we call it by the name "fate," unless perchance fate be understood as derived from *fari*, that is, from speaking.[3] For we cannot deny that it is written in the Scriptures: "Once God has spoken; twice have I heard this, that power belongs to God, and that to thee, O Lord, belongs mercy, for thou dost requite each man according to his work."[4] The words "Once God has spoken" mean "God has spoken immoveably," that is, unchangeably, even as he knows unchangeably all things that will come to pass and all things that he himself will do. With this explanation we might use the word fate as derived from *fari*, "to speak," if the word were not already commonly understood in another sense, to which we would not have the minds of men directed. Moreover, even if there is in God's mind a definite pattern of causation, it does not follow that nothing is left to the free choice of our will. For in fact, our wills also are included in the pattern of causation certainly known to God and embraced in his foreknowledge. For the wills of men are among the causes of the deeds of men, and so he who foresaw the causes of all things cannot have been ignorant of our wills among those causes, since he foresaw that these wills are the causes of our deeds.

Moreover, even the concession that Cicero makes, that nothing happens unless preceded by an efficient cause, is enough to refute him in this debate. He says that nothing happens without a cause, but that not every cause is a matter of fate, since there is also a fortuitous cause, a natural cause and a voluntary cause. But how does this help him? It is enough when he admits that everything that happens happens only by virtue of a preceding cause. As for those causes which he calls fortuitous (the word fortune is derived from the same root), we do not say that they are nonexistent, but that they are hidden, and we ascribe them to the will of the true God, or to the will of spirits of any sort you please. We by no means disconnect even the natural causes from the will of him who is the Author and Creator of all nature. Finally the voluntary causes belong either to God's will or to that of angels or men or animals, if indeed we may speak of wills in reference to those movements of irrational animals in which they act according to their nature when moving to get or to escape something. When I speak of the wills of angels, I include both good angels, whom we call angels of God, and wicked angels, whom we call angels of the devil or also demons. So too we include in wills of men both those of good and of bad men.

We draw from this the conclusion that the only efficient causes of all things that come to pass are voluntary causes, derived, of course, from that Being who is the breath (*spiritus*) of life. To be sure, this air or wind around us is also called " breath," but since it is a material thing, it is not the breath of life. The breath of life, accordingly, which gives life to all things and is creator of every body and of every created spirit, is God himself, the absolutely uncreated spirit. In his will lies the supreme power that strengthens the good wills of created spirits, judges the evil wills, and subjects them all to his divine order. To some he grants powers, to others he does not; for just as he is the creator of all beings, so he is the giver of all powers, but not of all wills. Bad wills of course do not come from him, since they are contrary to the strand of our nature that does come from him. Bodies, in turn, are rather subject to wills, some to our wills (that is, wills of all living, mortal creatures, and they are more subject to the wills of men than they are to those of beasts), some to the wills of angels, but all are subject to him, for they have no power except what he has granted. Hence God is the first cause, which causes and is not caused. Other causes, among them created spirits, especially rational spirits, both cause and are caused. But material causes, which are more passive than active, are not to be counted among efficient causes, for their only power is to do what the wills of immaterial beings do with them.

How, then, can the order of causes that is fixed in God's foreknowledge deprive us of all use of our will, when our wills play an important part in the order of causes itself? So let Cicero argue the case with those who say that this order of causes is determined by fate, or rather, call the order itself fate. We refuse to do this, because the word is commonly used to refer to a false notion. As for Cicero's denial that the order of all causes is perfectly defined and perfectly visible to the foreknowledge of God, that is an abomination to us, even more than to the Stoics. Either he is denying the existence of God, as he essayed to do in the speech that he gave to a disputant in the dialogue *On the Nature of the Gods,* or if he agrees that God exists, but denies his knowledge of the future, even so it amounts to nothing more than what "the fool has said in his heart, There is no God."[5] For one who does not know all future things is surely not God. Hence our acts of will also have just so much power as God chose to give them and also foresaw. Therefore, whatever power they have, they have it most assuredly. They themselves will in any case do what they are going to do, because he whose foreknowledge cannot be mistaken foresaw that they would have the power to do it, and that they would do it. Hence if I saw fit to apply the word fate to anything, I would rather say that the fate of the weaker is the will of the stronger, who has the other in his power, than to admit that the order of causes which the Stoics call fate (in their own, but not the common usage of the word) does away with our free will.

"WHETHER NECESSITY REIGNS OVER THE WILLS OF MEN"

Hence we need not fear that necessity which the Stoics feared so much that they took pains to discriminate among causes by exempting some from the decree of necessity while leaving others subject to it. Under the heading of causes that they would not leave in the realm of necessity they put our acts of will, obviously thinking that they would not be free if they were made subject to necessity. If the term necessity should be used of what is not in our power, but accomplishes its end even against our will, for example, the necessity of death, it is clear that our wills, by which we live rightly or wrongly, are not under such necessity. For we do many things that we certainly should not do if we were unwilling. To this class of things belongs first of all the will itself. If we will, the will exists; if not, it does not. For we should not will if we were unwilling.

But if the term necessity is used in the sense that it is necessary for something to be as it is, or happen as it does, I do not know why we should fear that it may destroy our freedom of will. In fact, we do not make the life of God, or the foreknowledge of God, subject to necessity if we say that it is necessary for God to live forever and to foreknow all things. Likewise his power is not lessened when we say that he cannot die, or be mistaken. In saying this we understand that he would rather have less power if he could die or be mistaken. Of course he is rightly called omnipotent, although he cannot die or be deceived, for he is omnipotent in that he does what he wills and does not suffer to be done what he does not will; otherwise he would certainly not be omnipotent. Hence it is because he is omnipotent that there are certain things he cannot do. The case is similar when we say that it is necessary, when we exercise will, to do so of our own free will. This that we say is undoubtedly true, yet we do not thereby put our free will under the necessity that takes away liberty.

Our wills, therefore, exist, and they do whatever it is that we do with a will, which would not be done if we were unwilling. Furthermore, when anyone suffers something against his will because of the will of other men, even so will is in control. Though it is not his own will, it is still a man's will, but its power is from God. If it were only a man's will, without the power to accomplish its will, the thing that held it fettered would be some more powerful will. Yet the will would still be a will, not another's, but the will of him who had a will, even if he could not carry it out. Hence what a man suffers against his will should be ascribed, not to the wills of men or angels or any created spirit, but rather to the will of him who bestows the power to realize the wish.

It is not true, then, that there is no reality in our will just because God foresaw what would be in our will. For when he foresaw this, he foresaw something. Further, he who foresaw what would be in our will certainly foresaw something real, not a mere nothing. Hence assuredly there is something in our will, even though God has foreknowledge of it. Therefore we are in no way compelled either to abolish free will when we keep the foreknowledge of God, or blasphemously to deny that God foreknows the future because we keep free will. Instead we embrace both truths; with faith and trust we assert both. The former is required for correct belief, the latter for right living. And there is no right living if there is no correct belief in God. Far be it then, from us, in order to enjoy free will, to deny the foreknowledge of him by whose assistance alone we are free, or shall ever be free. Consequently laws, reprimands, exhortations, praise and denunciation are not useless, for God knew that they would be used, and they are most effective as far as he foreknew that they would be. Prayers too are effective for obtaining those things which he foreknew he would grant to those who pray. And it accords with justice that rewards are provided for good deeds and punishments for sins. For man does not in fact fail to[6] sin because God foresaw that be would sin. Nay, it is precisely because of foreknowledge that there is no doubt that man himself sins when he sins. For he whose foreknowledge cannot be mistaken foresaw that neither fate, nor fortune, nor anything else but the man himself would sin. If he chooses not to sin, he certainly does not sin, and this choice not to sin was also foreseen by God.

"ON THE FALL OF THE FIRST MAN"

(2) But God foreknew all things and must therefore also have been aware that man would sin. For this reason, we must base any doctrine of the holy city on his foreknowledge and dispensation and not on that which could not have come to our knowledge because it was not a part of God's dispensation. Man could not possibly upset the divine plan by his sin, as if he could have compelled God to change what he had decreed, for God through his foreknowledge had anticipated both the coming events, that is, both how bad the man whom he himself had created good would become and what good he himself would use him to effect even so.

God, it is true, is said to change his decrees, and hence we read in Scripture the statement in figurative speech even that God repented.[7] But such a statement is based on man's expectation or on the prospect implicit in the, orderly course of natural causes, not on the Almighty's foreknowledge of what he will do. Thus, as Scripture tells us, God made man upright[8] and consequently of good will, for man would not have been upright without a good will. Good will then is the work of God, since man was created in possession of it by him.

On the other hand, the first evil act of will, preceding, as it did, all evil works in man, was rather a falling away from the work of God to the will's own works than any one work; and those works were evil because they followed the will's own pattern and not God's. Thus the will itself, or man himself in so far as he was possessed of an evil will, was the evil tree, as it were, that bore the evil fruit[9] that those works represented. Further, although an evil will is not in accordance with nature but contrary to nature because it is a defect, nevertheless it belongs to the natural being of which it is a defect, for it can exist only in a natural substance. But it must exist in the natural substance that God created out of nothing, not in that which the Creator begot from himself, as he begot the Word through which all things were made.[10] For, although God fashioned man from the dust of the earth,[11] this very earth and all earthly matter are derived from nothing at all, and he gave to the body when man was created a soul that was made out of nothing.

But the good things prevail over the bad, so much so in fact that, although bad things are permitted to exist in order to show how the righteous Creator with his perfect foresight can make good use even of them, nevertheless good things can exist without bad, for example, the true and supreme God himself or again all visible and invisible creations in the heaven above our murky air. On the other hand, evil cannot exist without the good since the created things in which it is found are certainly good as created. Moreover, an evil is eliminated not by the removal of some substance, or any part of it, which had supervened, but by the healing and restoration of the substance that had become morbid and debased.

Accordingly, the decision of the will is truly free only when it is not a slave to faults and sins. It had that freedom when God first gave it, but, having lost such freedom by its own fault, it can regain it only from him in whose power it was to grant it originally. Truth says on this point: "If the Son sets you free, then you will be truly free."[12] This is tantamount to saying: "If the Son saves you, then you will be truly saved." For the same act makes a savior a deliverer too.

Thus man lived according to God in a paradise that was both corporeal and spiritual. This paradise was not merely corporeal to supply the good things of the body without also being spiritual to supply the good things of the mind, nor was it merely spiritual for man to enjoy through his inner senses without also being corporeal for him to enjoy through his outer senses. It was clearly both for the good of both. Then, however, came that proud angel, whose very pride made him envious and also caused him to turn from God to follow himself. With the arrogance, as it were, of a tyrant he chose to rejoice over subjects rather than to be a subject himself; and consequently he fell from the spiritual paradise. I have discoursed as best I could in the eleventh and twelfth books of this work[13] on the fall of this angel and of those leagued with him, the former angels of God who became his angels. After his fall he sought by corrupting guile to work his way into the heart of man, whose unfallen state surely he envied since he himself had fallen. For this purpose he chose as his mouthpiece a serpent in the corporeal paradise, where along with those two human beings, male and female, there dwelt also all the other terrestrial animals, who were tame and harmless. This slippery animal, of course, which moves in twisting coils, was a suitable tool for his work. By his stature as an angel and his superior being he made it subject to him in spiritual wickedness, and misusing it as his instrument he conversed deceitfully with the woman. In so doing he no doubt began with the lower member of that human couple in order to arrive gradually at the whole. Presumably he did not think that the man was readily gullible or that he could be snared by his own mistake, but only if he gave way to the mistake of another.

So was it with Aaron, for he did not agree with the mistaken multitude to construct an idol because he was persuaded, but he yielded to it because he was under pressure.[14] Nor is it credible that Solomon mistakenly thought that he should serve idols; he was driven to such acts of irreligion by the blandishments of women.[15] Similarly, when we consider the situation of that first man and his woman, two fellow human beings all alone and married to each other, we must suppose that he was not led astray to transgress the law of God because he believed that she spoke the truth, but because he was brought to obey her by the close bond of their alliance. For the Apostle was not speaking idly when he said: "And Adam was not deceived, but the woman was deceived."[16] He must have meant that Eve had accepted what the serpent said to her as though it were true, while Adam refused to be separated from his sole companion even in a partnership of sin. Yet he was no less guilty if he sinned with knowledge and forethought. This also explains why the Apostle does not say: "He did not sin," but: "He was not deceived." For he surely refers to him where he states: "Sin came into the world through one man";[17] and a little later when he says more explicitly: "Like the transgression of Adam."[18]

The Apostle meant us to understand the deceived as being those who do not think that what they do is sin. Adam, however, knew; otherwise, how can it be true to say: "Adam was not deceived"? But since he was not yet acquainted with the strict justice of God, he might have been mistaken in believing that his offence was pardonable. Hence, though he did not suffer the same deception as the woman, yet he was mistaken about the verdict that would inevitably be pronounced on this plea that he would make: "The woman whom thou gavest to be with me, she gave it to me, and I ate."[19] To put it briefly then, we may say that although they were not both deceived by believing, yet both were taken captive by sinning and ensnared in the devil's toils.

NOTES

1. *On the Nature of the Gods*, 3.95.
2. *De fato*, 40.
3. This etymology is today accepted as correct.
4. Psalm 62.11–12.
5. Psalm 14.1.
6. Some manuscripts omit non: "does not in fact sin."
7. Cf. Genesis 6.6; Exodus 32.14; 1 Samuel 15.11; 2 Samuel 24.16.
8. Cf. Ecclesiastes 7.29.
9. Cf. Matthew 7.17–18.
10. Cf. John 1.3.
11. Cf. Genesis 2.7.
12. John 8.36.
13. Cf. above, 11.13; 12.1 (sections preceding our selections, Ed.).
14. Cf. Exodus 32.1–6.
15. Cf. 1 Kings 11.4.
16. 1 Timothy 2.14.
17. Romans 5.12.
18. Romans 5.14.
19. Genesis 3.12.

[St. Augustine, "On the Free Will," *The City of God*, tr. W. M. Green (Cambridge, Mass.: Harvard Univ. Press, 1978). (1) Bk. V, ch. 9, p. 167 to end of ch. 10, p. 187. (2) Bk. IV, ch. 11, pp. 323–33.]

(2d2)
St. Anselm
1033–1109

"On Freedom of Choice"
(Freedom as Rectitude)

Anselm, the most powerful thinker between St. Augustine and St. Thomas Aquinas, framed the ontological argument (*q.v.* D, and R, vol. 8). In the following passage he develops the argument, defining and defending freedom as rectitude, more powerfully than either his predecessor or successor in this line of saints. The first section, below, announces the argument of the essay in 14 chapter headings. In presenting Anselm's argument material is selected from seven of these chapters.

(1) CHAPTER HEADINGS AND DENIAL THAT
FREE WILL IS THE POWER TO SIN OR NOT TO SIN.

Chapters

1. That the power of sinning does not pertain to free will
2. Both the angel and man sinned by this capacity to sin and by free will and, though they could have become slaves of sin, sin did not have the power to dominate them
3. How free will is had after they have made themselves slaves of sin and what free will is
4. How those who do not have rectitude have the power to preserve it

1. *"That the power of sinning does not pertain to free will"*

Student. Since free will seems to be repugnant to grace, predestination and God's foreknowledge, I want to understand freedom of will and know whether we always have it. For if 'to be able to sin and not to sin' is due to free will, as some are accustomed to say, and we always have it, why do we sometimes need grace? But if we do not always have it, why is sin imputed to us when we sin without free will?

Teacher. I do not think free will is the power to sin or not to sin. Indeed if this were its definition, neither God nor the angels, who are unable to sin, would have free will, which it is impious to say.

S. But what if one were to say that the free will of God and the angels is different from ours?

T. Although the free will of men differs from the free will of God and the angels, the definition of freedom expressed by the word ought to be the same. For although one animal differs from another either substantially or accidentally, the definition attached to the word 'animal' is the same for all. That is why we must so define free will that the definition contains neither too little nor too much. Since the divine free will and that of the good angels cannot sin, to be able to sin does not belong in the definition of free will. Furthermore, the power to sin is neither liberty nor a part of liberty. Pay attention to what I am going to say and you will fully understand this.

S. That is why I am here.

T. Which free will seems more free to you, that which so wills that it cannot sin, such that it can in no way be deflected from the rectitude constituted by not sinning, or that which can in some way be deflected to sinning?

S. I do not see why that which is capable of both is not freer.

T. Do you not see that one who is as he ought to be, and as it is expedient for him to be, such that he is unable to lose this state, is freer than one who is such that he can lose it and be led into what is indecent and inexpedient for him?

S. I think there is no doubt that this is so.

T. And would you not say that it is no less doubtful that to sin is always indecent and harmful.

S. No one of healthy mind would think otherwise.

T. Therefore a will that cannot fall from rectitude into sin is more free than one that can desert it.

S. Nothing seems to me more reasonable to say.

T. Therefore, since the capacity to sin when added to will diminishes liberty, and its lack increases it, it is neither liberty nor a part of liberty.

S. Nothing is more obvious.

2. *"Both the angel and man sinned by this capacity to sin and by free will and, though they could have become slaves of sin, sin did not have the power to dominate them"*

T. What is extraneous to freedom does not pertain to free will.

S. I can contest none of your arguments, but I am not a little swayed by the fact that in the beginning both the angelic nature and ours had the capacity to sin, since without it, they would not have sinned. Wherefore, if by this capacity, which is alien to free will, both natures sinned, how can we say they sinned by free will? But if they did not sin by free will, it seems they sinned necessarily. That is, they sinned either willingly or necessarily.

But if they sinned willingly, how so if not by free will? And if not by free will, then indeed it seems that they sinned necessarily.

And there is something else that strikes me in this ability to sin. One who can sin, can be the slave of sin, since 'he who commits sin, is the slave of sin' [John 8.34]. But he who can be the slave of sin, can be dominated by sin. How was that nature created free then, and what kind of free will is it that can be dominated by sin?

T. It was through the capacity to sin willingly and freely and not of necessity that ours and the angelic nature first sinned and were able to serve sin, yet they cannot be dominated by sin in such a way that they and their judgement can no longer be called free,

S. You must expand on what you said since it is opaque to me.

T. The apostate angel and the first man sinned through free will, because they sinned through a judgement that is so free that it cannot be coerced to sin by anything else. That is why they are justly reprehended; when they had a free will that could not be coerced by anything else, they willingly and without necessity sinned. They sinned through their own free will, though not insofar as it was free, that is, not through that thanks to which it was free and had the power not to sin or to serve sin, but rather by the power it had of sinning, unaided by its freedom not to sin or to be coerced into the servitude of sin.

What seemed to you to follow does not, namely, that if will could be a slave to sin it could be dominated by sin, and therefore neither it nor its judgement are free. But this is not so. For what has it in its power not to serve cannot be forced by another to serve, although it can serve by its own power: for as long as the power uses that which is for serving and not that which is for not serving, nothing can dominate it so that it should serve. For if the rich man is free to make a poor man his servant, as long as he does not do so, he does not lose the name of freedom nor is the poor man said to be able to be dominated or, if this is said, it is said improperly, for this is not in his power but in another's. Therefore nothing prevents either angel or man from being free prior to sin or from having had free will.

3. "How free will is had after they have made themselves slaves of sin and what free will is"

S. You have satisfied me that nothing certainly prevents this prior to sin, but how can they retain free will after they have made themselves slaves of sin?

T. Although they subjected themselves to sin, they were unable to lose natural free will. But now they cannot use that freedom without a grace other than that which they previously had.

S. I believe that, but I want to understand it.

T. Let us first consider the kind of free will they had before sin when they certainly had free will.

S. I am ready,

T. Why do you think they had free will: to attain what they want or to will what they ought and what is expedient for them to will?

S. The latter.

T. Therefore they had free will for the sake of rectitude of will. As long as they willed what they ought, they had rectitude of will.

S. That is so.

(2) ONE RETAINS THE RECTITUDE OF THE WILL FOR THE SAKE OF THIS RECTITUDE ITSELF.

T. You have responded well to what was asked, but we must still consider for what purpose a rational nature ought to retain that rectitude, whether for the sake of the rectitude itself, or for the sake of something else.

S. If that liberty were not given to such a nature in order that it might preserve rectitude of will for the sake of rectitude, it would not avail for justice. Justice seems to be the retention of rectitude of will for its own sake. But we believe that free will is for the sake of justice. Therefore without a doubt we should assert that the rational nature receives liberty solely to preserve rectitude of will for its own sake.

T. Therefore, since all liberty is a capacity, the liberty of will is the capacity for preserving rectitude of the will for the sake of rectitude itself.

S. It cannot be otherwise.

T. So it is now clear that free judgement is nothing other than a judgement capable of preserving the rectitude of will for the sake of rectitude itself.

(3) THE WILL PREVAILS WHEN IT PRESERVES ITS RECTITUDE.

T. Would you deny that every free being is such that it can only be moved or prevented willingly?

S. I do not see how I could.

T. Tell me how right will prevails and how it is conquered.

S. To will the preservation of rectitude for its own sake is for it to prevail, but to will what it ought not is for it to be conquered.

T. I think that temptation can only stop right will or force it to what it ought not to will willingly, such that it wills the one and not the other.

S. I do not see any way in which that could be false.

T. Who then can say that the will is not free to preserve rectitude, and free from temptation and sin, if no temptation can divert it save willingly from rectitude to sin, that is, to willing what it ought not? Therefore when it is conquered, it is not conquered by another power but by itself.

S. That demonstrates what has been said.

T. Do you see that from this it follows that no temptation can conquer right will? For if it could, it would have the power to conquer and would conquer by its own power. But this cannot be, since the will can only be conquered by itself Wherefore temptation can in no way conquer right will, and it is only improperly said to conquer it. For it only means that the will can subject itself to temptation, just as conversely when the weak is said to be able to be conquered by the strong, he is said to be able, not by his own power but by another's, since it only means that the strong has the power to conquer the weak.

(4) NOT EVEN GOD CAN TAKE AWAY THE RECTITUDE OF ONE'S WILL, AND NOTHING IS FREER THAN THE "RIGHT WILL."

8. *"That not even God can take away the rectitude of will"*

S. Can even God take away rectitude from the will?

T. This cannot happen. God can reduce to nothing the whole substance that he made from nothing, but he cannot separate rectitude from a will that has it.

S. I am eager to have the reason for an assertion I have never before heard.

T. We are speaking of that rectitude of will thanks to which the will is called just, that is, which is preserved for its own sake. But no will is just unless it wills what God wants it to will.

S. One who does not will that is plainly unjust.

T. Therefore to preserve rectitude of will for its own sake is, for everyone who does so, to will what God wants him to will.

S. That must be said .

T. Should God remove this rectitude from anyone's will, he does this either willingly or unwillingly.

S. He could not do so unwillingly.

T. If then he removes this rectitude from someone's will he wills to do what he does.

S. Without any doubt.

T. But then he does not want the one from whom he removes this rectitude to preserve the rectitude of will for its own sake.

S. That follows.

T. But we already said that to preserve in this way the rectitude of will is for one to will what God wants him to will.

S. Even if we had not said it, it is so.

T. Hence if God were to take from something that rectitude of which we have so often spoken, he does not will one to will what he wants him to will.

S. An inevitable and impossible consequence.

T. Therefore nothing is more impossible than that God should take away the rectitude of will. Yet he is said to do this when he does not impede the abandonment of this rectitude. On the other hand, the devil and temptation are said to do this or to conquer the will and to remove from it the rectitude it has when they offer something or threaten to take away something that the will wants more than rectitude, but there is no way they can deprive it of that rectitude as long as the will wants it.

S. What you say is clear to me and I think nothing can be said against it.

9. That nothing is more free than right will

T. You can see that there is nothing freer than a right will since no alien power can take away its rectitude. To be sure, if we say that, when it wills to lie lest it lose life or safety, it is forced by the fear of death or torment to desert the truth, this is not true. It is not forced to will life rather than truth, but since an external force prevents it from preserving both at the same time, it chooses what it wants more—of itself that is and not unwillingly, although it would not of itself and willingly be placed in the necessity of abandoning both. It is not less able to will truth than safety, but it more strongly wills safety. For if it now should see the eternal glory which would immediately follow after preserving the truth, and the torments of hell to which it would be delivered over without delay after lying, without any doubt it would be seen to have a sufficiency for preserving the truth.

S. This is clear since it shows greater strength in willing eternal salvation for its own sake and truth for the sake of reward than for preserving temporal safety.

(5) TO DEFINE FREE WILL IN TERMS OF RECTITUDE IS TO PROVIDE THE PERFECT DEFINITION OF FREE WILL.

13. That the power of preserving the rectitude of will for its own sake is a perfect definition of free will

S. There is still something that troubles me. For we often have the power of preserving something which yet is not free because it can be impeded by another power. Therefore when you say that freedom of will is the power of preserving rectitude of will for the sake of rectitude itself, consider whether perhaps it should be added that this power is free in such a way that it can be overwhelmed by no other power.

T. If the power of preserving the rectitude of will for the sake of rectitude itself could sometimes be found without that liberty that we have succeeded in seeing clearly, your proposed addition would be fitting. But since the foregoing definition is perfected by genus and difference such that it can contain neither more nor less than what we call freedom, nothing should be added or subtracted from it. For 'power' is the genus of liberty. When 'of preserving' is added it separates it from every power which is not one of preserving, such as the power to laugh or walk. By adding 'rectitude' we separate it from the power of preserving gold and whatever else is not rectitude. By the addition of 'will' it is separated from the power of preserving the rectitude of other things, such as a stick or an opinion.

By saying that it is 'for the sake of rectitude itself' it is distinguished from the power of preserving rectitude for some other reason, for example for money, or just naturally. A dog preserves rectitude of will naturally when it loves its young or the master who cares for it. Therefore since there is nothing in this definition that is not necessary to embrace the free judgement of a rational creature and exclude the rest it sufficiently includes the one and excludes the other, nor is our definition too much or lacking anything.

[(1) Saint Anselm of Canterbury, "On Freedom of Choice," from *Truth, Freedom, and Evil: Three Philosophical Dialogues*, ed. and trans. Jasper Hopkins and Herbert Richardson, 1965, 1967 (New York: Harper Torchbooks, Harper and Row, 1967), ch. headings, ch. 1—first 16 ll. of ch. 3, pp. 175–78. (2) *Ibid.*, ch. 3, 18 ll., p. 179. (3) *Ibid.*, 27 ll. from end of ch. 5, pp. 183–84. (4) *Ibid.*, chs. 8 and 9, pp. 186–88. (5) *Ibid.*, first 3 pars. ch. 13, p. 191.]

St. Thomas Aquinas
1225–1274

Summa Theologica,
selections from ques. 59 and 83

Although Aquinas, in our view, is basically fourth definition, he includes the other three definitions as well. Reason and desire cooperate in acting freely. Choice requires both, and this is first definition. In the second reading we are told: "...whenever there is intellect, there is free-will," Will, however, is second, third, and fourth definition. Reason is natural to man and so a third-definition power. There are rational desires, so desire is sometimes third definition as well as second definition (one can irrationally oppose one's reason). And the good is what ought to be, and thus is fourth definition. He agrees with both of the points made in the St. Augustine reading.

OF FREE-WILL

(1) We now inquire concerning free-will. Under this head there are four points of inquiry: (1) Whether man has free-will ? (2) What is free-will—a power, an act, or a habit? (3) If it is a power, is it appetitive or cognitive? (4) If it is appetitive, is it the same power as the will, or distinct?

First Article. Whether Man Has Free-Will?

We proceed thus to the First Article:-

Objection 1. It would seem that man has not free-will. For whoever has free-will does what he wills. But man does not what he wills; for it is written (Rom. vii.19): *For the good which I will I do not, but the evil which I will not, that I do.* Therefore man has not free-will.

Obj. 2. Further, whoever has free-will has in his power to will or not to will, to do or not to do. But this is not in man's power: for it is written (Rom. ix.16): *It is not of him that willeth*—namely, to will—*nor of him that runneth*—namely, to run. Therefore man has not free-will.

Obj. 3. Further, what is *free is cause of itself,* as the Philosopher says (*Metaph.* i. 2). Therefore what is moved by another is not free. But God moves the will, for it is written (Prov. xxi.1): *The heart of the king is in the hand of the Lord; whithersoever He will He shall turn it;* and (Phil. ii.13): *It is God Who worketh in you both to will and to accomplish.* Therefore man has not free-will.

Obj. 4. Further, whoever has free-will is master of his own actions. But man is not master of his own actions: for it is written (Jer. x.23): *The way of a man is not his: neither is it in a man to walk.* Therefore man has not free-will.

Obj. 5. Further, the Philosopher says (*Ethic.* iii.5): *According as each one is, such does the end seem to him.* But it is not in our power to be of one quality or another; for this comes to us from nature. Therefore it is natural to us to follow some particular end, and therefore we are not free in so doing.

On the contrary, It is written (Ecclus. xv.14): *God made man from the beginning, and left him in the hand of his own counsel;* and the gloss adds: *That is of his free-will.*

I answer that, Man has free-will: otherwise counsels, exhortations, commands, prohibitions, rewards and punishments would be in vain. In order to make this evident, we must observe that some things act without judgment; as a stone moves downwards; and in like manner all things which lack knowledge. And some act from judgment, but not a free judgment; as brute animals. For the sheep, seeing the wolf, judges it a thing to be shunned, from a natural and not a free judgment, because it judges, not from reason, but from natural instinct. And the same thing is to be said of any judgment of brute animals. But man acts from judgment, because by his apprehensive power he judges that something should be avoided or sought. But because this judgment, in the case of some particular act, is not from a natural instinct, but from some act of comparison in the reason, therefore he acts from free judgment and retains the power of being inclined to various things. For reason in contingent matters may follow opposite courses, as we see in dialectic syllogisms and rhetorical arguments. Now particular operations are contingent, and therefore in such matters the judgment of reason may follow opposite courses, and is not determinate to one. And forasmuch as man is rational is it necessary that man have a free-will.

Reply Obj. 1. As we have said above (Q. LXXXI., A. 3, *ad* 2), the sensitive appetite, though it obeys the reason, yet in a given case can resist by desiring what the reason forbids. This is therefore the good which man does not when he wishes—namely, *not to desire against reason*, as Augustine says (*ibid.*).

Reply Obj. 2. Those words of the Apostle are not to be taken as though man does not wish or does not run of his free-will, but because the free-will is not sufficient thereto unless it be moved and helped by God.

Reply Obj. 3. Free-will is the cause of its own movement, because by his free-will man moves himself to act. But it does not of necessity belong to liberty that what is free should be the first cause of itself, as neither for one thing to be cause of another need it be the first cause. God, therefore, is the first cause, Who moves causes both natural and voluntary. And just as by moving natural causes He does not prevent their acts being natural, so by moving voluntary causes He does not deprive their actions of being voluntary: but rather is He the cause of this very thing in them; for He operates in each thing according to its own nature.

Reply Obj. 4. Man's way is said *not to be his* in the execution of his choice, wherein he may be impeded, whether he will or not. The choice itself, however, is in us, but presupposes the help of God.

Reply Obj. 5. Quality in man is of two kinds: natural and adventitious. Now the natural quality may be in the intellectual part, or in the body and its powers. From the very fact, therefore, that man is such by virtue of a natural quality which is in the intellectual part, he naturally desires his last end, which is happiness. Which desire, indeed, is a natural desire, and is not subject to free-will, as is clear from what we have said above (Q. LXXXII., AA. 1, 2). But on the part of the body and its powers man may be such by virtue of a natural quality, inasmuch as he is of such a temperament or dis-position due to any impression whatever produced by corporeal causes, which cannot affect the intellectual part, since it is not the act of a corpo-real organ. And such as a man is by virtue of a corporeal quality, such also does his end seem to him, because from such a disposition a man is inclined to choose or reject something. But these inclinations are subject to the judgment of reason, which the lower appetite obeys, as we have said (Q. LXXXI., A. 3). Wherefore this is in no way prejudicial to free-will.

The adventitious qualities are habits and passions, by virtue of which a man is inclined to one thing rather than to another. And yet even these inclinations are subject to the judgment of reason. Such qualities, too, are subject to reason, as it is in our power either to acquire them, whether by causing them or disposing ourselves to them, or to reject them. And so there is nothing in this that is repugnant to free-will.

Second Article. Whether Free-Will Is a Power?

We proceed thus to the Second Article:-

Objection 1. It would seem that free-will is not a power. For free-will is nothing but a free judgment. But judgment denominates an act, not a power. Therefore free-will it not a power.

Obj. 2. Further, free-will is defined as *the faculty of the will and reason.* But faculty denominates a facility of power, which is due to a habit. Therefore free-will is a habit. Moreover Bernard says (*De Gratia et Lib. Arb. 1, 2*) that free-will is *the soul's habit of disposing of itself.* Therefore it is not a power.

Obj. 3. Further, no natural power is forfeited through sin. But free-will is forfeited through sin; for Augustine says that *man, by abusing free-will, loses both it and himself.* Therefore free-will is not a power.

On the contrary, Nothing but a power, seemingly, is the subject of a habit. But free-will is the subject of grace, by the help of which it chooses what is good. Therefore free-will is a power.

I answer that, Although free-will[1] in its strict sense denotes an act, in the common manner of speaking we call free-will, that which is the principle of the act by which man judges freely. Now in us the principle of an act is both power and habit; for we say that we know something both by knowl-edge and by the intellectual power. Therefore free-will must be either a power or a habit, or a power with a habit. That it is neither a habit nor a power together with a habit, can be clearly proved in two ways. First of all, because, if it is a habit, it must be a natural habit; for it is natural to man to have a free-will. But there is no natural habit in us with respect to those things which come under free-will: for we are naturally inclined to those things of which we have natural habits—for instance, to assent to first principles: while those things to which we are naturally inclined are not subject to free-will, as we have said of the desire of happiness (Q. LXXXII., AA. 1, 2). Wherefore it is against the very notion of free-will that it should be a natural habit. And that it should be a non-natural habit is against its nature. Therefore in no sense is it a habit.

Secondly, this is clear because habits are defined as that *by reason of which we are well or ill disposed with regard to actions and passions* (*Ethic.* ii. 5); for by temperance we are well-disposed as regards concupiscences, and by intemperance ill-disposed: and by knowledge we are well-disposed to the act of the intellect when we know the truth, and by the contrary habit ill-disposed. But the free-will is indifferent to good or evil choice: wherefore it is impossible for free-will to be a habit. Therefore it is a power.

Reply Obj. 1. It is not unusual for a power to be named from its act. And so from this act, which is a free judgment, is named the power which is the principle of this act. Otherwise, if free-will denominated an act, it would not always remain in man.

Reply Obj. 2. Faculty sometimes denominates a power ready for operation, and in this sense faculty is used in the definition of free-will. But Bernard takes habit, not as divided against power, but as signifying a certain aptitude by which a man has some sort of relation to an act. And this may be both by a power and by a habit: for by a power man is, as it were, empowered to do the action, and by the habit he is apt to act well or ill.

Reply Obj. 3. Man is said to have lost free-will by falling into sin, not as to natural liberty, which is freedom from coercion, but as regards freedom from fault and unhappiness. Of this we shall treat later in the treatise on Morals in the second part of this work (I.–II. Q. LXXXV. *seqq.*; Q. CIX.).

Third Article. Whether Free-Will Is an Appetitive Power?

We proceed thus to the Third Article:-

Objection 1. It would seem that free-will is not an appetitive, but a cognitive power. For Damascene (*De Fid. Orth.* ii. 27) says that *free-will straightway accompanies the rational nature.* But reason is a cognitive power. Therefore free-will is a cognitive power.

Obj. 2. Further, free-will is so called as though it were a free judgment. But to judge is an act of a cognitive power. Therefore free-will is a cognitive power.

Obj. 3. Further, the principal function of the free-will is to choose. But choice seems to belong to knowledge, because it implies a certain comparison of one thing to another, which belongs to the cognitive power. Therefore free-will is a cognitive power.

On the contrary, The Philosopher says (*Ethic.* iii. 3) that choice is *the desire of those things which are in us.* But desire is an act of the appetitive power: therefore choice is also. But free-will is that by which we choose. Therefore free-will is an appetitive power.

I answer that, The proper act of free-will is choice: for we say that we have a free-will because we can take one thing while refusing another; and this is to choose. Therefore we must consider the nature of free-will, by considering the nature of choice. Now two things concur in choice: one on the part of the cognitive power, the other on the part of the appetitive power. On the part of the cognitive power, counsel is required, by which we judge one thing to be preferred to another: and on the part of the appetitive power, it is required that the appetite should accept the judgment of counsel. Therefore Aristotle (*Ethic.* vi. 2) leaves it in doubt whether choice belongs principally to the appetitive or the cognitive power: since he says that choice is either *an appetitive intellect or an intellectual appetite.* But (*Ethic.* iii., *loc. cit.*) he inclines to its being an intellectual appetite when he describes choice as a *desire proceeding from counsel.* And the reason of this is because the proper object of choice is the means to the end: and this, as such, is in the nature of that good which is called useful: wherefore since good, as such, is the object of the appetite, it follows that choice is principally an act of the appetitive power. And thus free-will is an appetitive power.

Reply Obj. 1. The appetitive powers accompany the apprehensive, and in this sense Damascene says that freewill straightway accompanies the rational power.

Reply Obj. 2. Judgment, as it were, concludes and terminates counsel. Now counsel is terminated, first, by the judgment of reason ; secondly, by the acceptation of the appetite: whence the Philosopher (*Ethic.* iii., *ibid.*) says that, *having formed a judgment by counsel, we desire in accordance with that counsel.* And in this sense choice itself is a judgment from which free-will takes its name.

Reply Obj. 3. This comparison which is implied in the choice belongs to the preceding counsel, which is an act of reason. For though the appetite does not make comparisons, yet forasmuch as it is moved by the apprehensive power which does compare, it has some likeness of comparison by choosing one in preference to another.

Fourth Article. Whether Free-Will Is a Power Distinct from the Will?

We proceed thus to the Fourth Article:-

Objection 1. It would seem that free-will is a power distinct from the will. For Damascene says (*De Fid. Orth.* ii. 22) that Θέλησις is one thing and βούλησις another. But Θέλησις is the will, while βούλησις seems to be the free-will, because βούλησις, according to him, is the will as concerning an object by way of comparison between two things. Therefore it seems that free-will is a distinct power from the will.

Obj. 2. Further, powers are known by their acts. But choice, which is the act of free-will, is distinct from the act of willing, because *the act of the will regards the end, whereas choice regards the means to the end* (*Ethic.* iii. 2). Therefore free-will is a distinct power from the will.

Obj. 3. Further, the will is the intellectual appetite. But in the intellect there are two powers—the active and the passive. Therefore, also on the part of the intellectual appetite, there must be another power besides the will. And this, seemingly, can only be free-will. Therefore free-will is a distinct power from the will.

On the contrary, Damascene says (*De Fid. Orth.* iii. 14) free-will is nothing else than the will.

I answer that, The appetitive powers must be proportionate to the apprehensive powers, as we have said above (Q. LXIV., A. 2). Now, as on the part of the intellectual apprehension we have intellect and reason, so on the part of the intellectual appetite we have will, and free-will which is nothing else but the power of choice. And this is clear from their relations to their respective objects and acts. For the act of *understanding* implies the simple acceptation of something; whence we say that we understand first principles, which are known of themselves without any comparison. But to *reason*, properly speaking, is to come from one thing to the knowledge of another: wherefore, properly speaking, we reason about conclusions, which are known from the principles. In like manner on the part of the appetite to *will* implies the simple appetite for something: wherefore the will is said to regard the end, which is desired for itself. But to *choose* is to desire something for the sake of obtaining something else: wherefore, properly speaking, it regards the means to the end. Now, in matters of knowledge, the principles are related to the conclusion to which we assent on account of the principles: just as, in appetitive matters, the end is related to the means, which is desired on account of the end. Wherefore it is evident that as the intellect is to reason, so is the will to the power of choice, which is free-will. But it has been shown above (Q. LXXIX., A. 8) that it belongs to the same power both to understand and to reason, even as it belongs to the same power to be at rest and to be in movement. Wherefore it belongs also to the same power to will and to choose: and on this account the will and the free-will are not two powers, but one.

Reply Obj. 1. βούλησις is distinct from Θέλησις on account of a distinction, not of powers, but of acts.

Reply Obj. 2. Choice and will—that is, the act of willing—are different acts: yet they belong to the same power, as also to understand and to reason, as we have said.

Reply Obj. 3. The intellect is compared to the will as moving the will. And therefore there is no need to distinguish in the will an active and a passive will.

WHETHER THERE IS FREE-WILL IN ANGELS?

(2) We Proceed thus to the Third Article:-²

Objection 1. It would seem that there is no free-will in the angels. For the act of free-will is to choose. But there can be no choice with the angels, because choice is *the desire of something after taking counsel,* while counsel is *a kind of inquiry,* as stated in *Ethic.* iii., 3. But the angels' knowledge is not the result of inquiring, for this belongs to the discursiveness of reason. Therefore it appears that there is no free-will in the angels.

Obj. 2. Further, free-will implies indifference to alternatives. But in the angels on the part of their intellect there is no such indifference; because, as was observed already (Q. LVIII., A. 5), their intellect is not deceived as to things which are naturally intelligible to them. Therefore neither on the part of their appetitive faculty can there be free-will.

Obj. 3. Further, the natural endowments of the angels belong to them according to degrees of more or less; because in the higher angels the intellectual nature is more perfect than in the lower. But free-will does not admit of degrees. Therefore there is no free-will in them.

On the contrary, Free-will is part of man's dignity. But the angels' dignity surpasses that of men. Therefore, since free-will is in men, with much more reason is it in the angels.

I answer that, Some things there are which act, not from any previous judgment, but, as it were, moved and made to act by others; just as the arrow is directed to the target by the archer. Others act from some kind of judgment; but not from free-will, such as irrational animals; for the sheep flies from the wolf by a kind of judgment whereby it esteems it to be hurtful to itself: such a judgment is not a free one, but implanted by nature. Only an agent endowed with an intellect can act with a judgment which is free, insofar as it apprehends the common note of goodness; from which it can judge this or the other thing to be good. Consequently, wherever there is intellect, there is free-will. It is therefore manifest that just as there is intellect, so is there free-will in the angels, and in a higher degree of perfection than in man.

Reply Obj. 1. The Philosopher is speaking of choice, as it is in man. As a man's estimate in speculative matters differs from an angel's in this, that the one needs not to inquire, while the other does so need; so is it in practical matters. Hence there is choice in the angels, yet not with the inquisitive deliberation of counsel, but by the sudden acceptance of truth.

Reply Obj. 2. As was observed already (A. 2), knowledge is effected by the presence of the known within the knower. Now it is a mark of imperfection in anything not to have within it what it should naturally have.

Consequently an angel would not be perfect in his nature, if his intellect were not determined to every truth which he can know naturally. But the act of the appetitive faculty comes of this, that the affection is directed to something outside. Yet the perfection of a thing does not come from everything to which it is inclined, but only from something which is higher than it. Therefore it does not argue imperfection in an angel if his will be not determined with regard to things beneath him; but it would argue imperfection in him, were he to be indeterminate to what is above him.

Reply Obj. 3. Free-will exists in a nobler manner in the higher angels than it does in the lower, as also does the judgment of the intellect. Yet it is true that liberty, insofar as the removal of compulsion is considered, is not susceptible of greater and less degree; because privations and negations are not lessened nor increased directly of themselves; but only by their cause, or through the addition of some qualification.

NOTES

1. *Liberum arbitrium*—i.e., free judgment.
2. Of question 59. See Endnotes below.

[St. Thomas Aquinas, *Summa Theologica*, tr. Fathers of the English Dominican Province (London: Burns Oates and Washbourne Ltd., 1922). (1) Vol. 4, ques. 83, pp. 147–55. (2) Vol. 3, ques. 59, art. 3, pp. 100–101.]

(2d4)

Governor John Winthrop

1588–1649

"The Little Speech on Liberty"

The occasion for the speech was Governor Winthrop's having been brought to court by the town of Hingham for appointing a militia captain disliked by the people. After his acquittal Winthrop, the first governor of the Massachusetts Bay Colony, "desired leave for a little speech" (accounting for the phrase by which the speech came to be known). In the speech he contrasts "natural liberty" (our second definition, "doing what you want to do") with "moral liberty" which is fourth definition, "doing what is good, just, and honest." The latter he identifies both with the authority of the state and that of Christ.

(1) I suppose something may be expected from me, upon this charge that is befallen me, which moves me to speak now to you; yet I intend not to intermeddle in the proceedings of the court, or with any of the persons concerned therein. Only I bless God, that I see an issue of this troublesome business. I also acknowledge the justice of the court, and, for mine own part, I am well satisfied, I was publicly charged, and I am publicly and legally acquitted, which is all I did expect or desire. And though this be sufficient for my justification before men, yet not so before the God, who hath seen so much amiss in my dispensations (and even in this affair) as calls me to be humble. For to be publicly and criminally charged in this court, is matter of humiliation, (and I desire to make a right use of it,) notwith-

standing I be thus acquitted. If her father had spit in her face, (saith the Lord concerning Miriam,) should she not have been ashamed seven days? Shame had lien upon her, whatever the occasion had been. I am unwilling to stay you from your urgent affairs, yet give me leave (upon this special occasion) to speak a little more to this assembly. It may be of some good use, to inform and rectify the judgments of some of the people, and may prevent such distempers as have arisen amongst us. The great questions that have troubled the country, are about the authority of the magistrates and the liberty of the people. It is yourselves who have called us to this office, and being called by you, we have our authority from God, in way of an ordinance, such as hath the image of God eminently stamped upon it, the contempt and violation whereof hath been vindicated with examples of divine vengeance. I entreat you to consider, that when you choose magistrates, you take them from among yourselves, men subject to like passions as you are. Therefore when you see infirmities in us, you should reflect upon your own, and that would make you bear the more with us, and not be severe censurers of the failings of your magistrates, when you have continual experience of the like infirmities in yourselves and others. We account him a good servant, who breaks not his covenant. The covenant between you and us is the oath you have taken of us, which is to this purpose, that we shall govern you and judge your causes by the rules of God's laws and our own, according to our best skill. When you agree with a workman to build you a ship or house, etc., he undertakes as well for his skill as for his faithfulness, for it is his profession, and you pay him for both. But when you call one to be a magistrate, he doth not profess nor undertake to have sufficient skill for that office, nor can you furnish him with gifts, etc., therefore you must run the hazard of his skill and ability. But if he fail in faithfulness, which by his oath he is bound unto, that he must answer for. If it fall out that the case be clear to common apprehension, and the rule clear also, if he transgress here, the error is not in the skill, but in the evil of the will: it must be required of him. But if the case be doubtful, or the rule doubtful, to men of such understanding and parts as your magistrates are, if your magistrates should err here, yourselves must bear it.

For the other point concerning liberty, I observe a great mistake in the country about that. There is a twofold liberty, natural (I mean as our nature is now corrupt) and civil or federal. The first is common to man with beasts and other creatures. By this, man, as he stands in relation to man simply, hath liberty to do what he lists; it is a liberty to evil as well as to good. This liberty is incompatible and inconsistent with authority, and cannot endure the least restraint of the most just authority. The exercise and maintaining of this liberty makes men grow more evil, and in time to be worse than brute beasts: omnes sumus licentia deteriores [we are worse through freedom]. This is that great enemy of truth and peace, that wild beast, which all the ordinances of God are bent against, to restrain and subdue it. The other kind of liberty I call civil or federal, it may also be termed moral, in reference to the covenant between God and man, in the moral law, and the politic covenants and constitutions, amongst men themselves. This liberty is the proper end and object of authority, and cannot subsist without it; and it is a liberty to that only which is good, just, and honest. This liberty you are to stand for, with the hazard (not only of your goods, but) of your lives, if need be. Whatsoever crosseth this, is not authority, but a distemper thereof. This liberty is maintained and exercised in a way of subjection to authority; it is of the same kind of liberty wherewith Christ hath made us free. The woman's own choice makes such a man her husband; yet being so chosen, he is her lord, and she is to be subject to him, yet in a way of liberty, not of bondage; and a true wife accounts her subjection her honor and freedom, and would not think her condition safe and free, but in her subjection to her husband's authority. Such is the liberty of the church under the authority of Christ, her king and husband; his yoke is so easy and sweet to her as a bride's ornaments; and if through frowardness or wantonness, etc., she shake it off, at any time, she is at no rest in her spirit, until she take it up again; and whether her lord smiles upon her, and embraceth her in his arms, or whether he frowns, or rebukes, or smites her, she apprehends the sweetness of his love in all, and is refreshed, supported, and instructed by every such dispensation of his authority over her. On the other side, ye know who they are that complain of this yoke and say, let us break their bands, etc., we will not have this man to rule over us. Even so, brethren, it will be between you and your magistrates. If you stand for your natural corrupt liberties, and will do what is good in your own eyes, you will not endure the least weight of authority, but will murmur, and oppose, and be always striving to shake off that yoke; but if you will be satisfied to enjoy such civil and lawful liberties, such as Christ allows you, then will you quietly and cheerfully submit unto that authority which is set over you, in all the administrations of it, for your good. Wherein, if we fail at any time, we hope we shall be willing (by God's assistance) to hearken to good advice from any of you, or in any other way of God; so shall your liberties be preserved, in upholding the honor and power of authority amongst you.

[*Winthrop's Journal, "History of New England," 1630–1649*, 2 vols., ed. J. K. Hosmer (New York: Charles Scribner's Sons, 1908), vol. 2. (1) Pp. 237–39.]

(2d5)

Montesquieu,
Charles de Secondat
1689–1775

Spirit of the Laws
selections from bks. XI, XII, XXVI

Montesquieu fits into the present grouping by defining freedom as "the power of doing what we ought to will, and in not being constrained to do what we ought not to will." Like Winthrop he identifies this "oughtness" with what the laws permit. We have included most of what he said on the subject in his *Spirit of the Laws*. Notice the separation of powers doctrine on p. 237.

"DIFFERENT SIGNIFICATIONS OF THE WORD LIBERTY"

(1) There is no word that admits of more various significations, and has made more varied impressions on the human mind, than that of liberty. Some have taken it as a means of deposing a person on whom they had conferred a tyrannical authority; others for the power of choosing a superior whom they are obliged to obey; others for the right of bearing arms, and of being thereby enabled to use violence; others, in fine, for the privilege of being governed by a native of their own country, or by their own laws. A certain nation for a long time thought liberty consisted in the privilege of wearing a long beard. Some have annexed this name to one form of government exclusive of others: those who had a republican taste applied it to this species of polity; those who liked a monarchical state

gave it to monarchy. Thus they have all applied the name of liberty to the government most suitable to their own customs and inclinations: and as in republics the people have not so constant and so present a view of the causes of their misery, and as the magistrates seem to act only in conformity to the laws, hence liberty is generally said to reside in republics, and to be banished from monarchies. In fine, as in democracies the people seem to act almost as they please, this sort of government has been deemed the most free, and the power of the people has been confounded with their liberty.

"In What Liberty Consists"

It is true that in democracies the people seem to act as they please; but political liberty does not consist in an unlimited freedom. In governments, that is, in societies directed by laws, liberty can consist only in the power of doing what we ought to will, and in not being constrained to do what we ought not to will.

We must have continually present to our minds the difference between independence and liberty. Liberty is a right of doing whatever the laws permit, and if a citizen could do what they forbid he would be no longer possessed of liberty, because all his fellow-citizens would have the same power.

"The Same Subject Continued"

Democratic and aristocratic states are not in their own nature free. Political liberty is to be found only in moderate governments; and even in these it is not always found. It is there only when there is no abuse of power. But constant experience shows us that every man invested with power is apt to abuse it, and to carry his authority as far as it will go. Is it not strange, though true, to say that virtue itself has need of limits?

To prevent this abuse, it is necessary from the very nature of things that power should be a check to power. A government may be so constituted, as no man shall be compelled to do things to which the law does not oblige him, nor forced to abstain from things which the law permits.

The political liberty of the subject is a tranquillity of mind arising from the opinion each person has of his safety. In order to have this liberty, it is requisite the government be so constituted as one man need not be afraid of another.

When the legislative and executive powers are united in the same person, or in the same body of magistrates, there can be no liberty; because apprehensions may arise, lest the same monarch or senate should enact tyrannical laws, to execute them in a tyrannical manner.

Again, there is no liberty, if the judiciary power be not separated from the legislative and executive. Were it joined with the legislative, the life and liberty of the subject would be exposed to arbitrary control; for the judge would be then the legislator. Were it joined to the executive power, the judge might behave with violence and oppression.

There would be an end of everything, were the same man or the same body, whether of the nobles or of the people, to exercise those three powers, that of enacting laws, that of executing the public resolutions, and of trying the causes of individuals.

As in a country of liberty, every man who is supposed a free agent ought to be his own governor; the legislative power should reside in the whole body of the people. But since this is impossible in large states, and in small ones is subject to many inconveniences, it is fit the people should transact by their representatives what they cannot transact by themselves.

"Of the Liberty of the Subject"

(2) Philosophic liberty consists in the free exercise of the will; or at least, if we must speak agreeably to all systems, in an opinion that we have the free exercise of our will. Political liberty consists in security, or, at least, in the opinion that we enjoy security.

This security is never more dangerously attacked than in public or private accusations. It is, therefore, on the goodness of criminal laws that the liberty of the subject principally depends.

The knowledge already acquired in some countries, or that may be hereafter attained in others, concerning the surest rules to be observed in criminal judgments, is more interesting to mankind than any other thing in the world.

Liberty can be founded on the practice of this knowledge only; and supposing a state to have the best laws imaginable in this respect, a person tried under that state, and condemned to be hanged the next day, would have much more liberty than a pasha enjoys in Turkey.

"The Same Subject Continued"

Those laws which condemn a man to death on the deposition of a single witness are fatal to liberty. In reason there should be two, because a witness who affirms, and the accused who denies, make an equal balance, and a third must decline the scale.

The Greeks and Romans required one voice more to condemn: but our French laws insist upon two. The Greeks pretend that their custom was established by the gods; but this more justly may be said of ours.

"That Liberty Is Favored by the Nature and Proportion of Punishments"

Liberty is in perfection when criminal laws derive each punishment from the particular nature of the crime. There are then no arbitrary decisions; the punishment does not flow from the capriciousness of the legislator, but from the very nature of the thing; and man uses no violence to man.

(3) Liberty consists principally in not being forced to do a thing, where the laws do not oblige: people are in this state only as they are governed by civil laws; and because they live under those civil laws, they are free.

[Montesquieu, *Spirit of the Laws*, tr. T. Nugent (New York: Hafner Publishing Co., 1949). (1) Vol. 1, bk. XI, sec. 2, pp. 149–54. (2) Vol. 1, bk. XII, sec. 2, pp. 183–85. (3) Vol. 2, bk. XXVI, sec. 20, p. 76.]

(3e1)

C. A. Campbell

1897–1974

"Is 'Free Will' a Pseudo-Problem?"

In "Is 'Free Will' a Pseudo-Problem?" Campbell argues that the position (which we identify as the second definition) where freedom is consistent with determinism, utilizes a sense of moral responsibility incompatible with what is usually meant by the phrase.

In mid-essay he distinguishes between the unreflective and the tolerably reflective person. The former is likely to agree with the second definition philosophers that freedom and determinism are consistent because acting otherwise means only that one could have acted otherwise if one had so chosen, and that proposition is compatible with determinism. The tolerably reflective person, on the other hand, will insist that one can act otherwise only if one has chosen otherwise, and that is not compatible with determinism. Near the end of the essay he analyzes one's inner situation when one's strongest desire is in conflict with what one takes to be one's duty. He relates creative activity to this inner standpoint, transcending one's character "as so far formed."

In the first passage from Campbell, Moritz Schlick's second definition view, in which free will is a pseudo-problem, is summarized. In material not quoted he argues that, in general, what Schlick means by moral responsibility (behavior which can be corrected by educative punishment) is inadequate: (1) We correct canine behavior without

240

regarding dogs as morally responsible. (2) We hold deceased people to be morally responsible, although their behavior cannot now be corrected. (3) We make allowances for people, citing bad heredity or environment, but the allowances make no sense if moral responsibility rests solely upon our ability to affect a person's future motives.

MORITZ SCHLICK'S VIEW

(1) I shall first summarize, as faithfully as I can, what I take to be the distinctive points in Schlick's argument.

The traditional formulation of the problem, Schlick points out, is based on the assumption that to have 'free will' entails having a will that is, at least sometimes, exempt from causal law. It is traditionally supposed, quite rightly, that moral responsibility implies freedom in *some* sense: and it is supposed, also quite rightly, that this sense is one which is incompatible with compulsion. But because it is further supposed, quite *wrongly*, that to be subject to causal or natural law is to be subject to compulsion, the inference is drawn that the free will implied in moral responsibility is incompatible with causal continuity. The ultimate root of the error, Schlick contends, lies in a failure to distinguish between two different kinds of Law, one of which does indeed 'compel,' but the other of which does *not*.[1] There are, first, *pre*scriptive laws, such as the laws imposed by civil authority, which presume contrary desires on the part of those to whom they are applied; and these may fairly be said to exercise 'compulsion.' And there are, secondly, *de*scriptive laws, such as the laws which the sciences seek to formulate; and these merely state what does as a matter of fact always happen. It is perfectly clear that the relation of the latter, the natural, causal laws, to human willing is radically different from the 'compulsive' relation of prescriptive laws to human willing, and that it is really an absurdity to talk of a species of natural law like, say, psychological laws, *compelling* us to act in this or that way. The term 'compulsion' is totally inept where, as in this case, there are no contrary desires. But the traditional discussions of Free Will, confusing descriptive with prescriptive laws, fallaciously assume 'compulsion' to be ingredient in Law as such, and it is contended accordingly that moral freedom, since it certainly implies absence of compulsion, implies also exemption from causal law.

It follows that the problem of Free Will, as traditionally stated, is a mere pseudo-problem. The statement of it in terms of exemption from causal law rests on the assumption that causal law involves 'compulsion.' And this assumption is demonstrably false. Expose the muddle from which it arises and the so-called 'problem' in its traditional form disappears.

But is it quite certain that the freedom which moral responsibility implies is no more than 'the absence of compulsion'? This is the premise upon which Schlick's argument proceeds, but Schlick is himself well aware that it stands in need of confirmation from an analysis of the notion of moral responsibility. Otherwise it might be maintained that although 'the absence of compulsion' has been shown not to entail a contra-causal type of freedom, there is nevertheless some *other* condition of moral responsibility that *does* entail it. Accordingly Schlick embarks now upon a formal analysis of the nature and conditions of moral responsibility designed to show that the *only* freedom implied by moral responsibility is freedom from compulsion. It was a trifle ambitious, however, even for a master of compression like Professor Schlick, to hope to deal satisfactorily in half a dozen very brief pages with a topic which has been so extensively debated in the literature of moral philosophy: and I cannot pretend that I find what he has to say free from obscurity. But to the best of my belief what follows does reproduce the gist of Schlick's analysis.

What precisely, Schlick asks, does the term 'moral responsibility' mean in our ordinary linguistic usage?[2] He begins his answer by insisting upon the close connexion for ordinary usage between 'moral responsibility' and *punishment* (strictly speaking, punishment and *reward*: but for convenience Schlick virtually confines the discussion to punishment, and we shall do the same). The connexion, as Schlick sees it, is this. In ordinary practice our concern with the responsibility for an act (he tells us) is with a view to determining *who is to be punished for it.* Now punishment is (I quote) 'an educative measure.' It is 'a means to the formation of motives, which are in part to prevent the wrong-doer from repeating the act (reformation), and in part to prevent others from committing a similar act (intimidation).'[3] When we ask, then, 'Who in a given case is to be punished?'—which is the same as the question 'Who is responsible?'—what we are really wanting to discover is some agent in the situation upon whose motives we can bring to bear the appropriate educative influences, so that in similar situations in future his strongest motive will impel him to refrain from, rather than to repeat, the act. 'The question of who is responsible' Schlick sums up, 'is ... a matter only of knowing who is to be punished or rewarded, in order that punishment and reward function as such—be able to achieve their goal.'[4] It is not a matter, he expressly declares, of trying to ascertain what may be called the 'original instigator' of the act. That might be a great-grandparent, from the consequence of whose behavior vicious tendencies have been inherited by a living person. Such 'remote causes' as this are irrelevant to questions of punishment (and so to questions of moral responsibility), 'for in the first place their actual contribution cannot be determined, and in the second place they are generally out of reach.'[5]

It is a matter for regret that Schlick has not rounded off his discussion, as one had hoped and expected he would, by formulating a precise definition of moral responsibility in terms of what he has been saying. I think, however, that the conclusion to which his argument leads could be not unfairly expressed in some such way as this: 'We say that a man is morally responsible for an act if his motives for bringing about the act are such as we can affect favorably in respect of his future behavior by the educative influences of reward and punishment.'

Given the truth of this analysis of moral responsibility, Schlick's contention follows logically enough that the only freedom that is required for moral responsibility is freedom from compulsion. For what are the cases in which a man's motives are *not* capable of being favorably affected by reward and punishment?—the cases in which, that is, according to Schlick's analysis, we do *not* deem him morally responsible? The only such cases, it would seem, are those in which a man is subjected to some form of external constraint which prevents him from acting according to his 'natural desires.' For example, if a man is compelled by a pistol at his breast to do a certain act, or induced to do it by an externally administered narcotic, he is not 'morally responsible'; or not, at any rate, in so far as punishment would be impotent to affect his motives in respect of his future behavior. External constraint in one form or another seems to be the sole circumstance which absolves a man from moral responsibility. Hence we may say that freedom from external constraint is the only sort of freedom which an agent must possess in order to be morally responsible. The 'contra-causal' sort of

freedom which so many philosophers and others have supposed to be
required is shown by a true analysis of moral responsibility to be irrelevant.

This completes the argument that 'Free Will,' as traditionally formulated, is a pseudo-problem. The only freedom implied by moral responsibility is freedom from compulsion; and as we have rid ourselves of the
myth that subjection to causal law is a form of compulsion, we can see that
the only compulsion which absolves from moral responsibility is the
external constraint which prevents us from translating our desires into
action. The true meaning of the question 'Have we free will?' thus becomes
simply 'Can we translate our desires into action?' And this question does
not constitute a 'problem' at all, for the answer to it is not in doubt. The
obvious answer is 'Sometimes we can, sometimes we can't, according to the
specific circumstances of the case.'

The "Errors" in the Common View of Moral Responsibility

(2) If we say that A morally ought to have done X, we imply that in our
opinion, he could have done X. But we assign moral blame to a man only for
failing to do what we think he morally ought to have done. Hence if we
morally blame A for not having done X, we imply that he could have done
X even though in fact he did not. In other words, we imply that A could have
acted otherwise than he did. And that means that we imply, as a necessary
condition of a man's being morally blameworthy, that he enjoyed a freedom
of a kind not compatible with unbroken causal continuity.

Now what is it that is supposed to be wrong with this simple piece of argument?—For, of course, it must be rejected by all these philosophers who tell us
that the traditional problem of Free Will is a mere pseudo-problem. The argument looks as though it were doing little more than reading off necessary
implications of the fundamental categories of our moral thinking. One's inclination is to ask 'If one is to think morally at all, how else than this *can* we think?'

In point of fact, there is pretty general agreement among the contemporary critics as to what is wrong with the argument. Their answer in general terms is as follows. No doubt A's moral responsibility does imply that
he could have acted otherwise. But this expression 'could have acted otherwise' stands in dire need of analysis. When we analyze it, we find that it
is not, as is so often supposed, simple and unambiguous, and we find that

in *some* at least of its possible meanings it implies *no* breach of causal continuity between character and conduct. Having got this clear, we can further discern that only in one of these *latter* meanings is there any compulsion upon our moral thinking to assert that if A is morally blameworthy for an act, A 'could have acted otherwise than he did.' It follows that, contrary to common belief, our moral thinking does *not* require us to posit a contra-causal freedom as a condition of moral responsibility.

So much of importance obviously turns upon the validity or otherwise of this line of criticism that we must examine it in some detail and with express regard to the *ipsissima verba* of the critics.

In the course of a recent article in *Mind*,[6] entitled 'Free Will and Moral Responsibility,' Mr. Nowell Smith (having earlier affirmed his belief that 'the traditional problem has been solved') explains very concisely the nature of the confusion which, as he thinks, has led to the demand for a contra-causal freedom. He begins by frankly recognizing that "It is evident that one of the necessary conditions of moral action is that the agent 'could have acted otherwise'" and he adds "it is to this fact that the Libertarian is drawing attention."[7] Then, after showing (unexceptionably, I think) how the relationship of 'ought' to 'can' warrants the proposition which he has accepted as evident, and how it induces the Libertarian to assert the existence of action that is 'uncaused,' he proceeds to point out, in a crucial passage, the nature of the Libertarian's error:

> The fallacy in the argument (he contends) lies in supposing that when we say 'A could have acted otherwise' we mean that A, *being what he was and being placed in the circumstances in which he was placed*, could have done something other than what he did. But in fact we never do mean this.[8]

What then *do* we mean here by 'A could have acted otherwise'? Mr. Nowell Smith does not tell us in so many words, but the passage I have quoted leaves little doubt how he would answer. What we really mean by the expression, he implies, is not a *categorical* but a *hypothetical* proposition. We mean 'A could have acted otherwise, *if he did not happen to be what he in fact was, or if he were placed in circumstances other than those in which he was in fact placed.*' Now, these propositions, it is easy to see, are in no way incompatible with acceptance of the causal principle in its full rigor. Accordingly the claim that our fundamental moral thinking obliges us to assert a contra-causal freedom as a condition of moral responsibility is disproved.

Such is the 'analytical solution' of our problem offered (with obvious confidence) by one able philosopher of today, and entirely representative of the views of many other able philosophers. Yet I make bold to say that its falsity stares one in the face. It seems perfectly plain that the hypothetical propositions which Mr. Nowell Smith proposes to substitute for the categorical proposition cannot express 'what we really mean' in this context by 'A could have acted otherwise,' for the simple reason that these hypothetical propositions have no bearing whatsoever upon the question of the moral responsibility of *A*. And it is *A* whose moral responsibility we are talking about—a definite person *A* with a definitive character and in a definitive set of circumstances. What conceivable significance could it have for our attitude to A's responsibility to know that someone with a *different* character (or *A* with a different character, if that collocation of words has any meaning), or A in a different set of circumstances from those in which A as we are concerned with him was in fact placed, 'could have acted otherwise'? No doubt this supposititious being *could* have acted otherwise than the definitive person A acted. But the point is that where we are reflecting, as we are supposed in this context to be reflecting, upon the question of *A's* moral responsibility, our interest in this supposititious being is precisely *nil.*

The two hypothetical propositions suggested in Mr. Nowell Smith's account of the matter do not, however, exhaust the speculations that have been made along these lines. Another very common suggestion by the analysts is that what we really mean by 'A could have acted otherwise' is 'A could have acted otherwise *if he had willed, or chosen, otherwise.'* This was among the suggestions offered by G. E. Moore in the well-known chapter on Free Will in his *Ethics.* It is, I think, the suggestion he most strongly favored: though it is fair to add that neither about this nor about any other of his suggestions is Moore in the least dogmatic. He does claim, for, I think, convincing reasons, that "we *very often* mean by 'could merely would, if* so-and-so had chosen.'" [9] And he concludes "I must confess that I cannot feel certain that this may not be all that we usually mean and understand by the assertion that we have Free Will."[10]

This third hypothetical proposition appears to enjoy also the support of Mr. C. L. Stevenson. Mr. Stevenson begins the chapter of *Ethics and Lan-*

guage entitled 'Avoidability-Indeterminism' with the now familiar pronouncement of his School that 'controversy about freedom and determinism of the will . . . presents no permanent difficulty to ethics, being largely a product of confusions.' A major confusion (if I understand him rightly) he takes to lie in the meaning of the term 'avoidable,' when we say 'A's action was avoidable'—or, I presume, 'A could have acted otherwise.' He himself offers the following definition of 'avoidable'—" 'A's action was avoidable' has the meaning of 'If A had made a certain choice, which in fact be did not make, his action would not have occurred.' "[11] This I think we may regard as in substance identical with the suggestion that what we really mean by 'A could have acted otherwise' is 'A could have acted otherwise if he had chosen (or willed) otherwise.' For clarity's sake we shall here keep to this earlier formulation. In either formulation the special significance of the third hypothetical proposition, as of the two hypothetical propositions already considered, is that it is compatible with strict determinism. If this be indeed all that we mean by the 'freedom' that conditions moral responsibility, then those philosophers are certainly wrong who hold that moral freedom is of the contra-causal type.

Now this third hypothetical proposition does at least possess the merit, not shared by its predecessors, of having a real relevance to the question of moral responsibility. If, *e.g.*, A had promised to meet us at 2 P.M., and he chanced to break his leg at 1 P.M., we should not blame him for his failure to discharge his promise. For we should be satisfied that he *could not* have acted otherwise, even if he had so chosen; or *could not*, at any rate, in a way which would have enabled him to meet us at 2 P.M. The freedom to translate one's choice into action, which we saw earlier is for Schlick the *only* freedom required for moral responsibility, is without doubt *one* of the conditions of moral responsibility.

But it seems easy to show that this third hypothetical proposition does not exhaust what we mean, and *sometimes* is not even *part* of what we mean, by the expression 'could have acted otherwise' in its moral context. Thus it can hardly be even part of what we mean in the case of that class of wrong actions (and it is a large class) concerning which there is really no question whether the agent could have acted otherwise, *if* he had chosen otherwise. Take lying, for example. Only in some very abnormal situation could it occur to one to doubt whether A, whose power of speech was evinced by his telling a lie, was in a, position to tell what he took to be the truth *if* he had so chosen. Of *course* he was. Yet it still makes good sense for one's moral thinking to ask whether A, when lying, 'could have acted otherwise': and we still require an affirmative answer to this question if A's moral blame-worthiness is to be established. It seems apparent, therefore, that in this class of cases at any rate one does not mean by 'A could have acted other-wise,' 'A could have acted otherwise *if* he had so chosen.'

What then *does* one mean in this class of cases by 'A could have acted otherwise'? I submit that the expression is taken in its simple, categorical meaning, without any suppressed 'if' clause to qualify it. Or perhaps, in order to keep before us the important truth that it is only as expressions of *will* or *choice* that acts are of moral import, it might be better to say that a con-dition of A's moral responsibility is that he could have *chosen* otherwise. We saw that there is no real question whether A who told a lie could have acted otherwise *if* he had chosen otherwise. But there is a very real question, at least for any person who approaches the question of moral responsibility at a tolerably advanced level of reflexion, about whether A could have *chosen* otherwise. Such a person will doubtless be acquainted with the claims advanced in some quarters that causal law operates universally: or/and with the theories of some philosophies that the universe is throughout the expres-sion of a single supreme principle ; or/and with the doctrines of some the-ologians that the world is created, sustained and governed by an Omniscient and Omnipotent Being. Very understandably such world-views awaken in him doubts about the validity of his first, easy, instinctive assumption that there are genuinely open possibilities before a man at the moment of moral choice. It thus becomes for him a real question whether a man could have chosen otherwise than he actually did, and, in consequence, whether man's moral responsibility is really defensible. For how can a man be morally responsible, he asks himself, if his choices, like all other events in the uni-verse, could not have been otherwise than they in fact were? It is precisely against the background of world-views such as these that for reflective people the problem of moral responsibility normally arises.

Furthermore, to the man who has attained this level of reflexion, it will in *no* class of cases be a sufficient condition of moral responsibility for an act that one could have acted otherwise *if* one had chosen otherwise— not even in these cases where there *was* some possibility of the operation of 'external constraint.' In these cases he will indeed expressly recognize freedom from external constraint as a *necessary condition*, but not as a *sufficient* condition. For he will be aware that, even granted *this* freedom, it is still conceivable that the agent had no freedom to choose otherwise than he did, and he will therefore require that the latter sort of freedom be added if moral responsibility for the act is to be established.

I have been contending that, for persons at a *tolerably advanced level of reflexion*, 'A could have acted otherwise,' as a condition of A's moral responsibility, means 'A could have chosen otherwise.' The qualification italicized is of some importance. The unreflective or unsophisticated person, the ordinary 'man in the street,' who does not know or much care what scientists and theologians and philosophers have said about the world, sees well enough that A is morally responsible only if he could have acted otherwise, but in his intellectual innocence he will, very probably, envisage nothing capable of preventing A from having acted otherwise except some material impediment—like the broken leg in the example above. Accordingly, for the unreflective person, 'A could have acted otherwise,' as a condition of moral responsibility, is apt to mean no more than 'A could have acted otherwise *if* he had so chosen.'

It would appear, then, that the view now favored by many philosophers, that the freedom required for moral responsibility is merely freedom from external constraint, is a view which they share only with the less reflective type of layman. Yet it should be plain that on a matter of this sort the view of the unreflective person is of little value by comparison with the view of the reflective person. There are some contexts, no doubt, in which lack of sophistication is an asset. But this is not one of them. The question at issue here is as to the kind of impediments which might have prevented a man from acting otherwise than he in fact did: and on this question knowledge and reflexion are surely prerequisites of any answer that is worth listening to. It is simply on account of the limitations of his mental vision that the unreflective man interprets the expression 'could have acted otherwise,' in its context as a condition of moral responsibility, solely in terms of external constraint. He has failed (as yet) to reach the intellectual level at which one takes into account the implications for moral choices of the world-views of science, religion, and philosophy. If on a matter of this complexity the philosopher finds that his analysis accords with the utterances of the uneducated he has, I suggest, better cause for uneasiness than for self-congratulation.

This concludes the main part of what it seems to me necessary to say in answer to the pseudo-problem theorists. My object so far has been to expose the falsity of those innovations (chiefly Positivist) in the way of argument and analysis which are supposed by many to have made it impossible any longer to formulate the problem of Free Will in the traditional manner. My contention is that, at least so far as these innovations are concerned, the simple time-honored argument still holds from the nature of the moral ought to the conclusion that moral responsibility implies a contra-causal type of freedom. The attempts to avoid that conclusion by analyzing the proposition 'A could have acted otherwise' (acknowledged to be implied in *some* sense in A's moral responsibility) into one or other of certain hypothetical propositions which are compatible with unbroken causal continuity, break down hopelessly when tested against the touchstone of actual moral thinking. It is, I think, not necessary to defend the procedure of testing hypotheses in the ethical field by bringing to bear upon them our actual moral thinking. If there is any other form of test applicable, I should be much interested to learn what it is supposed to be. Certainly 'logical analysis' *per se* will not do. That has a function, but a function that can only be ancillary. For what we are seeking to know is the meaning of the expression 'could have acted otherwise' not *in the abstract,* but in the context of the question of man's *moral responsibility.* Logical analysis *per se* is impotent to give us this information. It can be of value only insofar as it operates within the orbit of 'the moral consciousness.' One may admit, with some qualifications, that on a matter of this sort the moral consciousness without logical analysis is blind: but it seems to me to be true without any qualification whatsoever that, on the same problem, logical analysis without the moral consciousness is empty.

THE PREDISPOSING INFLUENCES

There are times when what seems to a critic the very strength of his case breeds mistrust in the critic's own mind. I confess that in making the criticisms that have preceded I have not been altogether free from uncomfortable feelings of this kind. For the arguments I have criticized, and more particularly the analyses of the conditions of moral responsibility, seem to me to be in many cases quite desperately unplausible. Such a state of affairs ought, I think, to give the critic pause. The thought must at least enter his mind (unless he be a total stranger to modesty) that perhaps, despite his best efforts to be fair, he has after all misrepresented what his opponents are saying. No doubt a similar thought will enter, and perhaps find lodgment in, the minds of many readers.

In this situation there is, however, one course by which the critic may reasonably hope to allay these natural suspicions. He should consider whether there may not be certain predisposing influences at work, extrinsic to the specific arguments, which could have the effect of blinding the proponents of these arguments to their intrinsic demerits. If so, he need not be too much disquieted by the seeming weakness of the case against him. For it is a commonplace that, once in the grip of general pre-possessions, even very good philosophers sometimes avail themselves of very bad arguments.

Actually, we can, I think, discern at least two such influences operating powerfully in the case before us. One is sympathy with the general tenets of Positivism. The other is the conviction already alluded to, that man does not in fact possess a contracausal type of freedom; whence follows a strong presumption that no such freedom is necessary to moral responsibility.

About the first of these influences I propose to say very little. I wish merely to indicate how strict adherence to Positivist tenets precludes one in principle from understanding moral responsibility as the ordinary man understands it, and how Positivists are therefore bound, when they attempt to define the conditions, of moral responsibility, to say things that seem monstrously unplausible.

That the Positivist—who has certainly not been drawn initially to this way of philosophizing by reflexion upon the phenomena of the moral life—should approach the problems of ethical analysis with certain strong prepossessions, is only to be expected. The most crucial of these is that (non-tautologous) statements in this field, as in every other field, can have no meaning—or at any rate no cognitive meaning—unless they are, at least in principle, sensibly verifiable. The consequence of that prepossession must be to close the mind in advance, more or less absolutely according to the extent to which the Verifiability principle is maintained as unshakeable dogma, against the common view of the moral ought—which happens also to be the view in terms of which the problem of moral responsibility historically and habitually arises. For on this view the moral ought as apprehended by the moral consciousness is most certainly an object neither of 'outer' nor of 'inner' sense. One need not wonder, therefore, that the Positivist should recommend analyses of the conditions of moral responsibility, such as the hypothetical propositions offered as the meaning of the expression 'could have acted otherwise,' which to anyone who understands the moral ought in the ordinary way seem little short of fantastic. By an *a priori* prejudice he has effectively debarred himself from appreciating what ordinary men mean by moral obligation and moral responsibility. I cannot forbear adding that in view of the doom which has so swiftly attended the very various attempts so far made to define moral obligation in Positivist terms, the case for at least a temporary suspension of belief in Positivist presuppositions in the ethical field would appear to be a strong one.

Of far wider and more permanent interest, in my judgment, is the second of the 'predisposing influences'—the conviction that there just *is* no contra-causal freedom such as is commonly alleged to be a condition of moral responsibility. A natural desire to 'save' moral responsibility issues, logically enough, in attempts to formulate its conditions in a manner compatible with unbroken causal continuity. The consequent analyses may be, as I have urged, very unsatisfactory. But there is no doubt that the conviction that motivates the analysis is supported by reasons of great weight: well-known arguments that are the property of no particular school and which most of us learned in our philosophical cradles. A very brief summary of what I take to be the most influential of these arguments will suffice for the comments I wish to make upon them.

A contra-causal I freedom, it is argued, such as is implied in the 'categorical' interpretation of the proposition 'A could have chosen otherwise than he did,' posits a breach of causal continuity between a man's character and his conduct. Now apart from the general presumption in favor of the universality of causal law, there are special reasons for disallowing the breach that is here alleged. It is the common assumption of social intercourse that our acquaintances will act 'in character'; that their choices will exhibit the 'natural' response of their characters to the given situation. And this assumption seems to be amply substantiated, over a wide range of conduct, by the actual success which attends predictions made on this basis. Where there should be, on the contra-causal hypothesis, chaotic variability, there is found in fact a large measure of intelligible continuity. Moreover, what is the alternative to admitting that a person's choices flow from his character? Surely just that the so-called 'choice' is not *that person's* choice at all: that, relatively to the person concerned, it is a mere 'accident.' Now we cannot really believe this. But if it *were* the case, it would certainly not help to establish *moral* freedom, the freedom required for *moral* responsibility. For clearly a man cannot be morally responsible for an act which does not express his own choice but is, on the contrary, attributable simply to chance.

These are clearly considerations worthy of all respect. It is not surprising if they have played a big part in persuading people to respond sympathetically to the view that 'Free Will,' in its usual contra-causal formulation, is a pseudo-problem. A full answer to them is obviously not practicable in what is little more than an appendix to the body of this paper; but I am hopeful that something can be said, even in a little space, to show that they are very far from being as conclusive against a contra-causal freedom as they are often supposed to be.

To begin with the less troublesome of the two main objections indicated—the objection that the break in causal continuity which free will involves is inconsistent with the predictability of conduct on the basis of the agent's known character. All that is necessary to meet this objection, I suggest, is the frank recognition, which is perfectly open to the Libertarian, that there is a wide area of human conduct, determinable on clear general principles, within which free will does not effectively operate. The most important of these general principles (I have no space to deal here with the others) has often enough been stated by Libertarians. Free will does not operate in these practical situations in which no conflict arises in the agent's mind between what he conceives to be his 'duty' and what he feels to be his 'strongest desire.' It does not operate here because there just is no occasion for it to operate. There is no reason whatever why the agent should here even contemplate choosing any course other than that prescribed by his strongest desire. In all such situations, therefore, he naturally wills in accordance with strongest desire. But his 'strongest desire' is simply the specific ad hoc expression of that system of conative and emo-

tive dispositions which we call his 'character.' In all such situations, therefore, whatever may be the case elsewhere, his will is in effect determined
by his character as so far formed. Now when we bear in mind that there are
an almost immeasurably greater number of situations in a man's life that
conform to *this* pattern than there are situations in which an agent is aware
of a conflict between strongest desire and duty, it is apparent that a Liber-
tarianism which accepts the limitation of free will to the *latter* type of situation is not open to the stock objection on the score of 'predictability.' For
there still remains a vast area of human behavior in which prediction on
the basis of known character may be expected to succeed: an area which
will accommodate without difficulty, I think, all these empirical facts about
successful prediction which the critic is apt to suppose fatal to Free Will.

The clash of strongest desire with duty, and creative activity.

So far as I can see, such a delimitation of the field of effective free will
denies to the Libertarian absolutely nothing which matters to him. For it is
precisely that small sector of the field of choices which our principle of
delimitation still leaves open to free will—the sector in which strongest
desire clashes with duty that is crucial for moral responsibility. It is, I
believe, with respect to such situations, and in the last resort to such situations alone, that the agent himself recognizes that moral praise and blame
are appropriate. They are appropriate, according as he does or does not
'rise to duty' in the face of opposing desires; always granted, that is, that he
is free to choose between these courses as genuinely open possibilities. If
the reality of freedom be conceded *here*, everything is conceded that the
Libertarian has any real interest in securing.

But, of course, the most vital question is, can the reality of freedom be
conceded even here? In particular, can the standard objection be met which
we stated, that if the person's choice does not, in these situations as elsewhere, flow from his *character*, then it is not *that person's* choice at all.

This is, perhaps, of all the objections to a contra-causal freedom, the
one which is generally felt to be the most conclusive. For the assumption
upon which it is based, viz. that no intelligible meaning can attach to the
claim that an act which is not an expression of the self's *character* may nevertheless be the *self's* act, is apt to be regarded as self-evident. The Liber-

tarian is accordingly charged with being in effect an *In*determinist, whose 'free will,' insofar as it does not flow from the agent's character, can only be a matter of 'chance.' Has the Libertarian who invariably repudiates this charge and claims to be a *Self*-determinist—any way of showing that, contrary to the assumption of his critics, we *can* meaningfully talk of an act as the self's act even though, in an important sense, it is not an expression of the self's 'character'?

I think that he has. I want to suggest that what prevents the critics from finding a meaning in this way of talking is that they are looking for it in the wrong way; or better, perhaps, with the wrong orientation. They are looking for it from the standpoint of the *external observer*; the standpoint proper to, because alone possible for, apprehension of the physical world. Now from the external standpoint we may observe processes of change. But one thing which, by common consent, cannot be observed from without is *creative activity*. Yet—and here lies the crux of the whole matter—it is precisely creative activity which we are trying to understand when we are trying to understand what is traditionally designated by 'free will.' For if there should be an act which is genuinely the self's act and is nevertheless not an expression of its character, such an act, in which the self 'transcends' its character as so far formed, would seem to be essentially of the nature of creative activity. It follows that to look for a meaning in 'free will' from the external standpoint is absurd. It is to look for it in a way that ensures that it will not be found. Granted that a creative activity of any kind is at least *possible* (and I know of no ground for its *a priori* rejection), there is one way, and one way only, in which we can hope to apprehend it, and that is from the *inner* standpoint, of direct participation.

It seems to me therefore, that if the Libertarian's claim to find a meaning in a 'free' will which is genuinely the self's will, though not an expression of the self's character, is to be subjected to any test that is worth applying, that test must be undertaken from the inner standpoint. We ought to place ourselves imaginatively at the standpoint of the agent engaged in the typical moral situation in which free will is claimed, and ask ourselves whether from *this* standpoint the claim in question does or does not have meaning for us. That the appeal must be to introspection is no doubt unfortunate. But he would be a very doctrinaire critic of introspection who declined to make use of it when in the nature of the case no other means of apprehension is available. Everyone must make the introspective experiment for himself: but I may perhaps venture to report, though at this late stage with extreme brevity, what I at least seem to find when I make the experiment myself.

In the situation of moral conflict, then, I (as agent) have before my mind a course of action X, which I believe to be my duty; and also a course of action Y, incompatible with X, which I feel to be that which I most strongly desire. Y is, as it is sometimes expressed, 'in the line of least resistance' for me—the course which I am aware I should take if I let my purely desiring nature operate without hindrance. It is the course toward which I am aware that my *character*, as so far formed, naturally inclines me. Now, as actually engaged in this situation, I find that I cannot help believing that I *can* rise to duty and choose X; the 'rising to duty' being effected by what is commonly called 'effort of will.' And I further find, if I ask myself just what it is I am believing when I believe that I 'can' rise to duty, that I cannot help believing that it lies with me here and now, quite absolutely, which of two genuinely open possibilities I adopt; whether, that is, I make the effort of will and choose X, or, on the other hand, let my desiring nature, my character as so far formed, 'have its way,' and choose Y, the course 'in the line of least resistance.' These beliefs may, of course, be illusory, but that is not at present in point. For the present argument all that matters is whether beliefs of this sort are in fact discoverable in the moral agent in the situation of 'moral temptation.' For my own part, I cannot doubt the introspective evidence that they are.

Now here is the vital point. No matter which course, X or Y, I choose in this situation, I cannot doubt, qua practical being engaged in it, that my choice is *not* just the expression of my formed character, and yet is a choice made by my *self*. For suppose I make the effort and choose X (my 'duty'). Since my very purpose in making the 'effort' is to enable me to act against the existing 'set' of desire, which is the expression of my character as so far formed, I cannot possibly regard the act itself as the expression of my *character*. On the other hand, introspection makes it equally clear that I am certain that it is *I* who choose: that the act is not an 'accident,' but is genuinely *my* act. Or suppose that I choose Y (the end of 'strongest desire'). The course chosen here is, it is true, in conformity with my 'character.' But since I find myself unable to doubt that I *could* have made the effort and chosen X, I cannot possibly regard the choice of Y as *just* the expression of my character. Yet here again I find that I cannot doubt that the choice is *my* choice, a choice for which *I* am justly to be blamed.

What this amounts to is that I *can* and *do* attach meaning, qua moral agent, to an act which is not the self's character and yet is genuinely the self's act. And having no good reason to suppose that other persons have a fundamentally different mental constitution, it seems to me probable that anyone else who undertakes a similar experiment will be obliged to submit a similar report. I conclude, therefore, that the argument, against 'free will' on the score of its 'meaninglessness' must be held to fail. 'Free Will' does have meaning; though, because it is of the nature of a creative activity, its meaning is discoverable only in an intuition of the practical consciousness of the participating agent. To the agent making a moral choice in the situation where duty clashes with desire, his 'self' is known to him as a creatively active self, a self which declines to be identified with his 'character' as so formed. Not, of course, that the self's character—let it be added to obviate misunderstanding—either is, or is supposed by the agent to be, devoid of bearing upon his choices, even in the 'sector' in which free will is held to operate. On the contrary, such a bearing is manifest in the empirically verifiable fact that we find it 'harder' (as we say) to make the effort of will required to 'rise to duty' in proportion to the extent that the 'dutiful' course conflicts with the course to which our character as so far formed inclines us. It is only in the polemics of the critics that a 'free' will is supposed to be incompatible with recognizing the bearing of 'character' upon choice.

"But what" (it may be asked) "of the all-important question of the *value* of this 'subjective certainty'? Even if what you say is sound as 'phenomenology,' is there any reason to suppose that the conviction on which you lay so much stress is in fact *true*?" I agree that the question is important; far more important, indeed, than is always realized, for it is not always realized that the only direct evidence there *could* be for a creative activity like 'free will' is an intuition of the practical consciousness. But this question falls outside the purview of the present paper. The aim of the paper has not been to offer a constructive defence of free will. It has been to show that the problem as traditionally posed is a real, and not a pseudo, problem. A serious threat to that thesis, it was acknowledged, arises from the apparent difficulty of attaching meaning to an act which is not the expression of the self's character and yet *is* the self's own act. The object of my brief phenomenological analysis was to provide evidence that such an act *does* have meaning for us in the one context in which there is any sense in *expecting* it to have meaning.

NOTES

1. *Problems of Ethics*, Ch. VIII. Section 2. (All references are to the English translation by David Rynin, published in New York in 1939.)

2. *Loc. cit.*, Ch. VII, Section 5.

3. *Ibid.*, p. 152.

4. *Ibid.*, p. 153.

5. *Ibid.*

6. January, 1948.

7. *Loc. cit.*, p. 49.

8. *Ibid.*

9. *Ethics*, p. 212.

10. *Loc. cit.*, p. 217.

11. *Ethics and Language*, p. 298.

[C.A. Campbell, "Is 'Free Will' a Pseudo-Problem?" *Mind*, vol. LX, no. 240, October, 1951. (1) Pp. 442–45. (2) Pp. 451–65.]

(5c)
Determinism

Pierre Simon De Laplace

1749–1827

selections from
Philosophical Essay on Probabilities

Laplace asks us to imagine a superhuman intelligence able to "comprehend all the forces by which nature is animated and the respective situation of the beings who compose it." For this being "nothing would be uncertain and the future, as the past, would be present to its eyes."

"Concerning Probability"

(1) All events, even those which on account of their insignificance do not seem to follow the great laws of nature, are a result of it just as necessarily as the revolutions of the sun. In ignorance of the ties which unite such events to the entire system of the universe, they have been made to depend upon final causes or upon hazard, according as they occur and are repeated with regularity, or appear without regard to order; but these imaginary causes have gradually receded with the widening bounds of knowledge and disappear entirely before sound philosophy, which sees in them only the expression of our ignorance of the true causes.

Present events are connected with preceding ones by a tie based upon the evident principle that a thing cannot occur without a cause which produces it. This axiom, known by the name of *the principle of sufficient reason*, extends even to actions which are considered indifferent; the freest will is

261

unable without a determinative motive to give them birth; if we assume two positions with exactly similar circumstances and find that the will is active in the one and inactive in the other, we say that its choice is an effect without a cause. It is then, says Leibnitz, the blind chance of the Epicureans. The contrary opinion is an illusion of the mind, which, losing sight of the evasive reasons of the choice of the will in indifferent things, believes that choice is determined of itself and without motives.

We ought then to regard the present state of the universe as the effect of its anterior state and as the cause of the one which is to follow. Given for one instant an intelligence which could comprehend all the forces by which nature is animated and the respective situation of the beings who compose it—an intelligence sufficiently vast to submit these data to analysis—it would embrace in the same formula the movements of the greatest bodies of the universe and those of the lightest atom; for it, nothing would be uncertain and the future, as the past, would be present to its eyes. The human mind offers, in the perfection which it has been able to give to astronomy, a feeble idea of this intelligence. Its discoveries in mechanics and geometry, added to that of universal gravity, have enabled it to comprehend in the same analytical expressions the past and future states of the system of the world. Applying the same method to some other objects of its knowledge, it has succeeded in referring to general laws observed phenomena and in foreseeing those which given circumstances ought to produce. All these efforts in the search for truth tend to lead it back continually to the vast intelligence which we have just mentioned, but from which it will always remain infinitely removed. This tendency, peculiar to the human race, is that which renders it superior to animals; and their progress in this respect distinguishes nations and ages and constitutes their true glory.

Let us recall that formerly, and at no remote epoch, an unusual rain or an extreme drought, a comet having in train a very long tail, the eclipses, the aurora borealis, and in general all the unusual phenomena were regarded as so many signs of celestial wrath. Heaven was invoked in order to avert their baneful influence. No one prayed to have the planets and the sun arrested in their courses: observation had soon made apparent the futility of such prayers. But as these phenomena, occurring and disappearing at long intervals, seemed to oppose the order of nature, it was supposed that Heaven, irritated by the crimes of the earth, had created them to announce its vengeance. Thus the long tail of the comet of 1456 spread terror through Europe, already thrown into consternation by the rapid successes of the Turks, who had just overthrown the Lower Empire. This star after four revolutions has excited among us a very different interest. The knowledge of the laws of the system of the world acquired in the interval had dissipated the fears begotten by the ignorance of the true relationship of man to the universe; and Halley, having recognized the identity of this comet with those of the years 1531, 1607, and 1682, announced its next return for the end of the year 1758 or the beginning of the year 1759. The learned world awaited with impatience this return which was to confirm one of the greatest discoveries that have been made in the sciences, and fulfil the prediction of Seneca when he said, in speaking of the revolutions of those stars which fall from an enormous height: "The day will come when, by study pursued through several ages, the things now concealed will appear with evidence; and posterity will be astonished that truths so clear had escaped us." Clairaut then undertook to submit to analysis the perturbations which the comet had experienced by the action of the two great planets, Jupiter and Saturn; after immense calculations he fixed its next passage at the perihelion toward the beginning of April, 1759, which was actually verified by observation. The regularity which astronomy shows us in the movements of the comets doubtless exists also in all phenomena.

The curve described by a simple molecule of air or vapor is regulated in a manner just as certain as the planetary orbits; the only difference between them is that which comes from our ignorance.

[Laplace, *Philosophical Essay on Probabilities*, tr. F. W. Truscott (New York: John Wiley and Sons, 1902). (1) Pp. 3–6.]

(5c2)

Brand Blanshard
1892–1987

"The Case for Determinism"

Identifying himself as a determinist, Blanshard argues that when mechanical is augmented by rational determinism, where causality is under the control of an immanent ideal (as in art, logic, science, and morality), the standard objections to determinism lose their power. In rational determinism, when everything is prompting us to do X, and yet we see that we ought to do Y, we have the power to do it.

(1) I am a determinist. None of the arguments offered on the other side seem of much weight except one form of the moral argument, and that itself is far from decisive. Perhaps the most useful thing I can do in this paper is explain why the commoner arguments for indeterminism do not, to my mind, carry conviction. In the course of this explanation the brand of determinism to which I am inclined should become gradually apparent.

But first a definition or two. Determinism is easier to define than indeterminism, and at first glance there seems to be no difficulty in saying what one means by it. It is the view that all events are caused. But unless one also says what one means by "event" and "caused," there is likely to be trouble later. Do I include among events not only changes but the lack of change, not only the fall of the water over the cataract's edge, but the persistence of ice in the frozen river? The answer is "Yes." By an event I mean any change or persistence of state or position. And what is meant by saying that an event is caused? The natural answer is that the event is so connected with some preceding event that unless the latter had occurred the former would not have occurred. Indeterminism means the denial of this. And the denial of this is the statement that there is at least one event to which no preceding event is necessary. But that gets us into trouble at once, for it is doubtful if any indeterminist would want to make such an assertion. What he wants to say is that his decision to tell the truth is undetermined, not that there is no preceding event necessary to it. He would not contend, for example, that he could tell the truth if he had never been born. No, the causal statement to which the indeterminist takes exception is a different one. He is not saying that there is any event to which some namable antecedents are not necessary; he is saying that there are some events whose antecedents do not make them necessary. He is not denying that all consequents have necessary antecedents; he is denying that all antecedents have necessary consequents. He is saying that the state of things just before he decided to tell the truth might have been exactly what it was and yet he might have decided to tell a lie.

By determinism, then, I mean the view that every event A is so connected with a later event B that, given A, B must occur. By indeterminism I mean the view that there is some event B that is not so connected with any previous event A that, given A, it must occur. Now, what is meant here by "must"? We cannot in the end evade that question, but I hope you will not take it as an evasion if at this point I am content to let you fill in the blank in any way you wish. Make it a logical "must," if you care to, or a physical or metaphysical "must," or even the watered-down "must" that means "A is always in fact followed by B." We can discuss the issue usefully though we leave ourselves some latitude on this point.

With these definitions in mind, let us ask what are the most important grounds for indeterminism. This is not the same as asking what commonly moves people to be indeterminists; the answer to that seems to me all too easy. Everyone vaguely knows that to be undetermined is to be free, and everyone wants to be free. My question is rather, When reflective people accept the indeterminist view nowadays, what considerations seem most cogent to them? It seems to me that there are three: first, the stubborn feeling of freedom which seems to resist all dialectical solvents; second, the conviction that natural science itself has now gone over to the indeterminist side; and, third, that determinism would make nonsense of moral responsibility. The third of these seems to me the most important, but I must try to explain why none of them seem to me conclusive.

One of the clearest heads that ever devoted itself to this old issue was Henry Sidgwick. Sidgwick noted that, if at any given moment we stop to think about it, we always feel as if more than one course were open to us, that we could speak or be silent, lift our hand or not lift it. If the determinist is right, this must be an illusion, of course, for whatever we might have done, there must have been a cause, given which we had to do what we did. Now, a mere intuitive assurance about ourselves may be a very weak ground for belief; Freud has shown us that we may be profoundly deceived about how we really feel or why we act as we do. But the curious point is that, though a man who hates his father without knowing it can usually be shown that he does and can often be cured of his feeling, no amount of dialectic seems to shake our feeling of being free to perform either of two proposed acts. By this feeling of being free I do not mean merely the freedom to do what we choose. No one on either side questions that we have that sort of freedom, but it is obviously not the sort of freedom that the indeterminist wants, since it is consistent with determinism of the most rigid sort. The real issue, so far as the will is concerned, is not whether we can do what we choose to do, but whether we can choose our own choice, whether the choice itself issues in accordance with law from some antecedent. And the feeling of freedom that is relevant as evidence is the feeling of an open future as regards the choice itself. After the noise of argument has died down, a sort of intuition stubbornly remains that we can not only lift our hand if we choose, but that the choice itself is open to us. Is this not an impressive fact?

No, I do not think it is. The first reason is that when we are making a choice our faces are always turned toward the future, toward the consequences that one act or the other will bring us, never toward the past with its possible sources of constraint. Hence these sources are not noticed. Hence we remain unaware that we are under constraint at all. Hence we feel free from such constraint. The case is almost as simple as that. When you consider buying a new typewriter your thought is fixed on the pleasure and advantage you would gain from it, or the drain it would make on your budget. You are not delving into the causes that led to your taking pleasure in the prospect of owning a typewriter or to your having a complex about expenditure. You are too much preoccupied with the ends to which the choice would be a means to give any attention to the causes of which your choice may be an effect. But that is no reason for thinking that if you did preoccupy yourself with these causes you would not find them at work. You may remember that Sir Francis Galton was so much impressed with this possibility that for some time he kept account in a notebook of the occasions on which he made important choices with a full measure of this feeling of freedom; then shortly after each choice he turned his eye backward in search of constraints that might have been acting on him stealthily. He found it so easy to bring such constraining factors to light that he surrendered to the determinist view.

But this, you may say, is not enough. Our preoccupation with the future may show why we are not aware of the constraints acting on us, and hence why we do not feel bound by them; it does not explain why our sense of freedom persists after the constraints are disclosed to us. By disclosing the causes of some fear, for example, psychoanalytic therapy can remove the fear, and when these causes are brought to light, the fear commonly does go. How is it, then, that when the causes of our volition are brought to light volition continues to feel as free as before? Does this not show that it is really independent of those causes?

No again. The two cases are not parallel. The man with the panic fear of dogs is investing all dogs with the qualities—remembered, though in disguised form—of the monster that frightened him as a child. When this monster and his relation to it are brought to light, so that they can be dissociated from the Fidos and Towsers around him, the fear goes, because its appropriate object has gone. It is quite different with our feeling of freedom. We feel free, it was suggested, because we are not aware of the forces acting on us. Now, in spite of the determinist's conviction that when a choice is made there are always causal influences at work, he does not pretend to reveal the influences at work in our present choice. The chooser's face is always turned forward; his present choice is always unique; and no matter how much he knows about the will and the laws, his present choice always emerges out of deep shadow. The determinist who buys a typewriter is as little interested at the moment in the strings that may be pulling at him from his physiological or subconscious cellars as his indeterminist colleague, and hence feels just as free. Thus, whereas the new knowledge gained through psychoanalysis does remove the grounds of fear, the knowledge gained by the determinist is not at all of the sort that would remove the grounds for the feeling of freedom. To make the persistence of this feeling in the determinist an argument against his case is therefore a confusion.

The second reason, I suggested, why so many thoughtful persons remain indeterminists is that they are convinced that science has gone indeterminist. Well, has it? If you follow Heisenberg, Eddington, and Born, it has. If you follow Russell, Planck, and Einstein, it has not. When such experts disagree it is no doubt folly for the layman to rush in. But since I am discussing the main reasons why people stick to indeterminism, and have admitted that the new physics is one of them, I cannot afford to be quite prudent. Let me say, then, with much hesitation that, as far as I can follow the argument, it provides no good evidence for indeterminism even in the physical world, and that, if it did, it would provide no good evidence for indeterminism in the realm of will.

First as to physical indeterminism. Physicists now tell us that descriptive statements about the behavior of bodies are really statistical statements. It was known long ago that the pressure that makes a football hard is not the simple quality one feels in pushing something: it is the beating on the inner surface of the football of millions of molecular bullets. We now know that each of these bullets is a swarm of atoms, themselves normally swarms of still minuter somethings, of which the proton and the electron are typical. The physicist admits that the behavior of an enormous mass of these particles, such as a billiard ball, is so stable that we may safely consider it as governed by causal law. But that is no reason, he adds, for assigning a like stability to the ultimate particles themselves. Indeed, there is good reason, namely the principle of indeterminacy, for saying that they sometimes act by mere chance. That principle tells us that whereas, when we are talking about a billiard ball, we can say that it has a certain momentum and direction at point B as a result of having a certain momentum and direction at point A, we can never say that sort of thing about an electron. Why? Because the conditions of observation are such that, when they allow us to fix the position exactly, they make it impossible to fix the momentum exactly. Suppose that we can determine the position of a moving particle with more accuracy the shorter the wave length of light we use. But suppose that the shorter the wave length, the more it interferes with the momentum of the particle, making it leap unpredictably about. And suppose there is no way of determining the position without in this way leaving the momentum vague, or of determining the momentum without leaving the position vague. It will then be impossible to state any precise law that govern's the particle's movement. We can never say that such-and-such a momentum at point *A* was necessarily followed by such-and-such a momentum at point *B*, because these statements can have no precise meaning, and can be given none, for either antecedent or consequent. Hence to speak any longer of nature as governed ultimately by causal laws—i.e., statements of precise connection between antecedent and consequent—is simply out of the question.

This argument, as Sir David Ross has pointed out, may be interpreted in different ways. It may be taken to say that, though the particle does have a certain position and momentum, we can never tell, definitely and for both at the same time, what they are. Many interpreters thus understand the theory. But so taken, there is of course nothing in it to throw the slightest doubt on the reign of causality. It is merely a statement that in a certain region our knowledge of causal law has limits. Secondly, the theory might be taken to mean that electrons are not the sort of things that have position and momentum at all in the ordinary sense, but are fields, perhaps, or widespreading waves. This, too, has no suggestion of indeterminism. It would not mean that general statements about the nature and behavior of electrons could not be made, but only that such statements would not contain references to position and momentum. Thirdly, the theory might mean that, though these particles do have a position and a momentum, the position or momentum is not definitely this rather than that. Even laymen must rise at this point and protest, with all respect, that this is meaningless. Vagueness in our thought of a position makes sense; vagueness of actual position makes none. Or, finally, the argument may mean that, though the particle does have a definite position and momentum, these cannot even in theory be correlated with anything that went before. But how could we possibly know this? The only ground for accepting it is that we do not know of any such correlates. And that is no reason for denying that any exist. Indeed, to deny this is to abandon the established assumption and practice of science. Science has advanced in the past precisely because, when things happened whose causes were unknown, it was assumed that they had causes nevertheless. To assume that a frustration of present knowledge, even one that looks permanent, is a sign of chance in nature is both practically uncourageous and theoretically a *non sequitur.*

But let us suppose that the Eddingtonians are right and that what has been called "free will among the electrons" is the fact. Would that imply indeterminism in the realm that most nearly concerns us, the realm of choice? I cannot see that it would. The argument supposed to show that it would is as follows: Psychical processes depend on physical processes. But physical processes are themselves at bottom unpredictable. Hence the psychical processes dependent on them must share this unpredictability. Stated in the abstract, the argument sounds impressive. But what does it actually come to? We are told that, even if there is inconstancy in the behavior of single particles, there is no observable inconstancy in the behavior of masses of them; the particles of a billiard ball are never able to get together and go on a spree simultaneously. Eddington admitted that they might, just as he admitted that an army of monkeys with a million typewriters might produce all the books in the British Museum, but he admitted also that the chances of a billiard ball's behaving in this way were so astronomically remote that he would not believe it if he saw it.

The question of importance for us, then, is whether, if acts of choice are dependent on physical processes at all, they depend on the behavior of particles singly or on that of masses of particles. To this there can be but one answer. They depend on mass behavior. An act of choice is an extremely complex process. It involves the idea of one or more ends, the association of that idea with more or less numerous other ideas, the presence of desires and repulsions, and the operation of habits and impulses; indeed, in those choices for which freedom is most demanded, the whole personality seems to be at work. The cortical basis for so complex a process must be extremely broad. But if it is, the great mass of cells involved must, by the physicist's admission, act with a high stability, and the correlated psychical processes must show a similar stability. But that is what we mean by action in accordance with causal law. So, even if the physicists are right about the unstable behavior of single particles, there is no reason whatever for translating this theory into a doctrine of indeterminism for human choice.

We come now to the third of the reasons commonly advanced in support of indeterminism. This is that determinism makes a mess of morality. The charge has taken many forms. We are told that determinism makes praise and blame meaningless, punishment brutal, remorse pointless, amendment hopeless, duty a deceit. All these allegations have been effectively answered except the one about duty, where I admit I am not quite satisfied. But none of them are in the form in which determinism most troubles the plain man. What most affronts him, I think, is the suggestion that he is only a machine, a big foolish clock that seems to itself to be acting freely, but whose movements are controlled completely by the wheels and weights inside, a Punch-and-Judy show whose appearance of doing things because they are right or reasonable is a sham because everything is mechanically regulated by wires from below. He has no objections to determinism as applied by physicists to atoms, by himself to machines, or by his doctor to his body. He has an emphatic objection to determinism as applied by anyone to his reflection and his will, for this seems to make him a gigantic mechanical toy, or worse, a sort of Frankenstein monster.

In this objection I think we must agree with the plain man. If anyone were to show me that determinism involved either materialism or mechanism, I would renounce it at once, for that would be equivalent, in my opinion, to reducing it to absurdity. The "physicalism" once proposed by Neurath and Carnap as a basis for the scientific study of behavior I could not accept for a moment, because it is so dogmatically antiempirical. To use empirical methods means, for me, not to approach nature with a preconceived notion as to what facts must be like, but to be ready to consider all kinds of alleged facts on their merits. Among these the introspectively observable fact of reflective choice, and the inference to its existence in others, are particularly plain, however different from anything that occurs in the realm of the material or the publicly observable or the mechanically controlled.

Now, what can be meant by saying that such choice, though not determined mechanically, is still determined? Are you suggesting, it will be asked, that in the realm of reflection and choice there operates a different kind of causality from any we know in the realm of bodies? My answer is: Yes, just that. To put it more particularly, I am suggesting (1) that even within the psychical realm there are different causal levels, (2) that a

causality of higher level may supervene on one of lower level, and (3) that
when causality of the highest level is at work, we have precisely what the
indeterminists, without knowing it, want.

1. First, then, as to causal levels. I am assuming that even the indeterminist would admit that most mental events are causally governed.
No one would want to deny that his stepping on a tack had something
to do with his feeling pain, or that his touching a flame had something
to do with his getting burned, or that his later thought of the flame had
something to do with his experience of its hotness. A law of association
is a causal law of mental events. In one respect it is like a law of physical events: in neither case have we any light as to *why* the consequent
follows on the antecedent. Hume was right about the billiard balls. He
was right about the flame and the heat; we do not see why something
bright and yellow should also be hot. He was right about association; we
do not understand how one idea calls up another; we only know that it
does. Causality in all such cases means to us little if anything more than
a routine of regular sequence.

Is all mental causation like that? Surely not. Consider a musician com-
posing a piece or a logician making a deduction. Let us make our musician
a philosopher also, who after adding a bar pauses to ask himself, "Why did
I add just that?" Can we believe he would answer, "Because whenever in the
past I have had the preceding bars in mind, they have always been followed
by this bar"? What makes this suggestion so inept is partly that he may
never have thought of the preceding bars before, partly that, if he had, the
repetition of an old sequence would be precisely what he would avoid. No,
his answer, I think, would be something like this: "I wrote what I did
because it seemed the right thing to do. I developed my theme in the
manner demanded to carry it through in an aesthetically satisfactory way."
In other words, the constraint that was really at work in him was not that
of association; it was something that worked distinctly against association;
it was the constraint of an aesthetic ideal. And, if so, there is a causality of
a different level. It is idle to say that the musician is wholly in the dark
about it. He can see not only *that B* succeeded *A*; as he looks back, he can
see in large measure *why* it did.

It is the same with logical inference, only more clearly so. The thinker
starts, let us say, with the idea of a regular solid whose faces are squares,

and proceeds to develop in thought the further characteristics that such a solid must possess. He constructs it in imagination and then sees that it must have six faces, eight vertices, and twelve edges. Is this association merely? It may be. It is, for example, if he merely does in imagination what a child does when it counts the edges on a lump of sugar. This is not inference and does not feel like it. When a person, starting with the thought of a solid with square faces, deduces that it must have eight vertices, and then asks why he should have thought of that, the natural answer is, Because the first property entails the second. Of course this is not the only condition, but it seems to me contrary to introspectively plain fact to say that it had nothing to do with the movement of thought. It is easy to put this in such a way as to invite attack. If we say that the condition of our thinking of B is the observed necessity between A and B, we are assuming that B is already thought of as a means of explaining how it comes to be thought of. But that is not what I am saying. I am saying that in thinking at its best thought comes under the constraint of necessities in its object, so that the objective fact that A necessitates B partially determines our passing in thought from A to B. Even when the explanation is put in this form, the objection has been raised that necessity is a timeless link between concepts, while causality is a temporal bond between events, and that the two must be kept sharply apart. To which the answer is: Distinct, yes; but always apart, no. A timeless relation may serve perfectly well as the condition of a temporal passage. I hold that in the course of our thinking we can easily verify this fact, and, because I do, I am not put off by pronouncements about what we should and should not be able to see.

2. My second point about these causal levels is that our mental processes seldom move on one level alone. The higher is always supervening on the lower and taking over partial control. Though brokenly and imperfectly rational, rational creatures we still are. It must be admitted that most of our so-called thinking moves by association, and is hardly thinking at all. But even in the dullest of us "bright shoots of everlastingness," strands of necessity, aesthetic or logical, from time to time appear. "The quarto and folio editions of mankind" can follow the argument with fewer lapses than most of us; in the texts of the greatest of all dramas, we are told, there was seldom a blot or erasure; but Ben Jonson added, and no doubt rightly, that there ought to have been a thousand. The effort of both

thought and art is to escape the arbitrary, the merely personal, everything that, casual and capricious, is irrelevant, and to keep to lines appointed by the whole that one is constructing. I do not suggest that logical and aesthetic necessity are the same. I do say that they are both to be distinguished from association or habit as representing a different level of control. That control is never complete; all creation in thought or art is successful in degree only. It is successful in the degree to which it ceases to be an expression of merely personal impulses and becomes the instrument of a necessity lying in its own subject matter.

3. This brings us to our last point. Since moral choice, like thought and art, moves on different causal levels, it achieves freedom, just as they do, only when is determined by its own appropriate necessity. Most of our so-called choices are so clearly brought about by association, impulse, and feeling that the judicious indeterminist will raise no issue about them. When we decide to get a drink of water, to take another nibble of chocolate, to go to bed at the usual hour, the forces at work are too plain to be denied. It is not acts like these on which the indeterminist takes his stand. It is rather on those where, with habit, impulse, and association prompting us powerfully to do X, we see that we ought to do Y and therefore do it. To suppose that in such cases we are still the puppets of habit and impulse seems to the indeterminist palpably false.

So it does to us. Surely about this the indeterminist is right. Action impelled by the sense of duty, as Kant perceived, is action on a different level from anything mechanical or associative. But Kant was mistaken in supposing that when we were determined by reason we were not determined at all. This supposition seems to me wholly unwarranted. The determination is still there, but, since it is a determination by the moral necessities of the case, it is just what the moral man wants and thus is the equivalent of freedom. For the moral man, like the logician and the artist, is really seeking self-surrender. Through him as through the others an impersonal ideal is working, and to the extent that this ideal takes possession of him and molds him according to its pattern, he feels free and is free.

The logician is most fully himself when the wind gets into his sails and carries him effortlessly along the line of his calculations. Many an artist and musician have left it on record that their best work was done when the whole they were creating took the brush or pen away from them and completed the work itself. It determined them, but they were free, because to be determined by this whole was at once the secret of their craft and the end of their desire. This is the condition of the moral man also. He has caught a vision, dimmer perhaps than that of the logician or the artist, but equally objective and compelling. It is a vision of the good. This good necessitates certain things, not as means to ends merely, for that is not usually a necessary link, but as integral parts of itself. It requires that he should put love above hate, that he should regard his neighbor's good as of like value with his own, that he should repair injuries, and express gratitude, and respect promises, and revere truth. Of course it does not guide him infallibly. On the values of a particular case he may easily be mistaken. But that no more shows that there are no values present to be estimated, and no ideal demanding a special mode of action, than the fact that we make a mistake in adding figures shows that there are no figures to be added, or no right way of adding them. In both instances what we want is control by the objective requirements of the case. The saint, like the thinker and the artist, has often said this in so many words. I feel most free, said St. Paul, precisely when I am most a slave.

We have now dealt, as best we can in a restricted space, with the three commonest objections to determinism. They all seem to admit of answers. To the objection that we always feel free, we answer that it is natural to feel so, even if we are determined, since our faces are set toward results and not toward causes, and the causes of present action always elude us. To the objection that science has gone indeterminist, we answer that that is only one interpretation of recent discoveries, and not the most plausible one, and that, even if it were true, it would not carry with it indeterminism for human choice. To the objection that determinism would reduce us to the level of mechanical puppets, we answer that though we are puppets in part we live, as Aristotle said, on various levels. And so far as causality in reflection, art, and moral choice involves control by immanent ideal, mechanism has passed over into that rational determinism that is the best kind of freedom.

[Brand Blanshard, "The Case for Determinism," in *Determinism and Freedom in the Age of Modern Science* (New York Institute for Philosophy), ed. Sidney Hook (Washington Square: New York University Press, 1958). (1) Pp. 3–13.]

Paul Edwards

b. 1923

"Hard and Soft Determinism"

Siding with the hard determinists, Paul Edwards relates to a number of the selections in this volume, *i.e.*, William James, Hume, Voltaire, and adds new material on the subject from Holbach, Schopenhauer, and C. A. Campbell. His account of "soft determinism" (a phrase introduced by William James, who called it a "quagmire of evasions"), is also noteworthy.

(1) In his essay "The Dilemma of Determinism," William James makes a distinction that will serve as a point of departure for my remarks. He there distinguishes between the philosophers he calls "hard" determinists and those he labels "soft" determinists. The former, the hard determinists, James tells us, "did not shrink from such words as fatality, bondage of the will, necessitation and the like." He quotes a famous stanza from Omar Khayyám as representing this kind of determinism:

> With earth's first clay they did the last man knead,
> And there of the last harvest sowed the seed.
> And the first morning of creation wrote
> What the last dawn of reckoning shall read.

Another of Omar's verses expresses perhaps even better the kind of theory that James has here in mind:

> Tis all a checker-board of nights and days,
> Where destiny with men for pieces plays;
> Thither and thither moves, and metes, and slays,
> And one by one back to the closet lays.

James mentioned no names other than Omar Khayyám. But there is little doubt that among the hard determinists he would have included Jonathan Edwards, Anthony Collins, Holbach, Priestley, Robert Owen, Schopenhauer, Freud, and also, if he had come a little earlier, Clarence Darrow.

James of course rejected both hard and soft determinism, but for hard determinism he had a certain respect: the kind of respect one sometimes has for an honest, straightforward adversary. For soft determinism, on the other hand, he had nothing but contempt, calling it a "quagmire of evasion." "Nowadays," he writes, "we have a *soft* determinism which abhors harsh words, and repudiating fatality, necessity, and even predetermination, says that its real name is 'freedom.'" From his subsequent observations it is clear that he would include among the evasionists not only neoHegelians like Green and Bradley but also Hobbes and Hume and Mill; and if he were alive today James would undoubtedly include Schlick and Ayer and Stevenson and Nowel-Smith, not to mention some of the philosophers present in this room.*

The theory James calls soft determinism, especially the Hume-Mill-Schlick variety of it, has been extremely fashionable during the last twenty-five years, while hardly anybody can be found today who has anything good to say for hard determinism. In opposition to this contemporary trend, I should like to strike a blow on behalf of hard determinism in my talk today. I shall also try to bring out exactly what is really at issue between hard and soft determinism. I think the nature of this dispute has frequently been misconceived chiefly because many writers, including James, have a very inaccurate notion of what is maintained by actual hard determinists, as distinct from the bogey men they set up in order to score an easy victory.

To begin with, it is necessary to spell more fully the main contentions of the soft determinists. Since it is the dominant form of soft determinism at the present time, I shall confine myself to the Hume-Mill-Schlick theory. According to this theory there is in the first place no contradiction

---

*This paper was read at the first New York University Institute of Philosophy, held on February 9 and 10, 1957. It was received with a great deal of hostility.

whatsoever between determinism and the proposition that human beings are sometimes free agents. When we call an action "free" we never in any ordinary situation mean that it was uncaused; and this emphatically includes the kind of action about which we pass moral judgments. By calling an action "free" we mean that the agent was not compelled or constrained to perform it. Sometimes people act in a certain way because of threats or because they have been drugged or because of a posthypnotic suggestion or because of an irrational overpowering urge such as the one that makes a kleptomaniac steal something he does not really need. On such occasions human beings are not free agents. But on other occasions they act in certain ways because of their own rational desires, because of their own unimpeded efforts, because they have chosen to act in these ways. On these occasions they are free agents although their actions are just as much caused as actions that are not deemed free. In distinguishing between free and unfree actions we do not try to mark the presence and absence of causes but attempt to indicate the *kind* of causes that are present.

Secondly there is no antithesis between determinism and moral responsibility. When we judge a person morally responsible for a certain action, we do indeed presuppose that he was a free agent at the time of the action. But the freedom presupposed is not the contracausal freedom about which indeterminists go into such ecstatic raptures. It is nothing more than the freedom already mentioned—the ability to act according to one's choices or desires. Since determinism is compatible with freedom in this sense, it is also compatible with moral responsibility. In other words, the world is after all wonderful: we can be determinists and yet go on punishing our enemies and our children, and we can go on blaming ourselves, all without a bad intellectual conscience.

Mill, who was probably the greatest moralizer among the soft determinists, recognized with particular satisfaction the influence or alleged influence of one class of human desires. Not only, for example, does such a lowly desire as my desire to get a new car influence my conduct. It is equally true, or so at least Mill believed, that my desire to become a more virtuous person does on occasion influence my actions. By suitable training and efforts my desire to change my character may in fact bring about the desired changes. If Mill were alive today he might point to contemporary psychiatry as an illustration of his point. Let us suppose that I have an intense desire to become famous, but that I also have an intense desire to become a happier and more lovable person who, among other things, does not greatly care about fame. Let us suppose, furthermore, that I know of a therapy that can transform fame-seeking and unlovable into lovable and fame-indifferent character structures. If, now, I have enough money, energy, and courage, and if a few other conditions are fulfilled, my desire may actually lead to a major change in my character. Since we can, therefore, at least to some extent, form our own character, determinism according to Mill is compatible not only with judgments of moral responsibility about this or that particular *action* flowing from an unimpeded desire, but also, within limits, with moral judgments about the *character* of human beings.

I think that several of Mill's observations were well worth making and that James's verdict on his theory as a "quagmire of evasion" is far too derogatory. I think hard determinists have occasionally written in such a way as to suggest that they deny the causal efficacy of human desires and efforts. Thus Holbach wrote:

> You will say that I feel free. This is an illusion, which may be compared to that of the fly in the fable, who, lighting upon the pole of a heavy carriage, applauded himself for directing its course. Man, who thinks himself free, is a fly who imagines he has power to move the universe, while he is himself unknowingly carried along by it.

There is also the following passage in Schopenhauer:

> Every man, being what he is and placed in the circumstances which for the moment obtain, but which on their part also arise by strict necessity, can absolutely never do anything else than just what at that moment he does do, Accordingly, the whole course of a man's life, in all its incidents great and small, is as necessarily predetermined as the course of a clock.

Voltaire expresses himself in much the same way in the article on "Destiny" in the *Philosophical Dictionary.*

> Everything happens through immutable laws. . . . everything is necessary. . . . "There are," some persons say, "some events which are neces-

sary and others which are not." It would be very comic that one part of the world was arranged, and the other were not; that one part of what happens had to happen and that another part of what happens did not have to happen. If one looks closely at it, one sees that the doctrine contrary to that of destiny is absurd; but there are many people destined to reason badly; others not to reason at all, others to persecute those who reason. . . .

. . . I necessarily have the passion for writing this, and you have the passion for condemning me; both of us are equally fools, equally the toy of destiny. Your nature is to do harm, mine is to love truth, and to make it public in spite of you.

Furthermore there can be little doubt that Hume and Mill and Schlick were a great deal clearer about the relation between motives and actions than the hard determinists, who either conceived it, like Collins, as one of logical necessity or, like Priestley and Voltaire and Schopenhauer, as necessarily involving coercion or constraint.

But when all is said and done, there remains a good deal of truth in James's charge that soft determinism is an evasion. For a careful reading of their works shows that none of the hard determinists really denied that human desires, efforts, and choices make a difference in the course of events. Any remarks to the contrary are at most temporary lapses. This, then, is hardly the point at issue. If it is not the point at issue, what is? Let me at this stage imagine a hard determinist replying to a champion of the Hume-Mill theory: "You are right," he would say, "in maintaining that some of our actions are caused by our desires and choices. But you do not pursue the subject far enough. You arbitrarily stop at the desires and volitions. We must not stop there. We must go on to ask where *they* come from; and if determinism is true there can be no doubt about the answer to this question. Ultimately our desires and our whole character are derived from our inherited equipment and the environmental influences to which we were subjected at the beginning of our lives. It is clear that we had no hand in shaping either of these." A hard determinist could quote a number of eminent supporters. "Our volitions and our desires," wrote Holbach in his little book *Good Sense*, "are never in our power. You think yourself free, because you do what you will; but are you free to will or not to will, to desire or not to desire?" And Schopenhauer expressed the same thought in the following epigram: "A man can surely do what he wills to do, but he cannot determine what he wills."

Let me turn once more to the topic of character transformation by means of psychiatry to bring out this point with full force. Let us suppose that both *A* and *B* are compulsive and suffer intensely from their neuroses. Let us assume that there is a therapy that could help them, which could materially change their character structure, but that it takes a great deal of energy and courage to undertake the treatment. Let us suppose that *A* has the necessary energy and courage while *B* lacks it. *A* undergoes the therapy and changes in the desired way. *B* just gets more and more compulsive and more and more miserable. Now, it is true that *A* helped form his own later character. But his starting point, his desire to change, his energy and courage, were already there. They may or may not have been the result of previous efforts on his own part. But there must have been a first effort, and the effort at that time was the result of factors that were not of his making.

The fact that a person's character is ultimately the product of factors over which he had no control is not denied by the soft determinists, though many of them don't like to be reminded of it when they are in a moralizing mood. Since the hard determinists admit that our desires and choices do on occasion influence the course of our lives, there is thus no disagreement between the soft and the hard determinists about the empirical facts. However, some hard determinists infer from some of these facts that human beings are never morally responsible for their actions. The soft determinists, as already stated, do not draw any such inference. In the remainder of my paper I shall try to show just what it is that hard determinists are inferring and why, in my opinion, they are justified in their conclusion.

I shall begin by adopting for my purposes a distinction introduced by C. A. Campbell in his extremely valuable article "Is 'Free Will' a Pseudo Problem?"[1] in which he distinguishes between two conceptions of moral responsibility. Different persons, he says, require different conditions to be fulfilled before holding human beings morally responsible for what they do. First, there is what Campbell calls the ordinary unreflective person, who is rather ignorant and who is not greatly concerned with the theories of science, philosophy, and religion. If the unreflective person is sure that the agent to be judged was acting under coercion or constraint, he will not hold him responsible. If, however, he is sure that the action was performed in accordance with the agent's unimpeded rational desire, if he is sure that the action would not have taken place but for the agent's decision, then the unreflective person will consider ascription of moral responsibility justified. The fact that the agent did not ultimately make his own character will either not occur to him, or else it will not be considered a sufficient ground for withholding a judgment of moral responsibility.

In addition to such unreflective persons, continues Campbell, there are others who have reached "a tolerably advanced level of reflection."

> Such a person will doubtless be acquainted with the claims advanced in some quarters that causal law operates universally; or/and with the theories of some philosophies that the universe is throughout the expression of a single supreme principle; or/and with the doctrines of some theologians that the world is created, sustained and governed by an Omniscient and Omnipotent Being.

Such a person will tend to require the fulfillment of a further condition before holding anybody morally responsible. He will require not only that the agent was not coerced or constrained but also—and this is taken to be an additional condition—that he "could have chosen otherwise than he actually did." I should prefer to put this somewhat differently, but it will not affect the main conclusion drawn by Campbell, with which I agree. The reflective person, I should prefer to express it, requires not only that the agent was not coerced; he also requires that the agent *originally chose his own character*—the character that now displays itself in his choices and desires and efforts. Campbell concludes that determinism is indeed compatible with judgments of moral responsibility in the unreflective sense, but that it is incompatible with judgments of moral responsibility in the reflective sense.

Although I do not follow Campbell in rejecting determinism, I basically agree with his analysis, with one other qualification. I do not think it is a question of the different senses in which the term is used by ignorant and unreflective people, on the one hand, and by those who are interested in science, religion, and philosophy, on the other. The very same persons, whether educated or uneducated, use it in certain contexts in the one sense and in other contexts in the other. Practically all human beings, no matter how much interested they are in science, religion, and philosophy, employ what Campbell calls the unreflective conception when they are dominated by violent emotions like anger, indignation, or hate, and especially when the conduct they are judging has been personally injurious to them. On the other hand, a great many people, whether they are educated or not, will employ what Campbell calls the reflective conception when they are not consumed with hate or anger—when they are judging a situation calmly and reflectively and when the fact that the agent did not ultimately shape his own character has been vividly brought to their attention. Clarence Darrow in his celebrated pleas repeatedly appealed to the jury on precisely this ground. If any of you, he would say, had been reared in an environment like that of the accused or had to suffer from his defective heredity, *you* would now be standing in the dock. I cannot refrain at this stage from reading a poem written by the hard determinist, A. E. Housman, which Darrow recited on such occasions. Its title is "The Culprit," and it is the soliloquy of a boy about to be hanged.

> The night my father got me
> His mind was not on me;
> He did not plague his fancy
> To muse if I should be
> The son you see.
>
> The day my mother bore me
> She was a fool and glad,
> For all the pain I cost her,
> That she had borne the lad
> That borne she had.
>
> My mother and my father
> Out of the light they lie;
> The warrant could not find them,
> And here 'tis only I
> Shall hang so high.
>
> Oh let not man remember
> The soul that God forgot,
> But fetch the county kerchief

And noose me in the knot,
And I will rot.

For so the game is ended
    That should not have begun.
My father and my mother
    They had a likely son,
    And I have none.[2]

Darrow nearly always convinced the jury that the accused could not be held morally responsible for his acts; and certainly the majority of the jurors were relatively uneducated.

I have so far merely distinguished between two concepts of moral responsibility. I now wish to go a step farther and claim that only one of them can be considered, properly speaking, a moral concept. This is not an easy point to make clear, but I can at least indicate what I mean. We do not normally consider just any positive or negative feeling a "moral" emotion. Nor do we consider just any sentence containing the words "good" or "bad" expressions of "moral" judgment. For example, if a man hates a woman because she rejected him, this would not be counted as a moral emotion. If, however, he disapproves, say, of Senator McCarthy's libelous speech against Adlai Stevenson before the 1952 election because he disapproves of slander in general and not merely because he likes Stevenson and dislikes McCarthy, his feeling would be counted as moral. A feeling or judgment must in a certain sense be "impersonal" before we consider it moral. To this I would add that it must also be independent of violent emotions. Confining myself to judgments, I would say that a judgment was "moral" only if it was formulated in a calm and reflective mood, or at least if it is supported in a calm and reflective state of mind. If this is so, it follows that what Campbell calls the reflective sense of "moral responsibility" is the only one that qualifies as a properly moral use of the term.

Before I conclude I wish to avoid a certain misunderstanding of my remarks. From the fact that human beings do not ultimately shape their own character, I said, it *follows* that they are never morally responsible. I do not mean that by reminding people of the ultimate causes of their character one makes them more charitable and less vengeful. Maybe one does, but that is not what I mean. I mean "follow" or "imply" in the same sense as, or in a sense closely akin to, that in which the conclusion of a valid syllogism follows from the premises. The effectiveness of Darrow's pleas does not merely show, I am arguing, how powerfully he could sway the emotions of the jurors. His pleas also brought into the open one of the conditions the jurors, like others, consider necessary on reflection before they hold an agent morally responsible. Or perhaps I should say that Darrow *committed* the jurors in their reflective nature to a certain ground for the ascription of moral responsibility.[3]

Notes

1. *Mind,* 1951.

2. From *The Collected Poems of A. E. Housman.* Copyright, 1922, 1940 by Henry Holt and Company, Inc. Copyright, 1950, by Barclays Bank, Ltd. By permission of the publishers.

3. I have been thinking a great deal about the questions discussed in this article since it was published in 1958. I hold substantially the same view but my treatment was incomplete. My present views are stated in the Appendix "Free Will and the Frankenstein Problem" in *God and the Philosophers* which will be published by Prometheus.

[Paul Edwards, "Hard and Soft Determinism" from *Determinism and Freedom,* ed. Sidney Hook (Washington Square: New York University Press, 1958). (1) Pp. 104–13.]

Appendix

The titles of the volumes constituting the 8-volume set of Study Guides and Readings in the projected 8-volume set, in addition to *Freedom* are *Value, Self, Truth, Beauty, Right and Wrong, Social Philosophy,* and *God and Immortality.* These are the unavoidable questions of philosophy from which all beginning range courses in philosophy are constructed. Individual students and classes are provided maximum flexibility in following out their adventures into philosophy in whatever order and combination they may find appropriate. While the books of readings can be used by themselves, or in any combination, they can also be used with the *Dictionary of Philosophy and Religion: Eastern and Western Thought* as companion volume, providing the student with a wealth of additional information on philosophy. The instructor can thus combine in depth, study of several problems through the Readings, while utilizing the *Dictionary* to provide mini-study guides for problems considered less fully. The *Dictionary* offers the following resources for the eight problems:

Freedom:

—Freedom entry. Thirty-one entry listings on philosophers who have held each of the four definitions with references (*q.v.*'s) to their own entries in the *Dictionary,* and relevant paragraphs of those entries. Such entry listings provide a summary of the important ideas on the given topic.

—Free Will (5 entry listings)
—Determinism (16 entry listings)

Value:

—Value (8 entry listings)
—Final Value (18 entry listings)
—Value Theory (11 entry listings)

Self:

—Person (15 entry listings)
—Self (10 entry listings)
—Soul (17 entry listings)

Truth:

—Truth (38 entry listings, 5 definitions)
—Epistemology (10 entry listings)
—Knowledge (16 entry listings)
—Skepticism (30 entry listings)
—Wisdom (17 entry listings)

Beauty:

—Aesthetics (37 entry listings)
—Art (8 entry listings)
—Poetry (3 *q.v.* references)

Right and Wrong:

—Good (12 entry listings)
—Right (6 entry listings)
—Ethics (44 entry listings)
—Evil (16 entry listings)
—Utilitarianism (13 entry listings)
—Axiology (4 entry listings)

Social Philosophy:

—Social Contract Theory (14 entry listings)
—Natural Rights (6 entry listings)
—Natural Law (12 entry listings)
—Sovereignty (6 entry listings)
—and entry listings for Hobbes, Locke, Marx, Plato, Rousseau, Jefferson, T. Paine, Rawls, Nozick.

God and Immortality:

—God (75 entry listings, divided among nature of God, arguments for God, and God as a projection of human awareness)
—Religion (27 entry listings, plus entries on basic faiths of the world)
—Immortality (11 entry listings)
—Reincarnation, and Metempsychosis (numerous *q.v.* references)
—Faith (16 entry listings)
—Myth (15 entry listings)
—Reason (15 entry listings)

Index